Great American Learning Adventures

Great American Learning Adventures

HARRIET WEBSTER

HarperPerennial
A Division of HarperCollins*Publishers*

For my teacher, Don Murray, with gratitude and respect

HarperCollins books may be purchased for educational, business, or sales promotional use. For information, please write to: Special Markets Department, HarperCollins Publishers, Inc., 10 East 53rd Street, New York, New York 10022.

FIRST HARPER PERENNIAL EDITION

DESIGNED BY HELENE BERINSKY

Library of Congress Cataloging-in-Publication Data
Webster, Harriet
   Great American learning adventures / Harriet Webster. — 1st ed.
     p. cm.
   Includes index.
   ISBN 0-06-273167-X
   1. Travel. 2. Vacations. I. Title.
G151.W425 1994
917.304'929—dc20
                                                          92-54674

---

94 95 96 97 98 ❖/RRD 10 9 8 7 6 5 4 3 2 1

Contents

3. Exploring the Arts 41

4. Outdoor Recreation 91

HIKING

BIKING

CLIMBING

SKIING AND DOGSLEDDING

FISHING

5. Natural History and Wilderness Challenges

222

COOKING

Introduction

Many of us approach travel expecting to be invigorated by the new experiences we anticipate. That's why we're thrown off base when a week after returning home from vacation we feel as though we never left. The trip is a memory, except for the bills, and we find ourselves feeling deflated but we can't quite articulate the source of our malaise. We vow that next year we'll go someplace more exotic, someplace flashier, someplace that will give us the sense of fulfillment we want from a vacation. Chances are we'll be disappointed again.

Fortunately, there's a solution, and it doesn't involve spending increasing amounts of money or traveling to the far corners of the earth. Often our dissatisfaction stems from the fact that we return from vacation unchanged. Maybe we're a little more rested, a little tanner, a bit better traveled, but basically we're the same. Instead of enriching our lives, our vacation has simply served as a respite from routine.

One good way to change that pattern is to purposefully look at vacations as opportunities to explore, expand, and challenge our own physical, spiritual, cultural, and intellectual resources. When we start using travel as a means for achieving growth, that's when we start coming back from vacation feeling strong and energized. *Great American Learning Adventures* can help make that happen.

This is a book for people who want their vacations to serve as a springboard to personal enrichment. The places and organizations listed here offer the opportunity to unearth a newfound talent or refine a familiar one, to expand our thinking on subjects that vary from social policy issues to exercise and nutrition. The suggestions delve into topics as diverse as whale ecology and southwestern cooking, hand-thrown pottery and white-water kayaking. Here you will find organizations, resorts, museums, and schools that will teach you to ride horseback, to fly fish and mountain climb, to take better photographs, to cultivate a wildflower garden, or to build a boat. Here are some examples:

Eager to introduce your children to the mountains? Spend two days participating in a family workshop offered by the Appalachian Mountain Club or sign up for one of the AMC's guided overnight family hikes led by a professional botanist. Fascinated by prehistoric human development? Join one of the twenty week-long traveling archaeological seminars offered by the Crow Canyon Archaeological Center in Cortez, Colorado. Itineraries include field visits to major archaeological sites in Colorado, New Mexico, Arizona, and Utah.

At the John C. Campbell Folk School in Brasstown, North Carolina, you can participate in workshops that last from a weekend to two weeks. There are sessions centering on self-sufficiency skills, folk dancing, woodcarving, and many other traditional and modern crafts. Challenge yourself intellectually by enrolling in a class at Cornell's Adult University in Ithaca, New York, where you'll live in campus housing while participating in a week-long seminar such as "Liking Ike and Loving Lucy: American Politics and Popular Culture in the 1950s" or "The Mathematics of Everyday Things."

Great American Learning Adventures is chock full of educational opportunities that range from modest to ambitious. You can make such an experience either the main component of your vacation or a brief highlight. Some of the programs last only a few hours, while others are structured around a full day, a weekend, a week, or even longer.

The United States offers such a broad range of experiential learning opportunities that you're likely to find an appealing option no matter what your temperament, talents, or tastes. Active or observant by nature, young or old, there are activities available for anyone who wants to do more than simply take it easy. The mission of this book is to highlight those places and activities that teach us something about ourselves and our world.

Learning ought not to stop at eighteen or even eighty. It's a lifelong process, and many of us begin to discover its joys long after we've completed our formal education. This book can help us design vacations that satisfy our need to know by helping us to become actively involved in experiencing this country's vast historical, cultural, and natural legacies. There are programs here for people who like to work with their hands, for those who want to explore a slice of the past or an aspect of the environment, and for others who want to work up a sweat mastering the fundamentals of a new sport or increasing their proficiency in a familiar one.

There are opportunities for people of all ages and personal circumstances—for those on tight budgets and those who aren't, for senior citizens, families with children, single travelers, midlifers in need of renewal, and just about everyone else. To help you find programs that complement your interests, *Great American Learning Adventures* is organized thematically. The chapters include Intellectual Adventures, History and Folk Arts, Exploring the Arts, Outdoor Recreation, Natural History and Wilderness Challenges, Mind and Body, and Traveling. Each chapter includes options diverse in age appeal, location, expense, and period of time involved.

This book is for those of us who have come to see vacations as opportunities to enrich our lives not only by traveling to different places but by satisfying our need to discover new parts of ourselves. One of the very best ways to do that is to learn more about the subjects and places that intrigue us. The programs, workshops, and activities included in this book will suggest hundreds of ways to do just that, no matter what your interests or abilities.

Great American Learning Adventures can help you plan your vacation around a learning opportunity. Soon you will find yourself returning home from vacation with a renewed sense of who you are and what you can do. You will probably also find yourself looking forward to your next vacation, still another opportunity to explore a special interest, expose yourself to new ideas, or master a new skill or improve an old one. Another opportunity to grow and change.

How to Use This Book

Great American Learning Adventures is a reference book. We hope you will use it as a starting point in your research as you seek out just the right learning vacation. As you read through the opportunities described, here are a few points to keep in mind.

The prices stated were current when we went to press, but in most cases they are no longer accurate. Use them as a guide, with the expectation that the real fees will be somewhat higher.

Specific courses, workshops, and tours change from year to year. Consider those described in the text as examples of the types of programs the organization offers.

The descriptions are representative but not exhaustive. An organization may offer options other than those we have highlighted. If you want to bring your twelve-year-old along on a wilderness-skills program dubbed "adults only," ask if there are any other options suitable for younger participants.

Some of the programs require registration six months or more in advance. To avoid disappointment, try to plan early.

Many of the categories listed in the book are related to one another. Each organization is classified according to its major activity, but there is lots of overlap. For example, while there is a category of programs called "Painting," you will also find painting classes offered at some of the craft centers listed under

"Crafts." Similarly, some of the schools listed under "Canoeing, Kayaking, and Rafting" also offer courses in mountain biking. It makes sense to browse generously.

Taking these points into account, a good way to organize your research is to make a list of the possibilities that complement your interests, budget, and time constraints. Then contact the organizations, requesting their brochures and other literature. Most are staffed by friendly people, committed to helping you make a wise choice. If you have questions about whether you can handle a particular physical challenge or whether your skill level is appropriate for a certain class, ask. If you want to know what it's really like to be a part of one of the programs, ask the staff to give you the names of previous participants you can contact.

We hope that this book will inspire you to visit parts of this country you have not visited before, to take some risks, to try what you have not tried, and to explore further the skills and activities you already love.

1

Exploring Ideas

THE ASIMOV SEMINAR AT THE RENSSELAERVILLE INSTITUTE

Rensselaerville, New York 12147
(518) 797-3783

Founded by noted writer, thinker, and scientist Isaac Asimov in 1972, the Asimov Seminar is a five-day event held each summer at a small conference center in the foothills of the Catskill Mountains. Asimov, who thought of the program as a thinking person's vacation, directed the sessions himself until his death in 1992.

The seminars are highly interactive, with an emphasis on group problem solving. Each year participants focus on a different subject. The topic is usually, but not always, related either to science fiction or futurism or to a scientific or technological theme. In the past, seminars have concentrated on the politics of global warming, artificial intelligence, bioengineering, and the governance of a closed, limited colony in space.

The 1993 session, titled "First Contact: The Human Impact," revolved around the assumption that extraterrestrials had just contacted humanity. Seminar participants took on the role of humans reacting to this initial contact, while seminar advisers took on the role of the alien emissaries, responding to the actions of the participants. Advisers included science fiction writer Ben Bova and experts from the fields of search for extraterrestrial intelligence (SETI) and cultural anthropology.

The seminar experience is structured to raise questions regarding the social, economic, and political implications of the topic at hand. Participants are assigned to small groups, and each group is given a specific role to play and an initial task to tackle. From then on, the seminar takes on a momentum of its own. Groups disperse, form, and reform throughout the week. The atmosphere fosters creative problem solving, but there are no right or wrong answers.

Although the intellectual and philosophical exercise is genuine, the mood is lighthearted. Throughout their stay, participants have plenty of opportunity for informal interaction with the expert advisers. They also enjoy swimming, hiking, boating, tennis, and other easily accessible recreational activities.

Each summer the seminar attracts a diverse group of about eighty participants, ranging in age from about fifteen to eighty. Single people attend and so do couples. Parents bring their adult children, and grandparents bring teenaged grandchildren. No special interest is required, simply an enthusiasm for group participation and a willingness to think and learn. Each year the group is composed of approximately equal numbers of returning alumni and newcomers.

COST: The fee for the Asimov seminar is $625 per person, which covers lodgings for four nights, meals, and tuition. A discount is available to those who register before April 1.

NEW YORK OPEN CENTER

83 Spring St.
New York, New York 10012
(212) 219-2527

The New York Open Center is committed to the exploration of ideas that support the emergence of a fresh world-view "characterized by a renewed sense of caring for the earth." A nonprofit holistic learning institution, the center presents courses, workshops, and events throughout the year.

Course offerings are divided into the following categories: health, body, psyche, spirit, sociocultural issues, and the arts. Most courses involve four to eight consecutive weekly meetings. The subjects vary widely, but share an emphasis on intellectual, physical, and spiritual development. For those visiting the city for a short time, there are many weekend workshops to consider. A recent fall catalog listed over ninety different offerings, with titles that ranged from "A Day with a Russian Healer" to "New Experiments in Poetry," "Mediation for Beginners," and "Overcoming Procrastination."

The center also offers holiday celebrations, lunch-time lectures, video showings, and arts events. A schedule of concerts and performances includes comedy, gospel music, storytelling, dance, and much more. Lectures are often presented by well-known writers interested in introspection and personal growth, such as Gloria Steinem and M. Scott Peck.

The Open Center is a lively place to explore new ideas, a place where there is something happening nearly every day and night of the week.

COST: Fees vary widely. A course that meets once a week for six 1¼ hour sessions runs about $70. The fee for most full-day workshops is $95. For two- and three-day workshops, it ranges from $160 to $200, depending upon the length of the sessions. The admission to most evening events and presentations is $12.

CORNELL'S ADULT UNIVERSITY

626B Thurston Ave.
Ithaca, New York 14850-2490
(607) 255-6260

You can go back to school as a college student next summer by enrolling in Cornell's Adult University (CAU) for a week or more, studying with university faculty members, living in a dormitory, and enjoying the university's cultural and recreational facilities. The largest, most diverse college vacation program of its kind, CAU operates for four weeks each July and attracts about three hundred people each week. Sixty-five percent are couples, 35 percent are singles, and nearly half bring children. About half graduated from college in the 1960s, 1970s and 1980s, while approximately one-third graduated before 1950.

The way the program works, you select one course for each week you attend. In a typical week, you might choose from the following subjects: "Motherland, Fatherland: Nationalism and the Modern World," "A Week at the Opera," "The Dead Sea Scrolls," "Fiction Writing Workshop," "The Mathematics of Everyday Things," "Home Landscape Design Workshop," and "Outdoor Skills and Challenges." The course meets each day from morning to midafternoon. After that, you are free to explore all the amenities Cornell and the Ithaca area have to offer.

If you have children, they can participate in a caring youth program that gives them a taste of college life, exposes them to a variety of learning activities, and at the same time gives parents an opportunity to pursue their own interests while knowing the kids are in good hands nearby. A staff of more than thirty instructors and counselors tend to the needs of 120–130 youngsters each week. Children are divided into five age groups, beginning at age three. (Babysitting is available for younger children.) L'il Bears (3–5-year-olds), Tykes (kindergarten graduates and six-year-olds), and Sprouts (seven- and eight-year-olds) enjoy a program that includes varied learning activities, crafts projects, music, games, hikes, and other outings.

Junior Cornellians (9–12-year-olds) choose a specific morning course for each week they attend. Typical subjects include printmaking, an introduction to veterinary medicine, horse care and riding, international cooking, sailing, and an introduction to entomology. Afternoon and evening activities include sports, swimming, crafts, cookouts, visits to campus facilities, and presentations by members of the university community.

Whenever possible, children 3–12 years old are matched up with roommates from their own age group and then assigned to rooms adjacent to their parents, with whom they eat breakfast and dinner. Older children (13–16 years) live and dine with their counselors in separate quarters from their parents. Teens spend their mornings in a specific course, choosing from subjects such as field geology, theater, board sailing, and a rapid-reading workshop. Afternoons and evenings are devoted to field trips, sports, parties, and other activities determined by the group. A special one-day wilderness skills minicourse taught by members of Cornell's Outdoor Education Program is also incorporated in the program.

COST: The fee is $665–$765 per adult per week, depending upon the choice of accommodations. This covers tuition (a few courses carry an additional instruction or studio fee), lodgings, meals, evening programs, and use of most campus facilities and the campus bus system. There is no charge for infants and toddlers. The fee is $235 for 3–5-year-olds, $300 for kindergarten graduates to twelve-year-olds, and $355 for teens.

CHAUTAUQUA INSTITUTION

Chautauqua, New York 14722
(800) 836-ARTS

A summer center dedicated to the philosophy of life-long learning, the Chautauqua Institution is a 750-acre complex bordering Chautauqua Lake. A national historic landmark, it encompasses a complete self-contained Victorian village. Here visitors of all ages come to explore educational, religious, recreational, and cultural opportunities. During a typical summer, 7,500 people are in residence and more than 180,000 attend public events.

When you visit Chautauqua, you will leave your car outside the village. Admission is by gate ticket, which enables you to attend most events, including those held in the 5,500-seat amphitheater. Within the village, transportation is on foot or by bike. The winding pathways and lanes are lined with gingerbread-trimmed Victorian cottages, most of which also offer accommodations to visitors.

Ecumenical in spirit and practice, responsive to changing social forces, Chautauqua is a distinctly American institution. Originally founded as a vacation school for Sunday School teachers, today Chautauqua presents leaders of many religious faiths, from this country and abroad. As an early Chautauquan once explained, "The root idea of Chautauqua was to develop more of religion in the head without having any less of it in the heart."

During the 1880s, Chautauqua developed a reputation as a national forum for the latest thinking in politics, economics, science, and religion, a reputation that persists today. Each of the nine summer weeks is devoted to a different theme. Recent examples include "Racism in America," "Emerging Democracies of the World: The Unfinished Agenda," "The Chautauqua Conference on Children," and "Business: Threats and Opportunities for Corporate America." The oldest continuous book club in the country, the Chautauqua Literary and Scientific Circle began here in 1878 and continues today as a vibrant intellectual institution in its own right. Recent speakers featured at the circle's Roundtable Lecture Series have included William Least Heat Moon, author of *PrairyErth*, and Vice President Al Gore. In addition to the world-famous lecture series, Chautauqua offers art exhibits and its own symphony orchestra and theater and opera companies.

One of the most enticing aspects of the "Chautauqua Experience" is the Chautauqua Summer School, which offers about 175 week-long special studies classes. Enrollment is open to visitors of all ages regardless of their length of stay. Attend for a day or a week. Subjects range from ceramics to "The Changing Role of Women in Society" to aerobics to "Three Outsiders: Pascal, Kirkegaard, Weil." Courses fall into sixteen general subject headings: art; basic skills; business and finance; the Chautauqua Classic Film Festival; dance; education; family; foreign languages; games, recreation, and fitness; handicrafts and hobbies; health; literature and writing; music; personal and professional growth; religion; and special interest.

Chautauqua also has extensive recreational facilities, including a twenty-seven-hole golf course, twelve tennis courts, and a lakefront sports club that offers lawn bowling, sailboat and canoe rentals, shuffleboard, bridge, and league play for softball and volleyball games. Bicycles are available for rental, and there are four public beaches and plenty of opportunity for fishing and jogging.

Truly a learning center for people of all ages, Chautauqua provides a supportive environment for young people as well as adults. Children are exposed to many new experiences and ideas, both with their families and on their own through the wealth of organized youth activities, including arts experiences, swimming instruction, water sports, nature studies, crafts, and team sports. There are structured morning and afternoon programs for children from 2½ to fifteen years old. Separate recreation centers meet the needs of junior and senior high school age Chautauquans and college-age youth, many of whom also participate in adult activities.

The institution issues an accommodations directory listing

privately owned rental properties within the village. The Chautauqua Accommodations Referral Service will assist you in finding lodgings that satisfy your time frame, location, and price range. Write to the service care of the Chautauqua Institution or call (716) 357-6204.

COST: Entrance to the Chautauqua Institution is by gate ticket, which covers admission to the grounds, lectures and exhibits, and events in the amphitheater. Tickets are available by the day, weekend, week, or entire season. Day tickets cost $8.25 (8:00 A.M.–8:00 P.M.), $17 (after 5:00 P.M.), and $25.25 (day/evening). Weekend tickets cost $37 for adults and $17 for minors (13–17 years old). A one-week adult ticket is $140 for adults and $54 for minors. Children twelve and under are always admitted free. Separate tickets are required to attend theater and opera performances. The tuition for special courses, which varies, is paid in advance for the week or at the door if attending just one session. There are separate fees for organized youth activities.

THE CHARLOTTE YIDDISH INSTITUTE AT WILDACRES

The Jewish Community Center of Charlotte
P.O. Box 13369
Charlotte, North Carolina 28270
(704) 366-5564

Each August the four-day-long Charlotte Yiddish Institute convenes at the Wildacres Retreat in Little Switzerland, North Carolina, a mountaintop conference center operated on a nonprofit basis for the betterment of human understanding. The institute welcomes men and women eager to enhance their knowledge and use of the Yiddish language and culture. The program is composed of faculty lectures, Yiddish language classes (beginning, intermediate, and advanced levels), Yiddish culture workshops, concerts, and folk singing and dancing. There are both daily and Shabbat services.

The spirit and feel of the institute are best described in the words of a veteran participant who writes, "Imagine one hundred men and women, Jews from all across the United States, spending four days together. . . . Imagine those one hundred people to be the kinds of warm, caring friends with whom you used to spend your summers at a very special camp. . . . They chat and smile and hug a lot. . . but they really can't wait to sing and dance and pray and study and learn together."

During the institute, participants are housed in one of Wildacres' two modern lodges. Located in the heart of the Blue Ridge Mountains, the fourteen-hundred-acre site has many scenic trails to explore, just perfect for contemplative nature walks.

COST: The fee of $195 covers tuition, shared double room with private bath, kosher meals, and gratuities.

ROWE CAMP & CONFERENCE CENTER

Kings Highway Road, Box 273
Rowe, Massachusetts 01367
(413) 339-4954

What's the purpose of attending a program at the Rowe Camp & Conference Center in rural western Massachusetts? The answer can be distilled into a simple series of words: retreat, relax, reflect, relate, revitalize. Rowe is affiliated with the Unitarian Universalist Association, whose values of respect for each person's belief system and unique view of the world and whose recognition of the importance of community in our lives as human beings form the foundation of the Rowe philosophy. Here, in a safe and supportive environment, visitors explore their own creativity, often discovering a purpose in life that extends beyond their personal concerns.

To facilitate self-discovery and the joy of learning what it feels like to experience a sense of community with others in a world that teaches us to stick it out on our own, Rowe offers a wide selection of weekend and holiday workshops and activities throughout the year. Many of them fashion a role for children, involving them in parts of the program and providing them with alternative activities at other times.

A sampling of weekend workshops described in a recent catalog gives you a feel for the Rowe experience. A rabbi teaches "Rosh Hashanah and the Days of Awe," leading participants on a search for authentic Jewish forms in the modern world. A distinguished composer helps us explore the relationship between the body's energy centers, color, scent, and sound in "Sounding the Inner Landscape: Music and Healing." A psychology and literature professor, a Unitarian Universalist minister, a native American, and a meditation expert join together for "Council for Men: From Isolation to Male Community."

During the summer, Rowe offers a number of camp sessions, each one geared toward a specific population. These include Young People's Camp (for children entering grades four, five, and six), Junior High Camp (entering grades seven, eight, and nine), and Senior High Camp (entering grades ten, eleven, and twelve). Adult sessions include Recovery Camp, Liberation Camp (open to men, women, and children, it explores issues raised by the women's liberation movement and encourages the liberation of men, children, and teenagers), Women's Circles (women exploring, redefining, and celebrating what it means to be a woman), and a Labor Day Retreat for Gay Men (men rediscovering creativity and joy). In addition to exercises, workshops, and rituals designed to foster self-awareness, all of the camps offer lots of just plain fun activities.

Accommodations at Rowe consist of dormitory housing in cabins and a farmhouse (bring your own bedding). A limited number of single- and double-occupancy private rooms are also available.

COST: Tuition (program cost) is charged on a sliding scale. For example, for those with a gross annual income of $20,000–$35,000, the fee for a weekend program is $145; for those with income above $35,000, the charge is $165. Housing and meals are charged at the same rate for everyone. A weekend in a winterized cabin, including all meals, is $90. There are substantial discounts for children.

VERMONT OFF BEAT

2 Church St.
Burlington, Vermont 05401
(802) 863-2535

Vermont Off Beat offers interactive vacation workshops based at country inns throughout the state. Each package focuses on a specific subject, using the state of Vermont—its people, environment, and social, cultural, and historical features—as a learning laboratory. The programs are designed for those who enjoy lively discussions with a group of like-minded people in an atmosphere that combines good food and pleasant lodgings with a lovely rural setting.

Most programs begin with dinner Friday evening and end by midafternoon Sunday. Groups generally consist of twelve to twenty people led by a group facilitator who is often joined by local residents with a special knowledge of the program topic. While topics change from year to year, typical sessions focus on building techniques, gardening, painting, crafts, music, and

Vermont businesses. Workshops are scheduled from May to October.

During "Gardens by Design," participants settle into the Old Tavern in Grafton to learn about the strategic planning that goes into producing an impressive garden. The workshop is led by a professional landscape artist and his wife, both of whom have written extensively on the subject. Activities begin with a slide show depicting English, French, and American gardens. During a walk to local gardens, participants study site analysis and property measurement. The group also travels fifteen miles from Grafton to visit two outstanding gardens, one of which is the creation of the program instructors. Participants are asked to bring with them photos of their own garden and a scaled drawing of the area that they would most like to improve.

Other workshop options include spending a weekend learning all about making wool from a woman who runs a home-based spinning and weaving business, learning the secrets of fly fishing and fly tying from an experienced fisherman, and learning about indigenous folk music from an innkeeper who also happens to be a concert pianist and singer. If you have ever fantasized about opening a country inn, "Innkeeping as a Career" offers an intensive behind-the-scenes look at the problems and pleasures of the business.

COST: The fee for the "Gardens by Design" workshop is $315, which covers tuition, double-occupancy room (single available at higher rate), and breakfasts and dinners from Friday evening to Sunday morning. The fee for "Innkeeping as a Career," including tuition, lodgings, and all meals Friday through Sunday, is $299.

THE BREAD LOAF WRITERS' CONFERENCE

Middlebury College
Middlebury, Vermont 05753-6125
(802) 388-371, ext. 5286

For twelve days each August, fledgling and established writers gather together in a lush Vermont setting to learn from one another and from an impressive lineup of professional writers through lectures, discussion groups, workshops, panels, and readings. Some of the better known writers who attended the conference in their formative years include Eudora Welty, Theodore Roethke, Anne Sexton, Joan Didion, and Tim O'Brien. Writers who have served on the faculty include John Irving, John Gardner, Stanley Elkin, Gail Godwin, and, again, Tim O'Brien.

The Bread Loaf Writers' Conference provides an opportunity for writers not to write but instead to talk with one another about writing, both as a craft and a profession. The faculty is composed of fourteen senior staff members and fourteen associate staff members, all of whom are both professional writers and professional teachers. Their efforts are supplemented by agents, editors, and publishers who frequently make short visits to participate on panels or to give lectures.

To be admitted to the conference as a contributor, you need to submit an application accompanied by samples of your writing (twenty pages of a novel or a nonfiction piece, 2–3 short stories, or 8–15 poems) in the genre in which you wish assistance. According to the conference admissions material, "Admission will be offered to those who, in the judgment of the Admissions Board, show serious intent and promise in their work." Each contributor meets privately for about one hour with a staff member who has read his or her manuscript and who is prepared to point out strengths and weaknesses and suggest possible improvements. If you wish to attend without bringing a manuscript, you can apply as an auditor.

Participants take meals together at the Bread Loaf Inn and

live in a cluster of country buildings within walking distance of one another on the the isolated mountain campus of Middlebury College. Most of the rooms are doubles, so you will probably be matched with a roommate. Tennis, volleyball, hiking, fishing, and swimming in chilly mountain streams all offer a break from the formal conference activities.

COST: Contributors pay $1,375 for tuition, room, and board. Auditors pay $1,305. Financial aid is available in the form of fellowships, tuition scholarships, and work-study scholarships. Write to the conference requesting application details by February 1 of the year in which you wish to apply.

LIFELONG LEARNING CENTER

Northland College
Ashland, Wisconsin 54806
(715) 682-1260

Each summer Northland College hosts "Wordscapes: Writing and the World of Nature," a writing institute for people from all over the country who love the outdoors and want to write about feelings and experiences related to the natural world. Sponsored by the college, the Sigurd Olson Environmental Institute, and *Backpacker* magazine, the twelve-day program is limited to thirty participants to assure maximum staff/student contact. To encourage younger writers, half of the places are reserved for those of high school and college age. The remaining places are filled by people ranging in age from their twenties into their mid-fifties and sometimes beyond.

Faculty members are published writers who assist students in all steps of the writing process, from generating ideas to composing the piece to finding a publisher. The highlight of the institute is a four-day writing adventure among the Apostle Islands in Lake Superior, twenty-five miles from the campus. Participants travel in small groups. Some board a sailboat, others paddle kayaks, and still others travel by voyageur canoe or ferry. Each participant works on a specific project during the trip, choosing from one of four genres: personal essay, environmental journalism, adventure/travel writing, and interpretive essay. On returning to the campus, students share and revise their first drafts together.

The institute runs from the end of July through the first week in August. Register early to be assured a place. The College for Lifelong Learning also offers a broad selection of other programs throughout the year. Some take the form of courses that run once or twice a week for four to eight weeks, but many others are structured as one- or two-day workshops. A catalog listing these opportunities, all of them scheduled for late afternoon hours, evenings, or weekends, is published twice a year. Some of the full-day workshops described in a recent issue included "The Internal Artist," "Dance You Can Grow With," and "The Art of Book Making." Half-day sessions were offered in "Juggling—All Levels" and "Bicycle Maintenance and Repair."

COST: Tuition for "Wordscapes" is $510. Participants register for meals and lodgings separately.

2 | History and Folk Arts

Folk Arts and Living History

THE CLEARING

P.O. Box 65
Ellison Bay, Wisconsin 54210
(414) 854-4088

Calling itself "A Private School for Contemplation and Study," the Clearing does not take its name from a field or open space in the forest. Instead, the name refers to "a clearing of the mind," reflecting the intentions of founder Jens Jensen, a renowned landscape architect who in 1935 retired at age seventy-five from a successful Chicago-area business and moved north to found a special school.

An early conservationist, Danish-born Jensen has been called a man ahead of his time. He firmly believed that the quality of one's life deepens the better one comes to know and respect the natural world. He believed that environments have a profound effect on people and that clear thinking derives from an understanding of one's own regional ecology and culture. Convinced there must be "natural" places where people can withdraw from the man-made world and experience a sense of renewal, he established the Clearing, a school in the woods. The campus is a wild place encompassing more than a hundred acres of meadows, deep woods, and towering bluffs overlooking the Green Bay waters of Lake Michigan.

Fashioned from native materials put together by hand, the log and stone buildings that serve as dormitories, dining room, and classrooms are listed on the National Register of Historic Places. Up to thirty students visit at a time, combining an escape from the stresses of a fast-paced world with a learning experience. Over the years, thousands have come to study the arts, nature, music, literature, writing, and other humanities in a setting that encourages "a better appreciation of the eternal cycle of life about them and about themselves."

An adult school of discovery, the Clearing was influenced by the folk schools of Jensen's native Denmark. Classes are small and students learn in a cooperative, familylike atmosphere. Most courses run for a week, although some are shorter. Courses are offered in watercolor and landscape painting, weaving, ecology, photography, writing, woodcarving, philosophy, and other subjects.

The Clearing is open from May through October. Representative courses include "Gardening with Herbs," "Introductory Geology," "Spring Birds of Northern Woods and Waters," "Norwegian Decorative Painting," "Navajo Silversmithing," "Chamber Music for String Instruments," "Aspects of Drama—From Script to Peninisula Stage," and "The Illustrated Journal."

COST: The fee for a week-long class, including tuition, room, and board (with the exception of Thursday evening supper) is $425 per person in a dormitory, $465 per person in a double room.

JOHN C. CAMPBELL FOLK SCHOOL

Route 1, Box 14-A
Brasstown, North Carolina 28902
(800) 562-2440

Modeled on the Danish folk-school concept, which stresses learning through the "living word" or personal exposure to the teacher, instead of through lectures, exams, books, and grades, the John C. Campbell Folk School attracts an average of four thousand students a year. They come from all over the country and abroad to participate in life-enrichment activities in a magnificent mountain setting. The mission of the school, "to awaken, enlighten, and enliven" each person who visits, is accomplished through a variety of hands-on experiences.

The school is well known for its craft, music, and dance instruction. It offers weekend, one-week, and two-week courses throughout the year in crafts, music, dance, gardening, and folklore. Classes are open to students of all abilities who are least eighteen years old. Participants register for one class per session. The experience is intense and specific.

There is no set curriculum, but course topics from recent years offer insight into the types of skills that are taught. During a week-long banjo-making workshop, participants learn to cut, shape, and construct a wooden banjo similar to one used in the Appalachian Mountains from before the Civil War until into the 1930s. A blacksmithing class focuses on the creation of early American hardware, while fiber classes are offered in broom making, knitting, bookbinding, bobbin lace making, smocking, weaving, and several types of basket making. Sessions are also offered in woodcarving and woodworking. More unusual workshops are devoted to hammock making, kaleidoscope making, and the creation of metal fetishes and images. A class called "Appalachian Music Week" emphasizes beginning and intermediate levels of clawhammer banjo, fiddle, mountain dulcimer, and rhythm guitar. There are also several special dance weeks, which combine instruction in traditional Appalachian square and big-circle dances with clogging and buck dancing, group singing, and an introduction to a variety of folk instruments. All in all, the selections are extremely extensive and there are options for all ability levels.

The courses, however, are just part of the experience. Beyond the specific subject they come to study, students get a taste of life in the Appalachian foothills and an introduction to mountain culture. Following the Danish tradition, each day begins with prebreakfast exercise and "morningsong," a time to share music and to discuss folklore, history, and or perhaps an instructor's work or philosophy. Students attend classes from 9:00 A.M. to 12:00 P.M. and 1:30 P.M. to 4:30 P.M. An assortment of events is scheduled for late afternoons and evenings: slide shows by instructors, videos of Appalachian entertainers, historical lectures, demonstrations, music programs, dances, and visits to a nearby planetarium. Students are also free to continue working on their projects after class.

The 365-acre campus has fully equipped studios and one of the finest hardwood dance floors in the country. Students live in one of the eight on-campus buildings set aside for guest housing. There is also a campground. Meals, with an emphasis on southern cooking, are served family style in the communal dining hall.

COST: Tuition is $110 for most weekend workshops and $200 for most one-week workshops. Room rates vary depending upon accommodations chosen. A double room with a shared bathroom is $75 per person for a weekend and $219 per person for a one-week workshop. Meals are included in the housing charge.

LANDIS VALLEY MUSEUM

2451 Kissel Hill Road
Lancaster, Pennsylvania 17601
(717) 569-0401

Dedicated to chronicling the history and traditions of Pennsylvania German rural heritage, the Landis Valley Museum encompasses more than twenty buildings, as well as adjoining farmsteads complete with historical breeds of animals and heirloom plants. During the 1700s, boatloads of German immigrants came ashore in Philadelphia, and by 1790 they accounted for 40 percent of the population of southeastern Pennsylvania. The vast majority of them earned a living by becoming farmers. They and their descendants developed folk traditions, decorative arts, and even a language (Pennsylvania German) based on their heritage. In interpreting and preserving the Pennsylvania German rural life, museum staffers demonstrate many of the traditional crafts and skills.

If you would like to try your own hand, you can enroll in one of the craft classes offered on Saturdays during the summer. Most of the classes take the form of a single full-day session, although several are divided into two half-day sessions scheduled for consecutive Saturday mornings. The subjects include tinsmithing, wood graining, blacksmithing, fraktur (a special form of decorative writing developed by the Pennsylvania Germans), redware pottery, leatherworking, rug hooking, cabinetmaking, woodcarving, bobbin lace making, and paper cutting. There are also special hands-on living-history sessions for children called "Stepping Back in Time."

In addition, each June the museum hosts the Institute of Pennsylvania Rural Life and Culture, a five-day-long educational program designed to pass on a working knowledge of eighteenth- and nineteenth-century American crafts. Participants register for either an all-day activity or for one morning and one afternoon workshop, and they stay with this choice throughout the institute. Subjects include many of those listed for the summer craft classes as well as others, such as fireplace cookery, gunstock carving, metal casting, bread baking, basketry, and eighteenth-century crewelwork. Class sizes are limited and many of the sessions are suitable for beginning, intermediate, and advanced students.

COST: The instruction fee for each summer adult craft class is $22. The fee for the children's course is $4.75. The fee for the five-day institute, which covers instruction and most meals, is $170. Most craft classes and institute workshops also carry a materials fee that is paid directly to the instructor.

OLD STURBRIDGE VILLAGE

1 Old Sturbridge Village Road
Sturbridge, MA 01566
(508) 347-5383

An outdoor living-history museum detailing everyday life in an early nineteenth century rural New England community, Old Sturbridge Village (OSV) covers over two hundred acres and includes more than forty buildings. Most visitors spend at least half a day exploring the farms, shops, houses, and meetinghouses, learning about life in the 1830s from historically costumed interpreters.

The museum's education department offers a number of workshops for visitors who want a hands-on experience or who want to get a more in-depth understanding of a particular aspect of nineteenth-century life. Winter Discovery Days, held on Saturdays from late February through March, are designed specifically for families. Children in grades three to eight, accompanied by an adult, can join in the 1½-hour-long Discovery Workshops, which combine hands-on activities in the Museum Education Building with a brief tour of the village. Subjects include "Fibers and Fashions," "Hearth and Home," and "Learning a Trade."

Kids and parents who want to explore a topic in greater detail can preregister for one of the three-hour-long Craftshops for Families. Recent subjects have included "Bandboxes: The Luggage of the 1830s," in which parent/child teams actually make a bandbox together, and "Shadows, Shades, and Silhouettes," where families make shadow puppets and recreate an 1830s entertainment.

Visitors fourteen years and older can enroll in Crafts-at-Close-Range. Although structured at an adult pace, many of these six-hour-long single-day workshops are geared toward people with little or no previous experience. Advanced sessions are also available. Each session is limited to four to ten participants, depending upon the craft in question. Subjects include coopering (learning to make wooden buckets), spinning, bandboxes, blacksmithing, sewing, tinsmithing, balloons (make and launch toy hot-air balloons), wool dying, and hearth cooking. The workshops are offered on Saturdays from November through April.

OSV also sponsors other educational activities throughout the year, including an annual Garden Planning Day early in March focusing on historic plants. Resident and guest horticulturists present workshops and illustrated lectures on subjects varying from medicinal herb gardens to garden structures (how to build your own trelliswork, arbors, and fences). A three-day-long Design and Decoration Weekend is also held in the spring, concentrating on the restoration of old houses.

With the exception of Garden Planning Day, all of the programs described above require preregistration. For more information on Winter Discovery Days, Crafts-at-Close-Range, Garden Planning Day, and the Design and Decoration Weekend, write to the Marketing Department at OSV requesting specific brochures and program dates.

COST: The fee for Crafts-at-Close-Range is $60 per class, plus a materials fee for some classes.

NORLANDS LIVING HISTORY CENTER

Route 2, Box 1740
Livermore Falls, Maine 04254
(207) 897-4366

A year-round working farm complete with oxen, horses, sheep, and cows, Norlands Living History Center offers an unusual weekend program for adults and families who want to experience life 1870s style. As a participant in a Norlands Adult Live-In, you will spend seventy hours immersed in nineteenth-century rural Maine life. For three days and three nights, you assume the role of a member of a Victorian-era farm family, tending to chores and experiencing the influence of nineteenth-century economics and social customs. You will live in Victorian-era quarters (complete with outhouses) and eat authentic farm fare.

The tasks you are assigned will be appropriate to a person of your age and gender living on a New England farm one hundred-plus years ago. There are animals to be cared for, wool to spin, quilts to stitch, and, of course, meals to cook. Depending upon the season, you might be involved in plowing, planting, haying, harvesting, cutting wood, or ice cutting. You will attend an 1870s vintage church service and learn about rural schooling of the period. You will stretch your imagination through role playing, storytelling, and creative dramatics, three of the tools used to enliven the Live-In experience.

Live-Ins are open to "teachers, adventure seekers, and families." Each session is limited to fourteen participants.

COST: The fee for the Live-In, which includes three nights' lodging, all meals, and instructional materials, is $195 for adults, $150 for teens, and $100 for children 8–12 years.

HANCOCK SHAKER VILLAGE

P.O. Box 898
Pittsfield, Massachusetts 01202
(413) 443-0188

Explore Shakerism and nineteenth-century culture and agriculture at Hancock Shaker Village, a restored site encompassing twenty buildings on twelve hundred acres of land. Occupied for 170 years by a celibate, communal, religious sect, the Village operates today as a museum of Shaker history, life, and work.

From late September through mid-December, the Village conducts a series of workshops designed to introduce Shaker crafts. Although specific topics vary, the range of crafts remains constant and includes blacksmithing, timber framing, chair caning and seat weaving, four-harness loom weaving, woodworking, working with dried flowers and herbs, and basket making. Sessions run from one to five days.

In February the Village opens for Winter Week, a series of activities including tours and talks, craft demonstrations, farm activities, and craft sessions. Learn how the Shakers passed the winter months by watching the farmers demonstrate flax breaking, bean flailing, and other nineteenth-century agricultural practices. Observe craftspeople at work indoors making baskets, oval boxes, and furniture. Listen to Shaker music and learn about Shaker worship practices.

The schedule also includes hands-on one-day workshops for children and for familiies. For example, kids ages 7–12 might sign up for an Easter-basket workshop, creating their own baskets from natural and dyed reed, while parents and kids ages 6–10 might choose to participate together in a weaving workshop, spinning wool and working on a loom. One- and two-day-long adult winter workshops are also offered.

COST: Sample workshop fees, including instruction and materials, run as follows: "Dried Flower and Herb

Garland," $25; "Shaker Chair Seat Weaving," $40; "Shaker Ash Trinket Basket," $65; "Basic Blacksmithing," $150; "Basic Shaker Oval Box Construction," $150.

DANEBOD FAMILY CAMPS

c/o Gerry Werth
3924 46th Ave.
Minneapolis, Minnesota 55406-3604
(612) 724-9564

True to the tradition of the Danish folk schools founded in Denmark in the nineteenth century, the Danebod Family Camps fosters personal growth in an atmosphere characterized by freedom of thought and mutual trust and concern. Held on the campus of the historic Danebod Folk School in Tyler, Minnesota, the camp is not affiliated with a religion or nationality, although many Danish Lutherans attend. People of all ages and backgrounds join together to share their interests, skills, and experiences in an activity-filled format that fosters friendship and fellowship.

The camp operates for three one-week sessions each summer. Mornings are filled with walking, biking, singing, and dancing, followed by games for the children and large-scale discussion groups for the adult campers, who zero in on subjects like "Mothers and Daughters" and "Moral Dilemmas."

After lunch, campers can try their hand at a variety of crafts. Specific activities vary from one session to another, but typical options include batik, woodcarving, making Danish paper hearts or hair ornaments, wheat weaving, copper enameling, mask making, leatherworking, snowshoe making, model rocket building, as well as crafts especially for children. Unlike some camps that cater to adults, Danebod does not require you to register for crafts in advance. Choose whatever looks interesting on the spot.

Evenings are filled with more singing and dancing, followed by stories and songs around the campfire, and then still another round of dancing for the truly energetic.

Campers are housed in the school dormitory. There is also space to set up your own camper or tent, if you prefer. Meals, including Danish specialties, are prepared and served by local cooks in the dining hall of the dormitory building. Babysitting is provided in the dorm nightly from 8:00 P.M. to midnight.

COST: The cost of the program includes tuition, housing (or camping space), and all meals. Fees run as follows: age 18 and up, $165; age 11–17, $140; age 6–10, $130; age 1–5, $85; below age 1, free. Local residents can participate in all programs for $5 (no meals).

COUNTRY DANCE AND SONG SOCIETY

**17 New South St.
Northampton, Massachusetts 01060
(413) 584-9913**

A national association of individuals and groups interested in traditional, historical, and contemporary English and American folk dance, song, and instrumental music, the Country Dance and Song Society sponsors week-long summer camps for adults, as well as several sessions for families. Participants spend a week in an outdoor setting, where the air is filled with the sounds of fiddle and flute, hammered dulcimer, mandolin, English concertina, and many other traditional musical instrments.

For the past sixty years the society has held its summer program at Pinewoods Camp near Plymouth, Massachusetts, where spacious wooden dance pavilions serve as classrooms, nestled in a woodland setting bordering two lakes. Each of the seven sessions has a different theme: Early Music Week, Folk Music Week, Family Week, American Dance Week, English Dance Week, English and American Dance Week, and Campers' Week. Each session is staffed by visiting singers, dancers, and musical ensembles from all around the country, many of whom serve as both instructors and performers.

The American Dance Week schedule features contras, squares, Cajun dance and clogging, and workshops in calling dancing, playing music, and singing. During Folk Music Week, the emphasis is on the music of the Irish, English, Anglo-American, and Scottish traditions and instruction is offered in instrumental and vocal music, songwriting, and dance, with evening dances designed to accommodate both beginning and experienced dancers.

For the past few years, the society has also run two camp sessions in West Virginia. The Buffalo Gap Camp for the Cultural Arts is sited on two hundred acres of woods and grassy slopes, highlighted by a huge open-air dance floor, swimming pool, and sauna. During English and American Dance Week, there are workshops in morris, garland, and step dancing, singing, instrumental music, band dynamics, leadership, and dance calling. During Family Week there are some times of the day when the whole camp gathers together, and other times when the group divides according to age and interests. Children three years old and up participate in craft, storytelling, music, and dance classes, while teenagers and adults choose from workshops such as English country dance, West Virginia squares, dance bands, clogging, and singing.

During camp, participants, who bring their own blankets and linens, live in shared houses, cabins, or small bunk rooms with bathrooms nearby. At Buffalo Gap, campers who prefer more privacy are welcome to bring a tent. Meals are prepared by professional cooks and are eaten together in the dining hall. There is a space on the registration form to indicate whether you prefer a meat or vegetarian menu. All campers, including children, are assigned a simple housekeeping job, which usually takes about half an hour each day.

COST: The fee for the adult weeks (with the exception of Campers' Week, which operates at a much reduced rate) ranges from $415 to $470, which covers room, board, and tuition. The fee for the Family Week Program varies according to age, ranging from $152 for a three-year-old to $435 for an adult at Buffalo Gap.

AUGUSTA HERITAGE CENTER

Davis Elkins College
Elkins, West Virginia 26241-3996
(304) 636-1903

Dedicated to the preservation and perpetuation of many different folk arts reflecting a variety of traditions, the Augusta Heritage Center is a leading educational program in the field of folk arts. Augusta (the name given to this part of West Virginia in Colonial times, when many of its cultural traditions developed) is dedicated to passing on the values, skills, and sense of craft of the early Appalachian settlers.

For seven weeks each year, the center, which is located on a wooded college campus, pulsates with excitement and energy as students of varied backgrounds explore Appalachian, Cajun, Irish, and other cultural traditions. Over two thousand participants from more than forty states and a dozen different countries traveled to West Virginia last summer to immerse themselves in the sights and sounds of the traditional arts at Augusta. Many of the instructors who travel here to teach traditional music, dance, and crafts are highly accomplished musicians and artisans who grew up in a particular cultural tradition, learning their skills from older members of their families.

The summer session runs for five weeks and offers nearly one hundred classes, accommodating all levels of expertise in music, dance, crafts, and folklore. A sampling of classes includes: quilt making; stone masonry; Appalachian literature; autoharp; treenware; woodslore, herbs, and foraging; reed making and pipe repair; Gaelic language and song; Scottish fiddle; old-time banjo; rag-rug weaving; English concertina; clogging; harmonica; traditional paper cutting; white-oak rib basketry; southern harmony; contradanse piano and fiddle; African-American storytelling; fiddle and bow repair; and Appalachian singing.

Each week begins with a Sunday evening orientation session, followed by a reception, square dance, and jam session. Participants enroll in one full-time class. With the exception of some craft classes that meet for two weeks, all classes are one week long. Classes are in session Monday through Friday and most meet for four to six hours daily. In addition, students can explore a different tradition by enrolling in late afternoon and evening mini-classes, which meet four times during the week. Evenings feature a lively assortment of concerts, dances, and informal music making.

A Folk Arts for Kids class, geared to boys and girls 8–13 years old, is offered each week of the summer session. Kids are in class six hours a day. A typical week offers an introduction to Appalachian folk arts, games, dances, crafts, storytelling, and songs. Augusta also runs a highly successful Elderhostel program. (Elderhostel is an organization that arranges learning vacations for people over 60 at various locations throughout the U.S. and abroad. For information write: Elderhostel, 80 Boylston St., Boston, MA 02116.)

Each April the center holds Spring Dulcimer Week, a mix of classes, jam sessions, and concerts, with workshops for beginning through advanced hammered dulcimer and mountain dulcimer players. In October, musicians gather for Old-Time Week to participate in small classes in old-time Appalachian fiddle, guitar and banjo, stringband ensemble playing, singing sessions, and bass workshops.

COST: Tuition for week-long courses is $230–$240. Tuition for most mini-courses is $30–$40. Cost of room and board (double-occupancy dormitory rooms and cafeteria meals) is $165 per week.

Historic Preservation and Archeology

CROW CANYON ARCHAEOLOGICAL CENTER

23390 County Road K
Cortez, Colorado
(800) 422-8975

Dedicated to archaeological research and education, Crow Canyon Archaeological Center has established a program that links laypersons with professional archaeologists in scientific research. The goal of the research is to reconstruct the cultural and natural environment of the Anasazi, the prehistoric people who lived in the "Four Corners Region," where Colorado, New Mexico, Utah, and Arizona meet, for over a thousand years until they vanished toward the end of the thirteenth century. By gathering information, scientists develop an understanding of the changes that evolved in ancient pueblo life.

Crow Canyon offers adult research programs in excavation and environmental archaeology. Both begin with a half-day activity called "Inquiries into the Past," a hands-on session during which participants are introduced to southwestern prehistory by examining artifacts, reconstructing the life ways they represent, and figuring out their chronological sequence. Participants in the excavation program spend the rest of their week excavating prehistoric Anasazi ruins in the field and analyzing artifacts in the lab, gathering information about community organization during the final occupation of the Mesa Verde region. The environmental archaeology program focuses on the Anasazis' relationship to the natural world. Participants contribute to one of several ongoing studies. Activities include documenting dead wood accumulation, measuring construction timbers, and monitoring the changing vegetative and reproductive status of key native plant resources.

Each August the center offers a family week. Children in the fourth grade and older can enroll in this week-long experience accompanied by parents or grandparents. Fourth through sixth graders excavate a simulated dig, participate in a simulated lab, tour the Anasazi Heritage Center, and learn to make pottery. Older children work beside adults in the field and in the lab. Everyone joins together for evening programs and a trip to Mesa Verde National Park, a repository of Anasazi cliff dwellings.

Crow Canyon also presents a series of cultural explorations led by native American scholars and specialists with the focus on native American culture and traditional crafts. Recent week-long workshops have included "Traditions from the Earth," in which participants collect local materials and construct Anasazi-style pottery, and "Woven Containers from the Natural World," in which they make baskets from sumac and explore the art of Anasazi weaving by working with yucca fibers. Other options include traveling seminars that visit many of the Southwest's most important archaeological sites and cultural areas.

COST: The program fee covers tuition, food, lodging, and transportation after arrival in Cortez. With the exception of the traveling programs, shared accommodations are provided in comfortable Navajo log hogans or in the Crow Canyon lodge. Both hogans and lodge have shared modern shower facilities. Participants in the cultural explorations workshops can choose to pay a supplementary fee if they prefer motel lodgings. The fee for the adult research programs is $750 per week. During family week the fee is $750 per adult, $350–$400 per child. The fee for the workshops in pottery and basketry is $1,095.

COLONIAL WILLIAMSBURG FOUNDATION

Department of Archaeological Research
P.O. Box 1776
Williamsburg, Virginia 23187
(804) 229-1000

Get some hands-on exposure to the basics of archaeological excavation and laboratory procedures by participating
in "Learning Weeks in Archaeology," a two-week course
designed to introduce individuals to the goals and methods of
archaeological research at Colonial Williamsburg.

Participants learn how to take field notes, do map finds,
and identify artifacts. They tour area archaeological sites and
museums accompanied by professional staff. These experiences
lead to an understanding of the ways in which scholars use
archaeology to reconstruct eighteenth-century and Colonial
daily life as it was lived in Virginia's Colonial capital. Specific
projects vary, but in the past participants have searched for the
remains of an eighteenth-century slave house and uncovered
evidence of a late eighteenth century blacksmithing operation.

The program is conducted several times each year between
May and October. Participation is open to anyone sixteen years
of age or older. Younger teens may attend with a participating
adult. Prior experience is not required.

COST: Tuition, which covers training, lectures, tours,
Sunday night reception, an evening at a Colonial tavern, and
admission to all Historic Area attractions, is $550. It is also
possible to attend for just the first week of any session. Tuition
for the one-week program is $350.

CENTER FOR AMERICAN ARCHEOLOGY

Box 366
Kampsville, Illinois 62053
(618) 653-4316

Some of the first inhabitants of the North American continent were drawn to the lower Illinois River valley by its abundant food resources as far back as twelve thousand years ago. The first visitors were nomadic, but several thousand years later, native populations began to establish year-round settlements. Located in the valley, the Center for American Archeology has become a major contributor to modern archeological theory and methods through its intensive studies of the vast resources at its doorstep.

The center currently provides students and professional archeologists an opportunity to participate in excavations of the Middle to Late Archaic quasar site, documenting the culture of the peoples who populated this location approximately 6,320 years ago. Participants who attend the center's programs develop insight into the cultural traditions of ancient America by becoming involved in an ongoing research effort supervised by professional scientists and educators.

Throughout June, July, and August, the Center offers week-long residential field schools, open to those high school age and up. Participants divide their daytime hours between site excavation and laboratory work, which involves cleaning, cataloging, and tabulating artifacts recovered at the dig site. One evening is usually devoted to an ecology hike, designed to introduce you to plant and animal resources important to the area's prehistoric residents. Other evenings are given over to lectures by staff members and visiting scientists. You'll also become familiar with the history of the region by manipulating artifacts and data from the center's collections and by using ancient technologies to reconstruct ceramics, lithics (stone tools), and prehistoric dwellings.

COST: The fee for a week of field school is $450 for adults, $375 for high school students. A week of field school begins on Sunday evening and ends Friday night. Tuition includes instruction, dormitory housing (through Saturday morning), and all meals, Monday through Friday.

NATIONAL TRUST FOR HISTORIC PRESERVATION

1785 Massachusetts Ave., N.W.
Washington, D.C. 20036
(202) 673-4138

Dedicated to the preservation and revitalization of America's historic environments, the National Trust for Historic Preservation offers volunteers the opportunity to assist in its mission by joining a National Trust Work-Study Project. As a volunteer, you will live and work at a National Trust property for a week, learning firsthand about the process of preservation while helping to save a national landmark.

Although specific projects change from year to year, the sites often stay the same as teams move on to different phases of the preservation work. An overview of three current projects typifies the kind of experience you can expect. The "Chesterwood Painting Project" recently brought volunteers to the longtime Massachusetts summer home of sculptor Daniel Chester French, best known for his statue of Abraham Lincoln in the Lincoln Memorial in Washington, D.C. The project focused on painting the house. Participants learned about paint color research and pigment analysis as they relate to historic buildings and artifacts. They also made a behind-the-scenes visit to a restoration workshop. The work involved scraping, applying a primer and two finish coats, and glazing and painting windows.

Ongoing projects include the "Belle Grove Archeology

Work-Study Project" at Belle Grove Plantation in Middletown, Virginia. Once at the center of a significant Civil War conflict, the Battle of Cedar Creek, this eighteenth-century plantation is the most important single site historically and architecturally for capturing the story of the lower Shenandoah Valley. The work-study project involves making an archeological survey of the yard surrounding Heater House, a property at Belle Grove central to the interpretation of the Battle of Cedar Creek and the plantation's role in it. Participants excavate small test units, recording soil color and changes, artifacts encountered, and other pertinent information.

Montpelier, where James Madison lived, is itself the site of two other work-study projects. The archeology project focuses on a continuing study of the main house yard. Participants do detailed excavation work. You will also wash, identify, and catalog discovered artifacts in the archeology lab, part of the Montpelier Research Center. The architectural research project centers on the garden temple built by President James Madison in about 1809. The work involves documenting the structure as it currently exists, removing deteriorated elements, and photographing the research process as well as the elements themselves. Other tasks involve laboratory analysis of the materials sampled.

Previous experience is not required for any of the projects. Some projects do, however, involve considerable bending and reaching, while others may involve working on scaffolding. All work takes place under the supervision of professional archeologists, anthropologists, and preservationists. What is important is that volunteers be willing to follow instructions and to recognize that the work sometimes may be long. An ability to adapt to changing conditions and a strong spirit of cooperation are the main qualifications required. Adults of all ages are welcome to participate.

COST: Fees, which cover lodgings and some meals, run as follows: Chesterwood project, $794; Belle Grove project, $657; Montpelier project, $585.

SMITHSONIAN RESEARCH EXPEDITIONS

490 L'Enfant Plaza S.W., Suite 4210
Washington, D.C. 20560
(202) 287-3210

Through its research expeditions program, the Smithsonian Institution offers its members and the general public the opportunity to become "citizen scholars," joining scientists, curators, and other researchers in their ongoing projects. Volunteers work in field settings, laboratories, and archives, collecting, organizing, and interpreting data. They deepen their personal understanding of science, history, and art while contributing to the body of research in areas that represent the museum's concerns. In the past, volunteer labor has assisted in the collection of valuable ethnographic information, the preservation of priceless artifacts, and the dissemination of new information on plants, animals, and minerals.

Some of the expeditions are physically demanding and some are not. Some involve long hours in the library, while others take place almost entirely out-of-doors. Previous training in specific field techniques is not required. The Smithsonian team leaders provide instruction in the necessary skills, although they also try to make good use of the special talents volunteers bring with them. Volunteers are expected to be cooperative, adaptable, and observant. The tasks can be taxing and tedious, requiring patience and a willingness to put in long hours. "This is not a tour program, not a vacation," the program manager explains. "It is a commitment of time, work, and energy."

The expeditions, which last one or two weeks, represent a two-way street. Volunteers contribute labor and financial support. In exchange, they are given the opportunity to work alongside leading experts from the Smithsonian on projects involving the natural sciences, social sciences, American history, native American studies, and photography.

For example, under the supervision of a historian from the

Smithsonian's National Museum of American History, volunteers contribute to a project called "Ethnic Images in Advertising" by surveying vast collections of materials in the museum's archives. They work with rare pamphlets, prints, sheet music, fruit-crate and cigar-box labels, posters, and other materials noting recurrent patterns of archetypes and stereotypes in commercial imagery over the last several hundred years.

Other U.S. expeditions are currently scheduled to projects underway in Virginia, Wyoming, Maine, Massachusetts, Montana, and Arizona. To be eligible for the program, participants must be eighteen years or older and in good health. Briefing packets containing specific directions, project goals, techniques, field conditions, related readings, a list of team members, and a packing list are distributed about four weeks before each expedition begins.

COST: To join an expedition, you first pay $22 to become a member of the Smithsonian Associates. The fee for participation in the two-week-long expedition "Ethnic Imagery in Advertising" is $1,460, which includes double-occupancy accommodation in a pleasant Washington, D.C., hotel and a welcome and farewell dinner.

WHITE MESA INSTITUTE FOR CULTURAL STUDIES

P.O. Box 211248
Salt Lake City, Utah 84121-8248
(801) 943-3702

A self-supporting, nonprofit organization, the White Mesa Institute for Cultural Studies (WMI) offers educational trips and workshops using the natural landscape of the

American Southwest as an outdoor classroom, laboratory, and museum. The instructors are recognized experts in the fields of history, the sciences, philosophy, and the arts. They are assisted by experienced guide-outfitters who take responsibility for trip logistics, cooking chores, and emergency care.

WMI programs explore Utah, Colorado, New Mexico, and Arizona. They are scheduled from April into October and most last four to six days. Programs are sometimes structured to retrace historic expeditions of the Southwest. Local residents, including native Americans, frequently join the instructors, enriching the experience by sharing their stories and traditions.

Each program is rated on a scale of zero to seven, indicating the nature of the physical activity involved. For example, a rating of zero indicates that no hiking or only optional hiking is involved. A rating of seven indicates total backpacking and strenuous hiking with new camps each night.

Typical of WMI's offerings is the four-day-long Arch Canyon Adopt-a-Ruin Program, which originates in Blanding, Utah. To assist the Bureau of Land Management in managing the archeological record on public lands in southeastern Utah, WMI has "adopted" the Arch Canyon ruin.

Each session begins with an evening orientation session. Participants then spend the next three days documenting the ruin and taking evening hikes to neighboring sites. You will be introduced to Anasazi archeology and to the archeological techniques of surface interpretation, site mapping, rock-art documentation, and Anasazi ceramic classification. The program is rated two ("moderate day hikes, vehicle or boat support, and camping").

Other recent programs have included "Past and Present Native American Cultures in Navajoland," "Slickhorn Canyon Rock Art Trek," "Navajo Mountain: Retracing the Bernheimer Expeditions," and "In the Footsteps of Early Archaeologists: Richard Wetherill and The Great Basketmaker Discovery." Most WMI programs can be taken for credit by arrangement through the College of Eastern Utah.

COST: The fee for the Arch Canyon Adopt-a-Ruin program is $633, which covers meals, van transportation, archeological supplies, permit fees, instruction, and outfitting service.

FOUR CORNERS SCHOOL OF OUTDOOR EDUCATION

East Route
Monticello, Utah 84535
(801) 587-2156

A nonprofit organization dedicated to increasing knowledge and appreciation of the 160,000-square-mile region known as the Colorado Plateau, the Four Corners School (FCS) "teaches outdoor skills, natural sciences, and land stewardship by creating a community of individuals who share their interests through informal, relaxed, hands-on experiences." The school operates learning vacations for small groups (8–25 students plus staff) of individuals interested in learning about both the natural and cultural history of the area and the logistics of low-impact camping.

FCS programs tend to attract adults ages 35–65, but younger and older people are welcome to join. Courses are divided into the following general subject areas: natural history, cultural studies, archeology, photography and writing, wilderness advocacy, and special interest. The staff is made up of leading experts in biology, archeology, geology, history, writing, and photography, many of whom have published books and other materials related to their field. To help you choose a course appropriate for your physical abilities, all programs are rated on a scale of one ("No camping or hiking. Motel lodging; touring or museum work.") to ten ("You must be crazy!").

Archeology is an FCS mainstay, with many courses to choose from, some involving participation in ongoing research projects. You might choose to sign on for a nine-day excavation program (rated 3–4) at Cedar Mesa, one of the least disturbed archeological areas in the Southwest. Under the direction of an expert archeologist, students excavate a dry cave site in search of remains dating back to 5,000–6,500 B.C. Evening lectures on the area's history and prehistory and a museum visit provide additional training.

During "The Teachings of San Juan: A Photo and Writing Workshop," an author/photographer team introduces principles and techniques related to field nature photography and natural history writing during a six-day float trip down the San Juan River. "Winter Wildlife and Geology at Yellowstone National Park" (rated 3–5) offers daily cross-country ski trips from the group's base at a comfortable lodge to the steaming geyser basins and hot springs where elk, moose, and bison gather. Participants learn animal-tracking skills and cross-country ski techniques and study the ecology and history of the park, as well as the mountain-building processes that shaped the region and created the world's largest thermal displays.

Courses run throughout the year and offer a tremendous variety of outdoor learning experiences. Accommodations for these programs vary from primitive base camps (remote location with no flush toilets) to clean, comfortable motels. FCS serves healthy, natural foods and a vegetarian choice is usually available. All programs originate in Monticello, Utah, unless otherwise noted.

COST: The fee for "Old Man Cave Excavation," the nine-day Cedar Mesa program, is $795; for "The Teachings of San Juan," $675. The fee for "Winter Wildlife and Geology in Yellowstone National Park," which originates in Bozeman, Montana, is $1,440. Fees cover all food, lodging, transportation from program start to end location, supplies, admissions, and group equipment.

3

Exploring the Arts

Painting

SKY LIGHT CONVERSATIONS

Route 4, Box 217
Santa Fe, New Mexico 87501
(505) 982-2393

Named for the incredible light that bathes the New Mexico landscape and the intimate studio discussions with working artists that form the core of the program, Sky Light Conversations offers an unusual travel/study experience that takes you behind the scenes of the Santa Fe art community as you explore the area's rich blend of native American, Hispanic, and Anglo traditions.

Sky Light Conversations are week-long sessions that combine visits to the city's wealth of art museums and galleries with side trips to nearby pueblos, Hispanic villages, and archaeological sites. Most important, by arranging studio visits with local potters, painters, printmakers, photographers, and sculptors to share in conversation and to watch them do their work, the seminars enable participants to gain insight into the uniqueness of the landscape and its people, as seen through the eyes of the artists.

Designed and led by Honey, who works at the Museum of

Indian Arts and Culture in Santa Fe, and Peter Chapin, painter and printmaker and former chairman of the Drew University Art Department, the seminars are both an intellectual and artistic journey. Participants receive a suggested reading list in advance and discussions of art, history, and multiculturalism are an integral part of the daily schedule. The program is offered three times a year and the group is always limited to twelve participants, who are housed in a pleasant hotel in downtown Santa Fe. The spring and summer sessions also include the opportunity to attend Pueblo ceremonial dances.

COST: The fee (approximately $1,100, depending upon the accommodations chosen) covers all program events, room, most meals, museum passes, and transportation between the Albuquerque Airport and Santa Fe as well as to the program activities.

MERLE DONOVAN'S MAINE COAST ART WORKSHOPS

P.O. Box 236
Port Clyde, Maine 04855
(207) 372-8200

If you would like to hone your painting skills using as subjects the offshore islands, tidal pools, working harbors, clam flats, and rocky cliffs of coastal Maine, consider enrolling in one of Merle Donovan's fifteen week-long workshops offered from June through September. The artists who teach the workshops represent a broad range of styles and approaches. The majority of workshops focus on watercolor techniques, although there are also options for those interested in oil painting and printmaking.

Each week begins with a Sunday evening get-together with your teacher and fellow artists. From Monday to Friday, the class gathers at 9:00 A.M. at the barn, which serves as the workshop headquarters. The barn is available to you at any time, so you can extend your painting day as long as you like. Some instructional sessions take place indoors, while others are held outside at locations that take advantage of the coastal landscape. On Tuesday evening, participants gather for dessert and Irish coffee at a local inn, where you enjoy good conversation along with a slide program and/or discussion presented by your workshop instructor. On Thursday evening, arrangements are made for the class to have dinner together. Artists at all levels are encouraged to attend and Ms. Donovan will be happy to suggest a session appropriate to your experience. Approximately twenty-two people attend each workshop, ranging in age from their twenties to their seventies and beyond.

COST: Tuition for each course is $320, which includes the Tuesday evening reception. Lodgings and meals are arranged on your own (some days you will be asked to bring along a brown-bag lunch depending upon the plans for the day).

HUDSON RIVER VALLEY ART WORKSHOPS

Route 1, Box 2
Greenville, New York 12083
(518) 966-5219

A series of five-day workshops taught by nationally recognized artists, the Hudson Valley Art Workshops are held from May to October each year at the Greenville Arms, a Victorian country inn located in the northern Catskills. Artists of all levels of accomplishment come to learn, to seek inspiration from the mountains and farmlands that inspired the artists of the renowned Hudson River Valley School of painting, and to enjoy the fellowship of others who share their interest. Throughout the week, students and teacher share breakfast and dinner together in the inn's dining room, providing plenty of opportunity for informal discussion.

Classes are held Monday through Friday, beginning after breakfast and continuing until about 4:00 P.M. Much of the instruction takes place out-of-doors, where the natural setting provides endless subjects. There are indoor facilities for studio classes and for respite in case of inclement weather. Slide presentations, talks, and critiques are given on several evenings during the week. Many students also like to return to their work after dinner.

A sampling of workshops offered during the season includes "Interpreting the Figure in Water Color," "Contemporary Art and Personal Expression," "Nature: Composition, Color, and Space," "Master Class: Advanced Experimental Techniques," "Inspirations from Nature," and "Portrait in the Landscape." There are classes for students who want to work in water-based media, oil, acrylics, pencil, pastel, and charcoal.

Several workshops are restricted to intermediate and advanced students but most are open to all levels. Except where a lower number is specified, class enrollments are limited to twenty students. After registering, each student receives a class supply list prepared by the workshop instructor. The Greenville Arms has a warm, old-fashioned feeling. When not in class, guests can swim in the pool, play shuffleboard, croquet, or ping-pong, or hike the area's many trails. The rooms are pleasant and comfortable, the breakfasts hearty and the dinners elegant, and a cookie and coffee break is provided each workshop day.

COST: The fee for most workshops is $599 per person for double occupancy, $699 for single occupancy, which covers tuition, wine and cheese reception, and coffee breaks, six nights' inn accommodations, and all breakfasts and dinners (lunch available at extra cost). Day students can enroll if space is available. Tuition is $250. Some workshops involve additional payments of $15–$30 to cover materials or models' fees.

WATERCOLOR PAINTING ON HOT-PRESSED SURFACES

160 West 71st St., Apt. 14D
New York, New York 10023
(212) 877-2270

Professional painter, teacher, graphic designer, and illustrator Marc Getter introduces serious artists to "the opportunity to explore and discover a new visual vocabulary" in his five-day workshop "Watercolor Painting on Hot-Pressed Surfaces."

Getter's technique involves replacing the textured and absorbent papers used by most watercolorists with hot-pressed papers or boards, which have been compressed under a heated plate during the final stage of the manufacturing process. As a result of the compression, the fibers are smoothed into a glasslike, nonabsorbent surface, a surface seldom associated with water-based media. During sessions that combine demonstrations with hands-on experience, participants discover the brilliance and vibrancy of colors as they appear on hot-pressed papers. Because the paint is so easy to remove and the surface so smooth, students learn to create subtle effects and textures. In addition to introducing special techniques, such as how to use an ordinary household sponge to produce results impossible to achieve on traditional papers, the instructor shares ideas for self-marketing and promotion. Throughout the workshop, which is open to intermediate and advanced painters, Getter stresses artistic achievement with an eye to reaching personal goals.

Getter offers his program, which he subtitles "The

Workshop that Shatters the Myths and Rules of Traditional Watercolor Painting," year-round at locations throughout the country. Most sessions average about twenty participants, with a maximum enrollment of twenty-five.

COST: Tuition for the five-day workshop ranges from $250 to $275.

FARMINGTON VALLEY ARTS CENTER

25 Arts Center Lane
Avon Park North
Avon, Connecticut 06001
(203) 678-1867, (203) 674-1877

Housed in a complex of mid-nineteenth-century brownstone factory buildings adjacent to a park, the Farmington Valley Arts Center (FVAC) encompasses studio space, classrooms, an art gallery, and a shop featuring hand-made crafts from hundreds of American artists. Part of the pleasure of taking a course or workshop here is the opportunity to chat with and observe the craftsmen at work in the twenty studios occupied by professional artists and artists' cooperatives.

FVAC offers a broad selection of classes and workshops, with options for beginning and advanced students as well as for children. Instruction is offered in the decorative arts, design and print, drawing, fiber arts, jewelry/metals and gems, painting, paper, photography, pottery, and sculpture. The teaching schedule is divided into four terms and most courses meet for eight consecutive weekly sessions. There is also a good selection of single-session workshops to choose from. To register for a course, you must be a member of the FVAC. Membership is not required for participation in the one-day workshops.

Typical workshops include "Stenciling," a six-hour session during which each participant designs and completes a two- by three-foot stenciled floor cloth and "An Introduction to Paper Making," a five-hour session where you will practice the basic steps involved in making paper by hand. Many other workshops are offered in subjects as varied as "Hand Coloring Black-and-White Photographs," "Eggs in the Ukrainian Tradition," "Illustrating Children's Books," and "Natural Dyeing."

COST: FVAC individual membership is $20. Tuition for most eight-session courses is $110–$145. Some classes carry additional materials fees. The fee for the stenciling workshop is $60 plus $40 for materials (students keep stencil brushes, stencil, and finished floor cloth). The fee for the workshop on illustrating children's books is $30.

DANGER ISLAND STUDIOS

5 Creek St.
Ketchikan, Alaska 99901
(907) 247-1330

Alaska's southernmost city, Ketchikan stretches along the southwestern shore of Revillagigedo Island in the Alexander Archipelago, an area of lush rainforests, rivers, lakes, and saltwater fjords teeming with wildlife. Bald eagles and killer whales are frequently sighted from the city's downtown area. In the summer the waterfront is filled with traffic—cruise ships, commercial fishing boats, and float planes—and the streets are alive with college students who come to work in the canneries, sightseers, campers, and fishermen. From the windows of Danger Island Studios, located on historic Creek Street, a boardwalk supported by pilings on the banks of

Ketchikan Creek, you can watch salmon swimming to their spawning grounds.

A newly renovated professional space incorporating an eleven-hundred-square-foot painting studio, a fine art gallery, and a private studio, Danger Island Studios is run by Mary Ida Hendrikson, who has taught painting and drawing at colleges in Washington, California, and Alaska. During the summer, Ms. Hendrikson offers seven-day workshops that focus on painting the features of the rainforest landscape. Each session is limited to twelve participants.

Your workshop begins with a Sunday evening orientation and slide show and a general discussion of the area. On Monday, equipped with sketching supplies, the class takes a day cruise into the Misty Fjords National Monument for a first-hand look at the mists and mosses of the rainforests and the sheer granite cliffs in what is often called southeast Alaska's Grand Canyon. Tuesday and Wednesday are devoted to all-day formal sessions in the studio. Ms. Hendrikson demonstrates rainforest mist, water reflection, and rock and tree painting techniques and provides individual instruction. The Thursday session features a live model in traditional Alaskan native regalia and instruction in draped-figure studies. On Friday, transportation is provided to Saxman Native Village, where the Tlingit people have lived since the 1880s. Ms. Hendrikson remains in the studio to provide informal instruction through-out the day. Saturday is devoted to the completion of projects and Sunday is departure day. All activities are optional and the studio remains open for your use from 9:00 A.M. to 6:00 P.M. every day except Sunday.

COST: The fee for the seven-day workshop is $1,400. This covers instruction, some equipment and supplies (easels, drawing horses, palettes, canvas boards, gesso solvents and mediums, and lockers), transportation to and from the ferry terminal or airport on arrival and departure days, the cruise, and housing. Participants live in modern units with private bathrooms within walking distance of the studio (rooms have queen-sized beds and you can share with a friend or spouse at no additional cost). Meals are not included.

CASTLE HILL

Truro Center for the Arts
Box 756
Truro, Massachusetts 02666
(508) 349-7511

At Castle Hill, students of all ages and ability levels work under the guidance of a faculty of professional artists, inspired by Cape Cod's ocean, bay, marshes, and dunes. The small nonprofit arts center is housed in an old horse barn that has been transformed into studio space, a darkroom, and gallery, with a spacious adjoining deck.

Courses vary from one-day workshops to month-long classes and include instruction and critiques in painting, drawing, printmaking, sculpture, ceramics, metal, fiber, photography, and writing. The focus is on individual development and students are encouraged to work at their own pace.

Sample classes include: "Frescoes" (six sessions in a two-week period), in which students learn the techniques involved in creating brilliantly colored and enduring plaster murals; "Drawing with Pastels" (four weekly sessions); "The Landscape in Watercolor" (5–10 sessions in a two-week period); "Vintage Photographs—Their Care and Evaluation" (one session); and "Clay Jewelry" (five sessions in one week), which focuses on the design and construction of beads, belts, and other art for the body and which requires no previous clay experience.

The writing program features a poetry workshop conducted here for the past fifteen years by poet Alan Dugan, winner of the National Book Award and the Pulitzer Prize. The workshop runs twice a week throughout the summer and participants can register for four, eight, or seventeen sessions.

Well-known writers who have offered their teaching services in nonfiction and fiction writing at the center in the past include *New Yorker* staff member E. J. Kahn, Jr., and novelist Anne Bernays.

COST: Tuition runs $160 plus a $10 materials fee for "Frescoes"; $115 for "Drawing with Pastels"; $130 for five sessions of "The Landscape in Watercolor"; $35 for "Vintage Photographs"; $140 plus a $10 lab fee for "Clay Jewelry"; and $90 for participation in four sessions of the poetry workshop.

ART NEW ENGLAND

425 Washington St.
Brighton, Massachusetts 02135
(617) 782-4218, (617) 782-4184

Held on the campus of Bennington College in the Vermont countryside, Art New England Summer Workshops draw together a community of accomplished artists and committed students eager to explore their creativity and expand their skills. For one week, participants are immersed in art in the company of others who share their passion. Although the specific workshop topics change each year, courses are always offered in painting, drawing, sculpture, ceramics, printmaking, and jewelry. A sampling of recent course titles includes "Alternative Watercolor," "Monotype: The Unique Print," "Jewelry and Beyond," "Bookworks," "Clay Sculpture: Vessels, Painting as Metaphor," "Video," and "Experimental Drawing." Three one-week sessions are offered and students may enroll in more than one session, but only in one course per session. These workshops are not for beginners. Participants should have some background in art.

The art complex is composed of a fully equipped printmaking studio, two ceramics studios with electric, gas-fired, and raku kilns, a sculpture studio, a well-equipped darkroom, and several studios for drawing and painting. Studios remain open around the clock, permitting uninterrupted work from morning to night. Come evening, many students return to the studios to continue working, while others attend faculty slide presentations or participate in the life drawing studios, which are open to all.

COST: The fee for a one-week workshop, including tuition, room, and board, is $680. The fee for students living off campus is $425, which covers tuition and lunch.

ART WORKSHOPS OF VERMONT

Box 57
Chittenden, Vermont 05737
(802) 483-6058

Spend a summer or fall week developing your watercolor technique at one of the four week-long sessions offered by Art Workshops of Vermont, each one taught by a different artist who shares his or her own technique and style. A typical day includes a demonstration or lecture, painting time, and a critique. Some classes take place outdoors, while others are taught in the studio.

If you have a desire to paint but have never tried, or if you are experienced in another medium and feel apprehensive about watercolor, resident artist Al Friedman's annual workshop may be just what you need to get started. He emphasizes the fundamentals, including use of basic materials, color mixing, design, and composition. By combining demonstrations, lectures, and hands-on painting exercises with individual attention at each student's own level, he helps students paint with confidence and control in a very short time.

The program is based at the Mountain Top Inn and Resort in Vermont's Green Mountains. Resort activities include golf and horseback riding (with instruction available for both), sailing, canoeing, fishing, tennis, mountain biking, trap shooting, and swimming in the heated pool or lake. You need not, however, stay at the inn to participate in the workshop sessions.

COST: Workshop tuition ranges from $200 to $285. A five-night lodging package at the inn is $338 for double occupancy.

Crafts

GRAND MARAIS ART COLONY

Box 626
Grand Marais, Minnesota 55604
(218) 387-2737

At the Grand Marais Art Colony, accomplished professional artists lead a series of intense week-long studio workshops each summer. Sessions meet daily from 9:00 A.M. to 4:00 P.M. and the studios remain open most evenings, providing participants with a highly concentrated art experience. Also in the evening, colony artists and instructors present slide lectures and prose and poetry readings.

Located forty miles from the Canadian border at the northeast entrance to the Boundary Waters Canoe Area Wilderness, near the rugged north shore of Lake Superior, the art colony is centered in an old church that serves as its main studio. Since 1947, artists have traveled here to improve their skills and nourish their creativity. A small art supply store and an attractive art gallery are part of the complex.

Although the specific topics vary from year to year, workshops are likely to be offered in painting and drawing, pottery, environmental sculpture, photography, clothing design, and writing. Approximately sixteen adult workshops are offered in a summer. Some programs are geared toward serious amateur artists and emerging professionals, while others are open to those with no previous experience or to artists and nonartists alike. A note labeled "Who Should Attend" accompanies each workshop description listed in the brochure.

The art colony also offers several workshops for elementary and middle-school students. In the past these have focused on drawing, painting, batik, and puppetry.

COST: Tuition for five-day adult workshops is $200. Some workshops have an additional materials fee.

CENTER FOR CREATIVE IMAGING

Eastman Kodak Company
51 Mechanic St.
Camden, Maine 04843
(800) 428-7400, (207) 236-7490

The Eastman Kodak Company Center for Creative Imaging calls itself "the world's most advanced showplace for the study and development of visual technology," an assessment that is not difficult to swallow after perusing its extremely handsome and informative fifty-page catalog. Located in a congenial setting in a striking Maine coastal town that offers optimal recreational opportunities, the center is housed in a renovated brass foundry next to a dramatic waterfall. Today the building contains an atrium, four computer laboratories, conference rooms, offices, a gallery, and a riverside cafe, but the original brick arches and powerful spruce beams remain.

The center opened its doors in May of 1991. Already more than twenty-five hundred students have arrived to study music, cyberart, electronic publishing, video, animation, corporate multimedia presentations, and related subjects. Here students use sophisticated electronic imaging equipment to explore the potential of digital technology, combining images, graphics, text, and sound under the guidance of an accomplished staff. In explaining the teaching approach, the catalog reads as follows: "There's no intimidating jargon, no reliance on workbooks or outmoded teaching techniques. The relationship is that between master and apprentice, with the magical intensity of one's first experience of learning."

Each student is given a computer workstation (Macintosh computer with twenty-four-bit color and thirteen-inch monitor, equipped with CD-ROM drive) to use during class (which usually runs from 9:00 A.M. to 4:00 P.M., with breaks) and as late into the evening as you wish. The center maintains an average of one instructor or teaching assistant to every four students, enabling even computer novices to progress rapidly. Assistance is available in the labs until 11:00 P.M. each evening.

Introductory, intermediate, and advanced courses, most lasting two to five days, are offered in the following areas: imaging, design and publishing, media and motion, business and technical, and photo compact disk. The center's core course, "Three-Day Creative Imaging," focuses on teaching students to control basic imaging tools. You will be introduced to color correction, color theory, resolution, image acquisition and reproduction, calibration, and image selection and manipulation tools.

The center also offers a group of one- to four-day courses collectively called "Artists' Vision," which differ from the other courses in that they do not involve hands-on computer instruction. Instead, accomplished artists assist participants in developing their ideas in preparation for later bringing their work into the digital realm. Examples of classes include collage, photographic sequence, landscape photography, page composition, and drawing for observation.

With the exception of the "Artist's Vision" courses, most introductory-level courses include a free one-day Macintosh computer fundamentals course for those who have no prior experience. The course will arm you with a clear, comprehensive understanding of how the Macintosh works and what it can do. Terms like "RAM," "ROM," and "windows" are clearly defined.

For those who would like to learn more before enrolling in a class, the center offers many free programs, including facility tours, critiques and discussions of student work in progress, demonstrations of different aspects of visual imaging, faculty lectures and presentations, and gallery exhibitions and receptions. The center is open year-round.

COST: Tuition for the "Three-Day Creative Imaging" course is $930 (off season) to $1,080. Tuition for the "Artists' Vision" courses is $100 per day (e.g., $200 for a two-day course in collage). All fees include lunch at the cafe throughout the course.

DILLMAN'S CREATIVE ARTS FOUNDATION

P.O. Box 98F
Lac du Flambeau, Wisconsin 54538
(800) 359-2511, (715) 588-3143

Based at Dillman's Sand Lake Lodge, a bustling family resort occupying its own peninsula jutting out into a lovely sand-bottom lake, Dillman's Creative Arts Foundation was founded in 1989 to encourage the development of the arts in northern Wisconsin. The foundation offers a continuing schedule of workshops featuring hands-on instruction in the visual arts, decorative arts, and photography. Recent topics have included "Portrait/Figure Painting in Multimedia," "Nature Scapes," "Beginning with Basics," "Waterfowl Carving/Painting," "Wearable Art/Scarves," and "Film: The Photographer's Canvas."

Classes normally run for five consecutive days, although there are some weekend sessions, and are taught by nationally known artists from around the country. During the sessions, students have twenty-four-hour access to the studio. The Foundation also offers a one-day family course, designed to make art fun for the whole family, and weekend courses in gourmet and native American cooking.

Dillman's is a good choice when you want to take a workshop but also want to enjoy a family vacation. Members of your family who are not participating in workshops will find plenty to do at the lodge. Activities include fishing, swimming, sailing, canoeing, water-skiing, hiking, biking, tennis, ping-pong, horseshoes, and shuffleboard. There's even a golf driving range. There's no additional charge for these activities or for the use of related resort equipment, including bikes, canoes, and kayaks. Supervised children's activities are offered throughout the day and some evenings, too.

COST: Package rates, including six nights' lodging, breakfasts, dinners, and five-day workshop tuition, begin at $585.

WAR EAGLE SEMINAR

Ozark Arts and Crafts Fair Association
War Eagle Mills Farm
Route 1, Box 157
Hindsville, Arkansas 72738
(501) 789-5398

For the past twenty-five years, top-flight craftsmen have gathered at War Eagle Mills Farm each June to share their talents by serving as instructors at the War Eagle Seminar. Sponsored by the Ozark Arts and Crafts Council, the seminar offers one- and two-week-long courses. Most classes meet Monday through Friday from 9:00 A.M. to 4:00 P.M.

Classes are taught beneath a cluster of colorful tents, inside a rustic exhibit building, and outdoors beside the old mill pond and on the banks of the War Eagle River. Courses are divided into two general categories, woodcarving and arts and crafts. Those who enroll in the two-week woodcarving course are assigned to a different instructor for each week. There is an introductory course for beginners as well as separate courses in carving animals, songbirds, and ducks. Other courses focus on general woodcarving, chip carving, relief carving, human form, knife making, and carving large figures.

Arts and crafts courses are usually offered in clay sculpture, drawing perspective, stone carving, chair caning, photography, painting, basket making, stained glass, dried-flower arranging, and lap quilting. Students can also register for bow making, where they learn to construct sinew-back American Indian bows and other styles, or a course in flint knapping and arrow making.

Students may camp on the site (a limited number of electrical hookups are available for motor homes) or find their own accommodations in nearby towns.

COST: The fee for a two-week course (ten days of instruction) is $110. The fee for a one-week course is $75. The fee for two one-week courses is $110. There are additional charges for materials.

TUSCARORA SCHOOL OF POTTERY

P.O. Box 7
Tuscarora, Nevada 89834
(702) 756-6598

From advanced beginners to professionals, potters come from all over the United States and abroad to study the simple, direct techniques taught at the Tuscarora School of Pottery by artist-in-residence Dennis Parks. Tuscarora sits sixty-four hundred feet up the side of Mount Blitzen in the northeastern corner of Nevada, an area classified climactically as high desert. Tuscarora started out as a mining town in 1872 and grew to a population of thirty-five hundred at its height in 1880. Today there are just twenty permanent inhabitants. It is quiet and isolated, fifty miles from the closest stores.

In addition to Dennis Parks's personal studio, facilities include two student studios equipped with kick wheels and hand-building tables, rooms for clay mixing and glazing, and a nineteenth-century rooming house where students live and help out with cleanup chores. The dining room houses an extensive collection of ceramic books and all the ceramic magazines published in the English language. With few distractions, students have time to read as well as time to work. The studios remain open twenty-four hours a day.

Students are attracted to the school by particular technical emphases that have evolved, which Parks describes as follows:

- All of the work is glazed raw and single fired;
- The kilns are fired with used crankcase oil;

- The kilns are constructed with one layer of insulating brick and an outer shell of rammed-earth bricks;

- Finally, the area is rich in minerals useful to the potter; therefore, gathering native materials for use in glazes has become common practice.

The six-week summer school runs from mid-June through the end of July and the minimum age for participants is eighteen.

COST: The fee for room, board, instruction, and firing is $1,925 for six weeks, $1,283 for four weeks, and $715 for two weeks.

SOUTHWEST CRAFT CENTER

300 Augusta
San Antonio, Texas 78205
(512) 224-1848

Housed in a cluster of historically significant nineteenth-century buildings that formerly served as a convent and girls' school, the Southwest Craft Center occupies a parklike riverside setting in downtown San Antonio. The center offers progressive educational programs in ceramics, fibers, metals, paper making, photography, and surface design.

Here students work side by side with professional artists, learning both the technical expertise related to an individual craft and the business nuts and bolts vital to making a living as an artist. More than sixty nationally recognized artists from all across the country join the center's six resident artists in teaching classes that vary from one-day workshops to fifteen-week courses. The center also hosts a Saturday morning program for children.

A recent schedule included such two- and three-day weekend workshops as "Using T-Max 3200 Film" ("This workshop is designed to pull back the curtain of misunderstanding by showing P-3200 to be an emulsion perfectly suited to subjects ranging from fine-art images to annual report photography"), "Japanese Containers/Unique Approaches to Packaging"

("... How to construct a variety of beautiful boxes, as well as special wrapping techniques. ... No prior papercraft experience is necessary."), and "Shining Cloth" ("Individuals will work with a variety of methods to pattern, print, and discharge dye cloth, and then work with the surfaces and imagery, incorporating metallic and shining pigments and additives.").

COST: The tuition for two- and three-day workshops ranges from $80 to $120. An additional lab fee of $20–$50 is also charged.

SIEVERS SCHOOL OF FIBER ARTS

Jackson Harbor Road
Washington Island, Wisconsin 54246-9723
(414) 847-2264

Accessible by ferry boat, the Sievers School of Fiber Arts enjoys a lovely rural setting on Wisconsin's Washington Island, surrounded by the waters of Lake Michigan. A remodeled schoolhouse and a refurbished barn blend modern studio facilities with old-fashioned charm. In good weather, students are just as likely to work outdoors as in, spreading out their work on the decks and on the lawn.

Classes, which run either a weekend, five days, or seven days, are scheduled from May to October. Most are limited to seven students. The majority of those who attend the Sievers School are beginners, but the selection of about fifty classes offers many options for intermediate and advanced fiber artists. Areas of instruction include basketry; handmade paper; quilting; spinning, dyeing, and felting; surface design; wearables; and weaving. Sample weekend courses include "Perfect Accents: Polymer and Clay Buttons and Beads," "Basic Rattan Wicker Basketry," and "Beginning Spinning."

If you have always wanted to learn to weave, sign on for "Basic Weaving Fundamentals: Four-Harness Floor Loom Weaving." During this five-day course you will become familiar with what the loom does and how it works. You will learn to "dress" or warp the loom, and you will learn about fiber selection, project planning, finishing techniques, and pattern drafting. You will have the opportunity to weave a sampler as well as the chance to design and weave a second small project if time allows. The school provides the floor looms and all necessary equipment, while students pay for their materials. Experienced weavers might choose to enroll in "Anything Goes! Design and Weave Wearable Art." As the week unfolds, each student designs a garment, then weaves it, sews it, and wears it.

Dormitory facilities outfitted with bunk beds and communal kitchen facilties are available at the school, but only for women. They are used by about half of the 450 students who attend annually. There is also a good selection of motels, hotels, campgrounds, and cottages on the island.

COST: Tuition is $280 for seven-day classes, $190 for five-day classes, and $90 for weekend classes. Dormitory housing costs $126 for a seven-day stay, $90 for a five-day stay, and $36 for a weekend stay.

PETERS VALLEY CRAFT CENTER

19 Kuhn Road
Layton, New Jersey 07581
(201) 948-5200

Each summer, experienced instructors from all over the United States arrive at the Peters Valley Craft Center in the lush Delaware Water Gap National Recreation Area to conduct a broad range of workshops, lectures, and demonstrations. There are programs for beginning, intermediate, and advanced students. Sessions vary from one to eighteen days, but most options are in the two- to five-day range.

Peters Valley produces a detailed catalog describing the summer workshops conducted in each of six areas: blacksmithing, ceramics, fibers, fine metals, photography, and wood. Sample offerings include a two-day session devoted to making Shaker oval boxes (beginners and intermediate woodworkers) and a five-day session devoted to marquetry techniques for the advanced woodworking student. If you are interested in fiber arts, you can choose from workshops that focus on basket making, paper making, rag weaving, batik, and spinning.

Workshops are open to those eighteen years and older. To ensure adequate work space, safety precautions, and instructor attention, most sessions are limited to 8–12 students. Applications are accepted on an ongoing basis, but spaces fill quickly. It is advisable to apply by April 15. Limited room-and-board arrangements are also available in Peters Valley's complex of historic buildings. Meals are served during the workshop sessions; they are included in the price of lodging and can also be purchased by day students.

COST: Tuition is $135 for "Shaker Oval Boxes," a two-day workshop; there is an additional materials fee of $35. Tuition for "Fundamentals of Blacksmithing," a five-day workshop, is $245; the materials fee is $40. The cost of room and board (semiprivate with shared facilities) is $55 for a two-day workshop, $185 for a five-day session.

OREGON SCHOOL OF ARTS & CRAFTS

8245 SW Barnes Road
Portland, Oregon 97225
(505) 297-5544

America's oldest continuously operating craft school, the Oregon School of Arts & Crafts offers year-round courses and workshops for both the aspiring professional crafts worker and the avocational artist. Programs are offered in book arts, ceramics, drawing, fibers, metal, photography, and wood. Sessions range from half a day to a week and many are scheduled to take place within a single weekend.

The school publishes a quarterly bulletin that describes current offerings and indicates which ones are suitable for beginning, intermediate, and advanced students. Some of the workshops featured recently include "Celtic Ornament" (learn how to apply Celtic designs to metal, wood, fabric, leather, stone, or paper), "Mask Making," "Making Paper for Printing, Calligraphy, and Bookbinding," and "Introduction to Furniture Making."

The school is located on a wooded campus in the hills west of Portland, just a little over an hour's drive from the Pacific Ocean and two hours away from the Cascade Mountains, making it easy to combine art studies with outdoor recreation. State-of-the-art studios and classrooms occupy a cluster of nine buildings constructed in a former filbert orchard in 1979. Designed for beauty as well as function, the facilities incorporate stained glass windows, handmade ceramic tiles, hand-carved doors, hand-wrought ironwork, and other custom details created by regional artists. There is, however, no on-campus housing, so you must make your own arrangements.

COST: The fee for the two-day "Celtic Ornament" workshop is $80, with a studio fee of $5. The fee for the week-long "Introduction to Furniture Making" workshop is $225, plus a $17 studio fee.

HAYSTACK MOUNTAIN SCHOOL OF CRAFTS

Deer Isle, Maine 04627-0518
(207) 348-2306

A unique campus composed of shingled buildings, decks, and walkways that seem an extension of the natural environment, Haystack overlooks the waters of Eggomoggin Reach. Located deep in the woods on a Maine coastal island connected to the mainland by a bridge, the school is remote from everyday distractions.

Here a community of about eighty students, faculty, and visiting artists gathers throughout the summer to develop their skills and nurture their creativity in an atmosphere that supports serious work and imaginative exploration of the ideas associated with art and craft. The school's philosophy respects traditional techniques and forms of expression while recognizing the rich potential of contemporary visual art.

The summer program is divided into six sessions of varying length, each of which features six intensive studio workshops. Participants register for one workshop, which lasts one, two, or three weeks, depending upon the session. Workshops are held in clay, fibers, glass, painting, mixed media, metals, wood, paper making, book arts, baskets, graphics, blacksmithing, quilts, surface design, and other subjects.

The studios are open around the clock seven days a week and classes are scheduled from Monday to Friday. The evenings are filled with slide lectures and presentations by faculty and visiting artists.

Most workshops are open to artists and crafts workers of all levels. In selecting applicants, the school seeks a diverse student body reflecting geographical distribution, a balance between alumni and first-timers, and a range of backgrounds from beginners to advanced professionals, all of whom share a clear sense of why they want to participate in the workshop they have chosen. Participants must be at least eighteen years of age. In addition to the summer programs, Haystack also sponsors shorter term workshops in May, September, and October.

COST: Tuition is $210 for a one-week session, $400 for two weeks, and $525 for three weeks. Additional shop fees run $5–$30 per week for most workshops; glassblowing and foundry fees are approximately $125. Supplies not provided for in the shop fee can be purchased at the school store. Room and board for a two-week session is $800 in a single room with bath and $385 in a twin bedroom near a central washroom. Several other accommodation arrangements are also available.

COUPEVILLE ARTS CENTER

P.O. Box 171
60 N.W. Coveland
Coupeville, Washington 98239
(206) 678-3396

Reached by bridge or ferry, the Coupeville Arts Center is located in a Victorian-era town on Whibey Island. Most programs take place at the Camp Casey Conference Center, which sits on a magnificent stretch of coastline overlooking Puget Sound. The center sponsors 3–5-day-long workshops in painting, photography, and fiber arts from May through September. Highly respected artists of national and international reknown travel to the island to teach beginning- to advanced-level students from all over the country.

Knitters, quilters, needlepointers, embroiderers, and beaders gather in March to participate in "Needleworks," two back-to-back series of unusual three-day workshops ranging from doll making to kimono design, loom beading to seamless garment construction. "Photo Focus," held in the spring, offers well over a dozen intensive photography workshops covering subjects such as nature photography, portrait work, platinum and palladian prints, and magazine and stock photography. The summer months are devoted to "Palettes Plus," varied classes in watercolor, oil, and related fine arts. The "Fiber Forum," a broad selection of workshops in weaving, spinning, dyeing, felting, basketry, Navajo weaving, color, and design, is featured in September.

The center publishes a series of detailed course description leaflets. While there are options for beginning, intermediate, and advanced students, many workshops are geared to a specific level of expertise, so it is wise to select carefully.

Participants arrange their own accommodations. The center does offer a limited amount of low-cost housing in the form of shared dormitory rooms in barracks buildings. Bring your own bedding and towels. Inexpensive meal packages are also available.

COST: Tuition is $145 for each "Needleworks" workshop and $185 for each "Fiber Forum" workshop. Tuition ranges from $225 to $325 for "Photo Focus" and "Palettes Plus". Materials fees are additional.

BROOKFIELD CRAFT CENTER, INC.

P.O. Box 122
Brookfield, Connecticut 06804
(203) 775-4526

At the Brookfield Crafts Center you can study almost any aspect of fine craftsmanship, choosing from an arts-and-crafts curriculum that has been called the most varied and comprehensive in the country. The center, open year-round, operates on a quarterly basis. More than four hundred classes and workshops are offered each year, with options for beginning, intermediate, and professional crafts workers. Many of the country's foremost artists and craftsmen come to the center to teach as visiting faculty members.

The *Brookfield Quarterly* provides detailed course descriptions and faculty biographies. There are dozens of one-, two-, and three-day workshops, as well as longer courses. Choose from an assortment of familiar and obscure topics, ranging from a two-day session devoted to learning basic stained glass techniques to a five-day workshop devoted to learning the art of building ultralight canoes. A sampling of other workshop topics includes letter-shape calligraphy, Andean pickup weaving, jewelry casting, ceramic tiles, decoy making, furniture restoration, and publicity for artists.

Classes are offered in two different locations and most are offered weekends or evenings. A complex of four Colonial-era buildings in rural Brookfield houses teaching studios, an exhibition gallery, and a retail shop featuring handmade functional artwork. Additional facilities, including a community photographic workshop and several resident artist studios, are located in Norwalk.

COST: Tuitions vary but are generally about $100 per full day.

Building Houses and Boats

SHELTER INSTITUTE

38 Center St.
Bath, Maine 04530
(207) 442-7938

Want to learn to build or renovate your own house? Pat and Patsy Hennin founded the Shelter Institute nearly twenty years ago to teach people to do just that. Since that time some twenty thousand students, representing every state in the United States and many foreign countries, have completed the institute's ninety-hour-long basic course in house design and construction.

Students run the gamut from the experienced carpenter who wants to learn the math behind framing to the marriage counselor interested in learning firsthand about the stress involved in building one's own home. Young and old, single, couples and groups, men and women—all have participated in the course. Whatever their building-related goals may be, they learn to map out a strategy of construction or renovation that allows them to do as little or as much of the work as they want, but always helps them envision the project as a whole, whether a complete house or a small addition. At the Shelter Institute students learn to design and build the house they want and to do it for 25–50 percent of the national average cost.

The intensive instruction mixes theory and lecture with practical application, suggesting a variety of solutions to design and building challenges encountered in both new construction and renovations. Students participate in a sixty-hour lecture sequence in which they become familiar with the basic physical principles involved in building construction.

Lectures are followed by skills workshops providing hands-on practice in tasks both simple (handling a circular saw) and complex (fabricating steel connectors). Students spend an additional thirty hours on site, exercising their new skills on houses being built in the area by Shelter graduates. The curriculum covers the following areas: design considerations ("recognizing the environmental, social, political, and familial parameters which make a house work"); climate; concept of heat; site; engineering; physics of materials; foundations; sheathing, insulation, and fasteners; plumbing; electricity; framing; and stone soup (insurance, financing, and other important odds and ends).

While enrolled in the basic course, students can also take a class called "Fine Art of House Cabinetry," which meets in the evening, twice a week, during the three weeks of the basic course. Participants hone their hand-tool skills while learning to make kitchen cabinets, butcher-block countertops, panel doors, and much more.

The institute also offers one- and two-day weekend workshops, which introduce a new skill by guiding participants through a specific project. Typical topics include veneering and wood finishing, woodcarving, furniture repair, and masonry demystified. Other options include a week-long program on post and beam construction.

COST: Tuition for the three-week course is $675 per person, $995 per couple. A two-week version is also offered and costs $625 per person, $900 per couple. Tuition for the evening cabinetry course is $175 per person. Tuition for most one-day weekend workshops is $45.

YESTERMORROW DESIGN/BUILD SCHOOL

Route 1, Box 97-5
Warren, Vermont 05674
(802) 496-5545

The Yestermorrow Design/Build School is rooted in the belief that the best-built environment depends on the close cooperation and involvement of designers, builders, and owners. In an ideal world, this philosophy comes to fruition when all three roles are played by the same person. At Yestermorrow, owners, designers, and builders become involved in all facets of creating the built environment. The school's name reflects its effort to combine yesterday's respect for quality craftsmanship and attention to detail with the technologies evolving for tomorrow.

There are about forty schools in the United States that teach people how to build their own house, but most pay short shrift to design, preferring instead to focus on building skills. In contrast, at Yestermorrow students spend at least as much time in the design studio as they do banging nails at the construction site. "Other schools are teaching how," explains founder John Connell. "We're teaching how and why.

"We try to put back into people's hands something they always used to have: responsibility for the built environment," Connell adds. "Architecture is basically problem solving. We teach students to figure out what they don't know how to do." The school offers courses lasting one to four weeks for both the layperson and the professional, as well as a series of one- and two-day mini-courses. Students come from diverse backgrounds and range in age from eighteen to sixty-five years old.

Geared to serve the layperson, the core curriculum is embodied in the two-week-long "Design/Build" course. During the studio component, the student is led through the design process, developing an individual program of wants and needs and then translating that program onto paper with floor plans, sections, elevations, and project models. During the site component, students get hands-on experience in a variety of construction techniques, including foundations and framing and plumbing and electrical systems. Related subjects such as estimating, permitting, and subcontracting are taught through lectures and slide shows.

The work begins each day at 8:00 A.M. and continues late into the night, when students head for their drawing boards to work on their own projects, which are presented to a jury of teachers and outside architects at the end of the course.

Some of the other options for laypersons include courses in landscape design, stone masonry, and renovation and restoration techniques. Novice, intermediate, and advanced courses in cabinetry improve individual woodworking skills. In the two-week "Workshop for Woodworkers," each student selects a specific project and takes it from the conceptual stage through completion under the watchful eye of the woodworking staff.

Young people who enjoy drawing, model making, and treehouse construction can enroll in Yestermorrow's special five-day summer programs, "Architecture for Kids" (ages 8–11) or "Architecture for Teens" (ages 12–14).

COST: Tuition, room, and board is $1,025 for a one-week course and $1,950 for a two-week course. Students are housed in double rooms at a local inn eight miles from the school. The tuition for a two-day mini-course (without room and board) is $150. Tuition for the five-day kids' courses (without room and board) is $215. All students are responsible for materials costs as well for the expense of crating and shipping their projects.

HEARTWOOD

Johnson Hill Road
Washington, Massachusetts 01235
(413) 623-6677

The staff at Heartwood has a mission. They want to empower students to become active participants in the creation of their own homes by arming them with the skills and knowledge needed to build an energy-efficient house. Whether you want to fill the role of designer or builder, Heartwood's instructors can help you build a place that respects the kind of life you want to live within its walls.

The program attracts people from a wide variety of backgrounds. What the majority of them have in common is little or no previous construction experience. Course enrollment averages about fifteen students, allowing for plenty of individual attention in a friendly atmosphere.

The core program is a three-week house-building course, designed to serve both those who plan to build their own home and those who wish to design their home and subcontract out all or part of the work. The course also accommodates those who want to make home building a career. Topics covered include: an introduction to tools, vocabulary, and materials; power-tool use and safety practices; site preparation and solar orientation; foundation types and how to build them; structural principles and calculating timber sizes; building code requirements; framing systems; roof framing and finishing; insulation and vapor barriers; interior and exterior finishes; installing doors and windows; building stairs; and plumbing and electrical systems.

Heartwood adheres to the philosophy that "the best way to learn to do something is to *do* it." To this end, the curriculum combines classroom sessions, demonstrations, and the use of mock-ups and models with student participation. Learning to frame a house, for example, starts with an explanation by an experienced builder, followed by a step-by-step slide show detailing the process and an examination of full-scale mock-ups of framing sections. After that, students head for the building yard to frame up a section, applying the techniques they have just learned. This process is followed throughout most of the morning sessions, whether the subject be orienting for a southern exposure, electricity, plumbing, or cutting rafters. Students spend the afternoons at a building site, working on the construction of a custom house. Throughout the course, emphasis is placed on developing problem-solving and visualization skills.

Heartwood also offers one-week-long workshops focusing on subjects such as designing your own home, site planning and landscape design, furniture making, finish carpentry, renovation, timber framing, cabinetmaking, contracting, and carpentry for women. In addition, the school has developed a series of one- and two-day-long weekend masonry workshops, each session devoted to a specific topic such as bricklaying, building with field stone, and fireplace construction. Each session is limited to six students, who enjoy eight hours of intensive instruction per day with a master craftsman.

COST: Tuition for the three-week house-building course is $800 per person, $1,400 per couple. Tuition for the one-week workshops is $375 per person, $650 per couple. Tuition for the masonry workshops is $100 per person per day. In all instances, lunch is included in the fee.

WOODENBOAT SCHOOL

P.O. Box 78
Brooklin, Maine 04616
(207) 359-4651

Started by *WoodenBoat* magazine in response to inquiries by readers itching to get some hands-on experience with the boat builders they read about, WoodenBoat School set up shop on a former saltwater farm in the tiny coastal town of Brooklin in 1981. More than eighty courses are now scheduled each year, extending from early June to mid-October. Most run for one or two weeks.

Courses are offered in both traditional and modern boat construction techniques, and in repair, maintenance, design, and boat handling. Many are well suited to the professional as well as the nonprofessional. Experienced amateur boat builders, woodworkers, and sailors will find a wide choice of subjects to study, as will outright novices eager to get started.

The core curriculum is presented in the school's most popular course, "Fundamentals of Boat Building." The course is open to all, although a familiarity with woodworking skills and the language of boat building are certainly useful. The course combines daily discussions with lots of practical, hands-on work. At the blackboard and on the workbench, students learn about various types of small boat construction, different methods for planking a boat, steam-bending tricks, lamination techniques, and much more. They hone their skills on real boats, working alongside others in classes that are limited to ten students.

Other courses focus on a specific aspect of boat building, such as lofting or lapstrake construction. There are also courses on boat repair and restoration. You can even take a course in which you build your own pram, kayak, or canoe. For those who want to sail, classes are offered at beginning, intermediate, and advanced levels, starting with the introductory "Elements of Seamanship." Several navigation courses are offered, too. Other options include sessions on marine painting and varnishing, rigging, troubleshooting outboards, and building half-models. Women who prefer to hone their skills in the company of other women can enroll in "Elements of Seamanship for Women" and "Woodworking Basics for Women."

COST: Tuition for one-week courses is $420–$550. Tuition for two-week sessions is $745–$785. In classes where each student works on his or her own project, the usual material cost is noted in the catalog. For example, the materials fee for "Building Your Own DK-14 Kayak" is $230. Room and board at the school is $265 per week. Students bring their own linens and live in simple rooms with shared baths. Campsites are available for $65 per week.

ARCOSANTI

HC 74, Box 4136
Mayer, Arizona 86333
(602) 632-7135

In 1956 Italian architect Paolo Soleri settled in Arizona with his family to begin a lifelong commitment to research and experimentation in urban planning. For more than twenty years, Soleri has devoted much of his energy to the design and construction of Arcosanti, a prototypical new town sited on 860 acres in the high desert of Arizona.

When fully realized, Arcosanti will provide work places, housing, and cultural centers for a population of five thousand. More than fifty residents make their home here now, hosting visitors in the gallery, café, and bakery, working in the foundry and ceramic studios, and building the town itself. At present, Arcosanti consists of ten buildings constructed by the thirty-five hundred people who have participated in the Arcosanti Workshop.

The first component of the workshop is a week-long seminar called "Arcosanti: An Urban Laboratory?" Participants receive an intensive introduction to the town through slide shows documenting the design, development, and construction of Arcosanti. They take site tours, explore silt as a sculpture medium, and sample work opportunities within the town. They also meet with Soleri several times to discuss his ideas. The seminar weeks begin the first Sunday of each month.

Those who successfully complete the seminar week are eligible to participate in the four-week-long construction workshop that immediately follows (with the exception of December). By living and working at Arcosanti, they become involved in current construction and maintenance projects as well as with the practical aspects of daily life. Classroom sessions involving surveying techniques, exposure to architectural drawings, and time to work on personal silt projects complement experiential learning on the site. Those who complete the initial seminar and the four-week construction workshop can apply for an extended stay combining residency and volunteer work.

Arcosanti also offers week-long programs for people over sixty, as well as intergenerational programs for grandparents and grandchildren. For more information about these options, contact Elderhostel, P.O. Box 1959, Wakefield, Massachusetts 01880-5959.

COST: The fee for the seminar week is $400. The fee for the four-week construction workshop is $260. This covers tuition, room, board, and use of site facilities. Accommodations are in "The Camp," which is equipped with electricity, toilets, showers, and simple living shelters. Participants bring their own sleeping bags. Guest rooms are available for the programs that run in conjunction with Elderhostel.

Photography

WILD HORIZONS PHOTOGRAPHIC SAFARIS

P.O. Box 5118
Tucson, Arizona 85703-0118
(602) 622-0672

"Wild Horizons was founded to enhance environmental appreciation through nature photography," writes company founder Thomas Weiwandt, who holds a doctoral degree in ecology and whose photographs have appeared in books and magazines published by the National Geographic Society, Time-Life, the Smithsonian Institution, and many other major organizations. Catering to the amateur who prefers to learn in an informal atmosphere, Wild Horizons Photographic Safaris offers a series of meticulously planned expeditions, each one limited to a maximum of eight participants. Because the groups are so small, it is possible to provide instruction geared to meeting each individual's goals. The major part of each safari is spent in the field taking pictures, with an emphasis on teaching you to get the most out of your equipment. Evening instructional programs are also incorporated in each itinerary.

The trips last one week (there are also longer excursions outside the United States) and focus on dramatic locations in the American West. Itineraries rotate from year to year. Typical trips include "Treasures of the Black Hills," a photographic journey to South Dakota's Mount Rushmore National Memorial, Custer State Park, Wind Cave National Park, Badlands National Park, and lesser known attractions, led by Thomas Wiewandt, assisted by a local paleontologist and a noted naturalist, and "Navajolands," an exploration of Arizona's stone monuments, pink sand dunes, sacred canyons, ancient cliff dwellings, and trading posts of the Old West, led by Weiwandt and native American guides. Both trips involve the use of four-wheel-drive vehicles for easy access to the back country.

Most of those who join the tours are active, well-educated professionals with a serious interest in photography as a hobby and a genuine curiosity about the natural world. Most are between thirty-five and sixty-five years of age and many sign on by themselves. Each safari combines first-class travel amenities with knowledgeable photographic instruction and the opportunity to learn about natural history and exotic cultures.

COST: The fee for "Treasures of the Black Hills," including seven nights' lodging, meals, ground transportation, instruction, and fees, is $1,375 per person, double occupancy. The all-inclusive fee for "Navajolands" is $1,480.

SIERRA PHOTOGRAPHIC WORKSHOPS

P.O. Box 214096
Sacramento, California 95821
(800) 925-2596, (916) 974-7200

Sierra Photographic Workshops offer personalized instruction in outdoor photography for photographers at all levels of experience, from the beginner to the working professional. The sessions are taught on location, a format that combines hands-on learning with a slice of adventure. Each workshop is limited to a maximum of ten participants to allow plenty of serious individual instruction in the techniques and discipline of creative photography. All of the workshops use magnificent natural settings as "outdoor classrooms." Some concentrate on landscape photography, while others focus on wildlife. All workshops combine field work with critique sessions honing in on participants' work. Programs run from five to ten days.

You might choose a spring landscape workshop based in Nevada's Death Valley, where you will photograph windswept dunes, desert creeks, ancient volcanoes, and multicolored hillsides from sunrise to sunset. Or you might decide to sign on for the Montana wildlife instructional tour, which offers the opportunity of photographing bear, lynx, wolf, bobcats, mountain lions, raccoons, and other mammals in totally natural settings within protective compounds. Other programs are held on location in Utah, Alaska, and in the Smoky Mountains of Tennessee during the height of the foliage season.

COST: The fee for Death Valley workshop is $945, which includes tuition, six nights' lodging, and ground transportation from Las Vegas. The fee for the Montana Wildlife Tour is $1,350, which includes tuition, five nights' lodging, and ground transportation to Kalispell, Montana.

NORTHLIGHT PHOTO WORKSHOPS

326 Bullville Road
Montgomery, New York 12549
(914) 361-1017

Catering to both the aspiring professional and the serious amateur, Northlight Photo Workshops specialize in high-quality small-group experiences. Eight week-long workshops are offered each year. Led by a photographer, each session is designed to maximize hands-on experience in the field. All of the workshops incorporate the opportunity for both group and individual crtiques, with on-site processing available so that work is ready for immediate review.

Workshops take place throughout the country. Examples of 1993 workshops include a week photographing winter snow scenics, waterfalls, and ice formations in Delaware Gap, Pennsylvania, a spring expedition to Arizona's Sonoran Desert, and an early-summer foray into the Great Smoky Mountains at the peak of rhodendendron season.

COST: Workshop fees cover on-location instruction and guide services. They do not cover ground transportation, meals, or lodging. Northlight attempts to arrange lodgings in comfortable hotels or country inns with meeting facilities for evening sessions. Participants can also arrange to stay at campgrounds. Workshop fees range from $495 to $600.

THE MAINE PHOTOGRAPHIC WORKSHOPS

Rockport, Maine 04856
(207) 236-8581

The Maine Photographic Workshops offers more than two hundred one- and two-week-long courses in photography, film, video, and television. Sessions are held from May to October, and last year more than two thousand students came to study at the school's campus in Rockport, Maine, a small coastal village. Of this number, 60 percent were working professionals in the field, while 40 percent were serious amateurs. Sixty-five percent of those who attended worked in film, television, or video, while 35 percent were photographers.

Although some courses are intended for novices, the workshop is best known for the courses and master classes it offers for advanced photographers and filmmakers on a career track. Acceptance into the advanced workshops and the master classes is made on the basis of portfolios and résumés. The master classes are taught by famous photographers and filmmakers, who have built their reputations in the worlds of commercial and fine-art photography, filmmaking, and television. The basic and intermediate workshops are taught by people who teach for a living. Most classes are limited to eighteen students to each instructor/assistant team.

David Lyman, founder and director of the Maine Photographic Workshops, notes that while a week here may be fun, it is not a vacation. "The Workshop is a magical place," he writes, "a place where creative people from around the world come each summer to renew their creative drive, set goals, learn new skills, develop their visual eye and be inspired to grow. . . . The Workshop is not for everyone. You must be committed to your craft, your art and your inner voice. This is not a place for dabblers and dilettantes. If you want to master your craft, this is the place to do it."

Workshop participants choose from a variety of local accommodations, including hotels, motels, and rooms in private homes. They share buffet-style meals together in the Homestead, a restored nineteenth-century farmhouse. For children, the school offers the "Young Filmmaker's Workshop" and the 'Young Photographer's Workshop." These two-week-long sessions are conducted twice each summer.

COST: Tuition for most one-week photography workshops ranges from $450 to $700, plus a $90 lab fee. Tuition for most film and video workshops ranges from $600 to $980 per week. Materials fees run $85–$150 per week. Depending upon the type of accommodation chosen, room and board ranges from $355 to $655.

JOSEPH VAN OS PHOTO SAFARIS

P.O. Box 655
Vashon Island, Washington 98070
(206) 463-5383

Joseph Van Os Photo Safaris organizes and conducts trips to dramatic areas of North America and far-flung parts of the world with the aim of providing superb opportunities for natural history and wildlife photography. The company also operates a series of photo workshops, designed for those who seek an intensive hands-on learning experience stressing photo techniques. While the photo safaris travel from one point of interest to another, the photo workshops are usually based at a single site. Both safaris and workshops are led by professional wildlife photographers whose work has been published extensively and many of whom have an academic background in biology, zoology, environmental science, and related fields.

Each workshop is limited to twenty participants and most run for five days. They are open to photographers at all levels who want to hone their techniques with expert instructors. Under the guidance of an experienced teacher, participants are taught through a combination of indoor slide lectures and field instruction. Some of the sessions involve advanced instruction. Workshop locations are subject to change from year to year, but they are always held in parts of North America with abundant wildlife and magnificent scenery. Sessions are often scheduled for the following locations: Olympic National Park, Washington; Palouse County of Eastern Washington; Saguaro National Monument, Arizona; Death Valley, California; and Sanibel Island, south Florida.

COST: The fee for each workshop is $645. This covers instruction, guide service, and specified ground transportation. Room and meals are not included.

GERLACH NATURE PHOTOGRAPHY

**P.O. Box 259
Chatham, Michigan 49816
(906) 439-5991**

Based in Michigan's Upper Peninsula, John and Barbara Gerlach operate one of the largest stock nature photography businesses in the country. They share their skills and their enthusiasm for nature photography through field workshops and a traveling seminar.

The seminar, "How to Shoot Beautiful Nature Photographs for Fun and Profit," is an intensive one-day instructional program offered in several different cities. It is intended for people who want to learn how to shoot in the wild with 35-mm cameras. Each session is limited to one hundred people. As a participant, you will learn how to use natural light to photograph birds, mammals, reptiles, dew, fog, spiderwebs, and other subjects found in nature. The program takes a practical approach, paying considerable attention to solving problems frequently encountered by nature photographers in the field. To illustrate key points, more than five hundred slides are projected during the course of the day.

At the seminar, each participant receives a packet of materials containing over forty pages of instructional notes and a copy of the Gerlachs' extensive document, "How to Shoot Perfect Natural Light Exposures on Color Transparency Film."

The Gerlachs also offer one-week summer nature photography field workshops, usually near their home in the Upper Peninsula. Typically, time is divided between the Pictured Rocks National Lakeshore, which derives its name from the colorful rock formations along this part of the southern shoreline of Lake Superior, and Hiawatha Forest. About 25 percent of each week is spent viewing instructional slide programs and the other 75 percent is spent in the field, learning how to choose good photo prospects and how to get the best possible pictures of your chosen subjects using techniques anyone can learn.

Each workshop is limited to sixteen participants and the

emphasis is on the effective use of 35-mm color slide film. Immediate processing is available and the Gerlachs will critique your slides as the week goes by. The program is suitable for beginning through professional photographers.

COST: The fee for the seminar is $65 per person. The fee for the one-week workshop is $375, which covers classroom and field instruction and instructional materials. Meals, lodgings, and film processing are not included. The workshops are based at the Timber Ridge Motel and Lodge, where accommodations are available in the $22–$39 per person per night range. Camping options are also available.

ANCIENT IMAGES

P.O. Box 1086
Moab, Utah 84532
(800) 388-7886

From January through November, Dan and Nan Norris, publishers of Ancient Images greeting cards, conduct four-day photographic workshop adventures in the Four Corners area of the Southwest. During the tour, you will learn about and photograph little-known Anasazi ruins and rock art in a magnificent high-desert landscape. You will learn about composition, exposure techniques, and equipment on site, surrounded by a panorama of bluffs, mesas, spires, arches, and domes whose colors change with the rising and setting of the sun.

The workshop convenes Friday afternoon in Moab. You will learn to take sunset photos at Arches National Park, which features the greatest concentration of natural stone arches and balanced rocks anywhere in the world. Saturday begins with a sunrise session. During the day the group will travel to several locations to see and photograph rock art representing prehistoric, historic, and contemporary cultures. You will also visit ancient Anasazi dwellings. Sunday is spent visiting more Anasazi sites in the Cedar–Mesa–Grand Gulch Primitive Area. These field trips provide many opportunities to photograph ancient architecture, rock art, and magnificent canyon scenery, including a sunset session at an ancient village.

On both days, the group remains in the field for sunset and dinner. Weather permitting, evenings are spent learning how to photograph star trails (the streaking of starlight caused by the rotation of the earth) with spectacular rock formations as foregrounds. Instruction centers on the use of moonlight, flash units, and other artificial lighting.

On Monday morning, you return to Moab, usually making a stop at Newspaper Rock Historical Monument, a conglomerate of rock art representing three thousand years of ancient cultures. The tours are led by Dan Norris, who provides instruction for all skill levels. The enrollment in each tour is limited to eight. The itinerary involves hiking to several of the sites, but in most cases the hikes are less than a mile long.

COST: The fee for the four-day photo tour/workshop is $595, based on double occupancy. This covers lodgings, eight meals, the services of the tour guide/instructor, and transportation from lodgings to field sites each day.

Music

INTERNATIONAL MUSIC CAMP

1725 11th St.
Minot, North Dakota 58701
(701) 838-8472

A staff of 150 artists/teachers, guest conductors, and clinicians from the United States, Canada, and Europe gathers each summer in the International Peace Garden, which straddles the border between North Dakota and Manitoba, to work with more than three thousand students and adults. The International Music Camp Summer School of Fine Arts offers intensive instruction in band, electronic music, handbells, drama, piano, dance, guitar, twirling and drum majoring, cheerleading, orchestra, string orchestra, chorus, barbershop chorus, vocal jazz, piping and drumming, marimba and vibes, and other areas.

Some of the programs are specifically designed for middle and high school students, while others are restricted to adults. Many programs are open to people of all ages. Instruction is available at all levels, with classes divided according to ability, not age.

The camp operates eight one-week-long residential sessions during June and July. Students live in dormitories supervised by adult counselors. Adults are housed in dormitories, too, one for men and one for women. There are no accommodations for couples but camping can be arranged. Meals are served cafeteria style.

The camp also hosts an Art School Week for all ages, featuring classes in oils and acrylics, watercolors, drawing, portraiture, and figure drawing. The International Music Camp School of Dance offers one- and two-week-long sessions featuring ballet, jazz, and modern dance classes for beginners with some dance experience, intermediate, and advanced students. Instruction in choreography and improvisation and demonstrations and lectures focusing on makeup and stage appearance are also part of the program. A student performance concludes each session.

In addition to the camp's general brochure, separate leaflets are available for each program, so be sure to state your area(s) of interest when you request information.

COST: The fee for most one-week sessions, including tuition, room, and board, is $175–$190.

CHAMBER MUSIC CONFERENCE

Interlochen Center for the Arts
P.O. Box 199
Interlochen, Michigan 49643-0199
(616) 276-9221

Internationally known for its superb arts programs for young people, Interlochen welcomes adult musicians to participate in its annual Chamber Music Conference held for one week each August at its twelve-hundred-acre wooded campus in northern Michigan, nestled between two large clearwater lakes. This is a unique opportunity for amateur, professional, and semiprofessional musicians to play chamber music in both coached and informal ensembles and to attend master classes featuring keyboard, wind, and string instruments.

Offerings include: multiple ensembles for strings; reading ensembles for winds; chamber music repertory class for pianists; organized ensembles for strings and winds; string master classes; piano solo repertoire class; duo-piano repertoire class; piano pedagogy class; free ensembles; and chamber music master class. Organized ensembles practice from 10:15 A.M. to 12:15 P.M. each day. Nightly chamber music concerts are presented each evening by renowned guest artists who also serve as faculty members during the conference.

Upon registering for the conference, participants complete a form noting principal and secondary instruments and including a self-rating (elementary to advanced on a scale of -1 to 6+).

COST: The fee for attending the conference is $180. On-campus housing is available. Single rooms range from $297.44 to $414.96 and doubles range from $435.76 to $560.56.

SUMMER CHAMBER MUSIC WORKSHOP

Gettysburg College
Music Department
Gettysburg, Pennsylvania 17325-1486
(717) 337-6000

The music department at Gettysburg College conducts an annual Summer Chamber Music Workshop each June. College students, music teachers, and other adults gather to study and perform string quartets together for a week in a noncompetitive, supportive atmosphere. Participants and faculty live in a college dormitory and share social as well as musical activities.

The application process is simple. You provide an objective assessment of your musical abilities by checking off the appropriate category from a list that includes statements varying from "able to perform works by Brahms, late Beethoven, Schubert, Schumann" to "able to read most Haydn and Mozart" to "have played very little chamber music, but am willing to give it my best try!" The application deadline is May 1.

COST: For full room, board, and tuition, $255; $165 for tuition only.

APPLE HILL SUMMER CHAMBER MUSIC PROGRAMS

Apple Hill Center for Chamber Music
Apple Hill Road
East Sullivan, New Hampshire 03445
(603) 847-3371

Whether you're a conservatory musician or an enthusiastic amateur, you'll find a comfortable niche at Apple Hill, where you can become immersed in chamber music in a noncompetitive intergenerational setting. Each summer fifty students of varied skill levels participate in a series of five ten-day-long workshops. Students range in age from twelve to ninety and their instruments include violin, viola, cello, double bass, piano, harpsichord, flute, oboe, clarinet, bassoon, horn, and voice.

Motivated musicians have flocked to this eighteenth-century New England farm setting for over twenty years, playing music they love and forging new friendships with those who share their passion. Participants receive music in advance of their session, so they can learn their parts ahead of time. On the basis of ability, not age, students are assigned to at least two ensembles, each of which meets for 1½ hours each day. Extensive coaching is provided by the resident musicians, the Apple Hill Chamber Players, as well as guest faculty artists. Many students also join in informal sight-reading groups.

Students at Apple Hill live in cabins equipped with electric lights, camp cots, and mattresses. Meals are served buffet style in the concert barn (vegetarian entrees available). There is also a rehearsal barn as well as several practice cabins, which offer greater privacy. Music seems always to be in the air—ensembles often play during or after a meal and each session culminates in a concert where all who wish to play perform in front of a supportive audience.

Students frequently take time out to join in volleyball and soccer games, play ping-pong, tennis, or basketball, or go for a swim in a nearby pond. Evening excursions to local concerts, festivals, and contredances are popular, too. In describing her experience at Apple Hill, one young participant observed, "You know that the music is serious but at the same time there's laughter and kindness surrounding you."

Application to Apple Hill involves filling out a form describing your chamber music experience and your reasons for wanting to attend. You will also need to submit a tape including selections representing three of the following four periods: baroque, classical, romantic, and twentieth century.

COST: An all-inclusive fee of $860 is charged per session.

ADULT CHAMBER MUSIC FESTIVAL

Montana State University
Music Department
Bozeman, Montana 59717-0008
(406) 994-3561

For more than twenty years, accomplished musicians have gathered at Montana State University to make music together in both assigned and impromptu groups. "Our players vary widely as to ability (we ask that they be at least intermediate but many are professionals), age (some high schoolers but the largest number are over sixty-five years old with a fair number between), vocations (many teachers of course, and music students, but an equal number of doctors, computer programmers, housewives, etc.)," writes festival director Mary Sanks, who describes the atmosphere as akin to the spirit of a huge family reunion. Many players return year after year, and newcomers are always welcome.

Last year over two hundred musicians attended the festival. Participants and coaches live together in the university dorms, where rooms are set aside for playing and where some people quite literally make music all night long. In fact, informal sessions or "freelancing" is a major part of the festival's attraction. During the structured part of the program, each musician participates in ten assigned groups during the week, experiencing variety in terms of stylistic period, instrumentation, group size, difficulty of music, familiarity of music, and personnel. "We explore the literature fearlessly," writes Sanks, "from late Renaissance to contemporary."

The festival takes place each June, but registration is required early in April to allow time to organize assignments.

COST: The fee for participation in the festival is $210. Inexpensive dormitory accommodations are $16 per night in a single room, $12 per night per person in a double room. Meals are not included.

4 | Outdoor Recreation

Sports Camps

THE CRAFTSBURY SPORTS CENTER

Box 31
Craftsbury Common, Vermont 05827
(802) 586-7767

Tucked away on a dirt road in Vermont's pastoral Northeast Kingdom, where it is not unusual to spot deer, mink, beaver, coyote, or fox, the Craftsbury Sports Center occupies a former boy's boarding school.

"We're a resort with modestly priced lodgings and meals specializing in offering active outdoor vacations ranging from highly structured sculling and running camps to relaxed multi-sport samplers," explains program director John Brodhead. Other camps focus on race walking, fitness walking, flat-water canoeing, orienteering, and triathalon participation. These three- to seven-day residential programs are geared toward both those interested in mastering a new skill and those who want to improve their proficiency in an old one. Guests are encouraged to train at their own pace.

The running camps include coached runs with videotaped analysis and a one-on-one coaching session to help each participant formulate a individualized six-week program.

Classroom sessions are devoted to mental training, nutrition, sports medicine, and physiology. Campers begin early each morning with coached ability group runs and then choose two workouts a day: cycle, hike, swim, run, or row. Interval work on the center's measured grass track is part of the plan, too. Campers also enjoy fun activities like canoeing, tennis, and swimming.

During the winter, the center is transformed into the Craftsbury Nordic Ski Center, featuring cross-country skiing on over one hundred kilometers of continuous groomed trail connected to seventy kilometers of back-country trail, making this the most extensive system in the East. Staff members provide instruction at all levels, beginner to expert, as well as guided wilderness and nature tours and free advice on waxing and equipment. Facilities include a lighted skating rink. Ice skate and ski rentals are available.

COST: The fee is $385 for a five-day running camp, including shared accommodations, all meals, and daily coaching/instruction program. A five-night midweek ski package, including lodging and all meals, one group ski lesson, trail passes, and organized evening activities, begins at $225 for adults, $127.50 for children 4–11. A similar two-night weekend package begins at $120 for adults, $60 for children 4–11.

SMITH COLLEGE ADULT SPORTS AND FITNESS CAMP

Scott Gymnasium
Smith College
Northampton, Massachusetts 01063
(413) 585-3971

Spend a week improving specific sports skills and strengthening your motivation to pursue a healthy lifestyle built on a foundation of good nutrition, appropriate exercise, and reduced stress. The Smith College Adult Sports and Fitness Camp is offered for several weeks each June. Well over half of those who have participated since the program began twelve years ago have returned for additional camp sessions.

Don't let the term *fitness camp* dissuade you. The emphasis here is equally as much on fun. You will spend the week in a variety of activities, learning new skills and refining old ones. Classes are taught at all levels in the following areas: aerobic dance, badminton, canoeing, croquet, diving, drown-proofing, orienteering, running, sculling, squash, step aerobics, stress management, swimming, t'ai chi, tennis, water-skiing, windsurfing, and yoga. Hiking, canoeing, and cycling trips are also scheduled.

Another important program component is the assessment opportunity. All participants are eligible (but not required) to take a fitness exam that tests pulmonary function, cardiovascular endurance, body composition, muscle strength, and flexibility. Each person is given an individualized computer exercise prescription based on the results of the exam. You can also elect to undergo nutritional assessment. Those who choose to do this complete a food-intake diary for computer analysis prior to camp. During the session, they meet individually with a nutritionist. Participants may also choose to have an individual evaluation by a sports-medicine specialist concerning orthopedic problems related to athletic participation.

During free time, campers have full use of the college's

athletic facilities, which include two gymnasiums, six squash courts, weight room, swimming pool, and provisions for indoor tennis and track. Outdoor facilities include twelve lighted tennis courts, two tracks, a pond, riverside boathouse, and croquet court.

While at camp, you will live in a single or double room in a student dormitory. Campers join together in a campus dining facility at the end of each day for a social hour, dinner, and evening recreational and educational programs.

COST: An all-inclusive fee of $600 covers tuition, room, and board.

Tennis

THE SEA PINES RACQUET CLUB

P.O. Box 7000
Hilton Head Island, South Carolina 29938
(803) 671-2494, ext. 4; (803) 785-3333;
(800) 845-6131

The Sea Pines Racquet Club has been the site of more nationally televised tennis events than any other location. Tennis greats who have won titles here include Rodney Laver, Bjorn Borg, Billie Jean King, Chris Evert, John Newcombe, Martina Navratilova, and Steffi Graf. Under the guidance of former world champion Stan Smith, who has served as Sea Pines' touring pro and tennis consultant for more than twenty years, the resort offers a complete instructional program that meets the needs of players at every level, from novice to tournament player.

The most effective way to improve your tennis is to sign up for a comprehensive four-day program based on the teaching method developed by Stan Smith. The Stan Smith Tennis

Academy starts off with a detailed video analysis of your strokes. Teaching pros provide stroke and strategy instruction to correct your errors and/or add new shots to your repertoire. To help you consolidate new skills, fast-action drills and ball-machine workouts are integral parts of the program. Attention is also paid to teaching you how to get the most out of your practice time. To further improve your game, you will work on court positioning and tactics designed to mentally prepare you for your matches. The program is open to players of all levels, who are grouped according to ability. Classes take place from 9:00 A.M. to 12:00 P.M. Tuesday through Friday. With an instructor-to-student ratio of 4:1, each student is assured ample individualized instruction.

If you want to concentrate on your doubles game, enroll in the "Stan Smith Weekend Workout." This program offers six hours of fast-action drills and ball-machine workouts designed to improve strokes and tactics important for better doubles play. The class meets Saturday and Sunday mornings from 9:00 A.M. to 12:00 P.M. and students are grouped by ability. Students are accepted for one or both days. Doubles clinics are also scheduled for Tuesday and Thursday afternoons.

From Monday to Friday Sea Pines also offers a 9:00 A.M. to 10 P.M. "Stroke of the Day Clinic." The focus is on a different stroke each day, with an emphasis on developing consistency, control, and spin. This is followed each day by a "Daily Drills Clinic," a 10:00 A.M. to 11:00 A.M. session during which you will learn and practice drills designed to focus on the stroke of the day. The clinics, designed for beginning and intermediate players, are open on a daily or weekly basis.

Sea Pines also offers a "Grand Slam Training Session" for high-intermediate to advanced competitive players who want to work hard. This clinic centers on advanced shot making, conditioning, footwork, and ball-machine drills and is held each afternoon from 3:30 P.M. to 5:00 P.M.

For children, the "Junior Instructional Program" includes clinics for those four years old and up, beginners to serious juniors. Adult programs are year-round while junior programs are offered holidays and from Memorial Day through Labor Day.

COST: The fee for the four-day "Stan Smith Tennis Academy," including all instruction, tennis manual, T-shirt, and midweek sailboat cruise, is $245. The fee for the "Stan Smith Weekend Workout" is $50 for a single session and $90 for a weekend. The fee for "Stroke of the Day" sessions and "Daily Drills Clinics" is $16 per day, $75 per week for either one; $30 per day and $140 per week for both.

THE VIC BRADEN TENNIS COLLEGE

The Green Valley Spa and Tennis Resort
1515 W. Canyon View Drive
St. George, Utah 84770
(801) 628-8060, (800) 237-1068

Located at a luxurious fitness spa poised on a mesa overlooking a spectacular canyon in the heart of Utah's red-rock country, the Vic Braden Tennis College (VBTC) features "Strokes to Strategies," a comprehensive program offered in two-, three-, and five-day versions. The curriculum combines classroom lessons with 4–5 hours of daily on-court instruction. Daily video analysis enables student and coach to verify improvement and to identify key areas requiring additional work.

The VBTC program is designed for players of all abilities, beginning to advanced. School begins each day in a modern classroom facility, equipped with demonstration stage, large rear-projection TV screen, and stop-action video equipment. After watching slow-motion videos of players hitting a variety of shots, the instructor demonstrates the day's strokes. Then the class marches outside to the courts, where members are grouped by ability. Four or five students are assigned to each teacher.

The two-day program covers backhand ground-stroke video analysis, forehand ground stroke, volleys and movement at the net, serve video analysis, service return, and approach shot. The three-day program covers all of the above plus forehand ground-stroke video analysis, overhead, lob, backhand ground-stroke review, serve and return review, approach-shot strategy for singles and doubles, and volley drills. The five-day program incorporates all of the above plus serve video analysis (second time), serve and volley, poaching, doubles position and play, a second forehand/backhand ground-stroke video analysis; ground-stroke drills/strategy, and coaches' evaluation of singles/doubles points.

During the first two days of each program, your backhand and serve are videotaped on special color-coded instructional courts. Using stop-action video and slow motion, your strokes are immediately analyzed in the school's playback rooms. Armed with practice tips, you return to the courts. As you progress, so too do the drills, leading eventually to match play. This progression takes place at three teaching stations: the video-analysis court, the drill-running court, and the Future Sport Teaching Lanes. The teaching lanes are a Vic Braden innovation that allow thirteen players to hit balls fed to them automatically; each lane is the width of an actual tennis court. With no time spent picking up balls, you can whack about nine hundred of them in an hour.

The VBTC program runs year-round. The emphasis is on having fun while improving play in a low-stress atmosphere. After class, you can swim in the resort's four swimming pools or enjoy the fitness facilities in the eighty-thousand-square-foot sports center.

COST: Fees for the tennis instruction program run as follows: two days, $250; three days, $375; five days, $500. These rates do not include lodging or meals, which vary according to arrangements chosen.

VAN DER MEER TENNIS CENTER

P.O. Box 5902
Hilton Head, South Carolina 29938
(800) 845-6138

Dennis Van der Meer has taught more people how to play and teach tennis than anyone else in the world. Facilities at the Van der Meer Tennis Center include twenty-four courts, eight lighted courts, and four covered/lighted courts. Daily, weekend, and week-long clinics are offered year-round to players at all skill levels. The center is associated with the adjoining Players Club, a full-service resort complete with ultramodern fitness and racquetball center, located just a block from the island's pristine beach. Accommodation rates are discounted for those participating in tennis clinics.

Dennis Van der Meer personally conducts the center's adult programs and the advanced adult clinics. The week-long adult programs are geared to the needs of intermediate and advanced intermediate players. The emphasis is on helping students build mastery of a variety of strokes, building stroke consistency, and developing mental skills for tennis. Students practice mobility drills and footwork and individualized tactics and strategy. In-depth video analysis with personal evaluation of strokes and match-play tactics is also part of the program. Weekend clinics, a shortened version of the adult program, are offered as well. Private and semiprivate lessons are another option.

The center also offers a variety of programs that are open to students on a day-by-day basis. These include 9:00 A.M. one-hour "Stroke of the Day" clinics. Monday is devoted to the serve, Tuesday is forehand day, Wednesday concentrates on the backhand, Thursday focuses on the volley, and Friday is for homing in on specialty shots. Each lesson is followed by a two-hour "Drills Session," open to intermediate players and above, which reinforces the Stroke-of-the-Day techniques. Daily drill sessions specifically geared to advanced-level players are also offered. The center also features a broad selection of junior programs, beginning with instruction for children as young as three years of age and continuing up to the "World-Class Training Program" for children ages twelve and up who have a ranking. Three- and five-day tennis camps for junior players are held during school vacation periods.

Five-day programs specifically designed for seniors are offered throughout the year. These clinics involve sixteen hours of instruction, including video analysis of strokes. A round-robin tournament and several social activities are also incorporated in this tennis experience. These clinics are suitable for both beginning and advanced players. Each participant is matched with partners and opponents of similar abilities.

You can also perfect your game at the Van der Meer TennisUniversity Midwest, based at the Lodge of Four Seasons Racquet Club in Lake Ozark, Missouri. The club offers stroke- and drill-of-the-day programs, ladies' clinics, private lessons, video analysis, and junior programs. In addition, players can participate in three-day adult clinics designed for all skill levels. The clinics, scheduled year-round, feature ten hours of instruction and in-depth video analysis with personal stroke evaluation.

Van der Meer summer camps, including adult and junior clinics, are also held at Sweet Briar College in the foothills of the Blue Ridge Mountains in Virginia.

COST: The fee for an adult clinic led by Dennis Van der Meer and including twenty-five hours of instruction over a five-day period is $415; the fee for the same format clinic led by a different pro is $315. Private lessons cost $35–$40 per hour; semiprivate lessons cost $23–$25 per person for two people, less for groups of three and four. The fee for the "Stroke of the Day" program is $10 per day or $45 for five days. The fee for the Seniors Tennis Clinics is $195.

Golf

THE ROLAND STAFFORD GOLF SCHOOL

P.O. Box 81
Arkville, New York 12406
(800) 447-8894, (914) 586-2915

The Roland Stafford Golf Schools adhere to a teaching philosophy rooted in the owner's belief that the most common mistake in golf instruction is overanalysis. Here the emphasis is on helping you develop your swing by concentrating on the fundamentals. As Stafford explains, "A rhythmic swing and a thorough understanding of the overall shape of the swing is the foundation of our teaching method. We cover the basics: the grip, connection of the swing, reading the course, and specialty shots designed to cut shots off your game." In addition, carefully developed drills are used to eliminate bad habits.

The Roland Stafford Golf Schools offer similar two-, three-, and five-day instructional programs at full-service resort locations in New York, Florida, Vermont, Canada, and abroad. Each school begins with a welcome reception the evening of your arrival, an opportunity to become acquainted with your instructors and fellow students. Participants are then grouped into classes according to ability, each one limited to four to six students, depending upon the program you choose. A lesson plan is developed for each class and the same instructor remains with the class throughout the program to ensure continuity of instruction.

The first day begins with a one-hour presentation detailing the Roland Stafford Golf Schools method. During the two-hour session that follows, each group is assigned to a particular practice area. After lunch, groups switch areas for another two-hour session. At 3:00 P.M. you are free to play on the course, practice, or take some time off.

Using information garnered from the first day, a schedule is established for subsequent days, with time set aside for rules-and-etiquette clinics and golf equipment talks and demonstrations. The schedule is flexible so the instructor can balance the class's needs—allowing time for playing the course, driving, practicing the short game, or watching a videotape. Students gather at 9:00 A.M. each morning for their daily assignments.

The two-day weekend package includes five hours of instruction daily on Saturday and Sunday, greens fees and cart after class, unlimited range balls, room for two nights, all meals, full use of resort facilities, video analysis, and rules clinic. The five-day midweek school includes twenty-three hours of instruction with on-course playing lessons, greens fees and cart during and after class, unlimited range balls, room for five nights, all meals, use of resort facilities, final-day tournament, video analysis, and rules, etiquette, and equipment clinics. Welcome receptions and golf school gifts are also part of the fun.

COST: For five-day midweek schools conducted at the Grand Palms Golf & Country Club Resort in Florida, the cost is $888 per person double occupancy, $1,033 single occupancy. For the two-day weekend schools conducted at the Inn at the Mountain/Mount Mansfield Resort in Vermont, the cost is $551 per person double occupancy, $637 single. Golf clubs are provided for beginners to use during the programs.

CRAFT-ZAVICHAS GOLF SCHOOL

600 Ditmer Ave.
Pueblo, Colorado 81005
(800) 858-9633

Owned and operated by LPGA Master Professional Penny Zavichas, the Craft-Zavichas School has been teaching golf since 1968. Students include men and women from their teens into their eighties, with an average age in the early fifties. Instruction emphasizes the development of effective fundamentals and is targeted toward men and women who want to play a respectable game but also want golf to be fun.

The school is staffed by full-time golf teachers and caters to both beginning and advanced golfers. Each student is assigned to the same instructor for the week, a method that speeds up learning. Because only five or fewer students are assigned to each teaching professional, the instruction is highly personalized. The school is committed to making your golf swing compatible with your natural body balance, using the dominant side of your body as a source of energy and consistency.

Classes are scheduled on a rotating basis, with a change every hour and fifteen minutes as you move from techniques for the long game to those required for the short game and every other situation in between. The rotation schedule conserves your energy by offering variety. At four- and five-day schools, classes run from 8:30 A.M. to 2:30 P.M. (only half a day of instruction on Wednesday during a five-day session), leaving plenty of time to get out on the course and play.

From January through April, the school is conducted at the Tucson National Golf & Conference Resort in Tucson, Arizona. In May and June, it is held at Pueblo West Golf Club & the Inn at Pueblo West in Pueblo West, Colorado. Both locations provide excellent golf with fine teaching facilities and full resort amenities.

All programs include welcome and farewell banquets/receptions, practice facilities and unlimited practice balls, club cleaning and storage, instruction manual, a personal split-screen analysis videotape to take home, greens fees and cart for unlimited play, accommodations, and lunches. Three- and five-day programs are offered in Tucson, incorporating a minimum of fifteen and twenty-five hours of golf instruction, respectively. A six-day program is offered in Pueblo West, which incorporates at least twenty hours of instruction. Both locations also offer "for women only" sessions.

COST: The per-person price for a three-day instructional package in Tucson, including three nights' resort lodging and program features as described above, is $1,585 for single occupancy, $1,325 for double occupancy. For the five-day package (six nights' lodging), the price is $2,075 for single occupancy and $1,685 for double occupancy. In Pueblo West, the per-person price for a six-day (five nights' lodging) package is $1,085 for single occupancy and $995 for double occupancy.

STRATTON GOLF SCHOOLS

Stratton Mountain, Vermont 05155
(800) 843-6867

STRATTON SCOTTSDALE GOLF SCHOOL

P.O. Box 6349
Scottsdale, Arizona 85258
(800) 238-2424

The Stratton Golf Schools cater to players at all levels, from rank beginnners to low handicappers. New golfers get off to a good start, while experienced players fine-tune their skills and correct problems. Each location has an extensive training facility complete with greens, fairways, bunkers, and chipping areas, where you can master your strokes apart from people playing on the golf courses around you. The Vermont school has indoor teaching facilities so that you can continue to improve your game even if it rains.

Videotape analysis and stop-action photography are used to help players identify and build on individual strengths. These sophisticated teaching aids also enable instructors to spotlight weaknesses and help correct bad habits. "Everyone is different," comments PGA pro Keith Lyford, director of the Stratton Golf Schools. "I like to videotape the student, analyze what he or she is doing, find one or two key elements and concentrate on those things."

Programs are offered from May through early October at the school's Vermont location. The two-day session includes two complete days of instruction plus complementary play on the twenty-seven-hole Stratton Mountain Country Club golf course on your day of arrival and after regular instruction hours. The five-day session includes four full days of instruction and a fifth day of play on the course, in addition to course time on your day of arrival and after instruction hours. Similar two-, three-, and five-day programs are available at the Stratton Scottsdale Golf School from November through early May. Both schools maintain a 5:1 or better student-to-instructor ratio to ensure intensive personalized instruction.

COST: Rates include luxury resort lodgings, lunch each day, and instruction and course time as described above. *Stratton Scottsdale:* The two-day program during prime season (mid-January through early May) runs $460; the five-day program runs $1,055. *Stratton Mountain:* The two-day program during prime season (May through Labor Day) runs $405 to $505, depending upon time of week; the five-day midweek program runs $850. Rates quoted are per person, per session, based on double occupancy.

THE LA COSTA GOLF SCHOOL

La Costa Resort and Spa
Costa Del Mar Road
Carlsbad, California 92009
(619) 438-9111

The La Costa Golf School, described by one golf magazine as "undoubtedly, the most comprehensive, effective and enjoyable golf school around," is located at the La Costa Resort and Spa, a luxurious 478-room complex complete with two PGA championship eighteen-hole golf courses. The resort hosts the annual Infiniti Tournament of Champions at La Costa each January.

School founder and director Carl Welty is recognized as a pioneer in the field of video swing analysis and as the top video instructor in the country today. His approach to instruction combines student interviews, videotaped play, and lab/workshop study focusing on areas that need improvement. To see if you're making contact with the ball in the right spot, impact tape is affixed to the head of each club you use.

Because the instruction is so highly personalized, it benefits everyone from rank beginners to the top touring professionals who come to brush up on specific facets of their game. A typical half-day instructional session begins with an interview. You will be queried about your golf history, worst and best parts of your game, shot patterns, goals, physical problems, and frequency of play. Next come stretching exercises, practicing the movements demonstrated on a video developed specifically for golfers. After a few warm-up shots on the driving range, head for the course to play several holes while a video camera documents the action. Then it's back to the studio for staff analysis of everything that can be examined in a golf swing. After that, it's time to head for the indoor mats to hit practice balls, applying the pointers you've just received. Again, the video camera records the action. Then it's out to the driving range to further apply the morning's lessons.

COST: The school offers half-day and full-day private sessions at a rate of $85 per hour for a single student, $100 per hour for two students. The La Costa Golf School package, which includes two nights at the resort and three days at the golf school, is $1,115 based upon double occupancy. Meals are purchased a la carte.

JOHN JACOBS' PRACTICAL GOLF SCHOOLS

7825 E. Redfield Road
Scottsdale, Arizona 85260-6977
(800) 472-5007, (602) 991-8243

Under the direction of cofounder Shelby Futch, the John Jacobs' Practical Golf Schools have become the largest golf school in the world, teaching more than ten thousand students each year. John Jacobs' welcomes beginners as well as players at all other levels. Because of the number of students enrolled, John Jacobs' can create "schools within a school," grouping students by handicaps and ability levels. Many students drop 8–10 strokes off their handicaps as a result of their participation in the program.

The school specializes in teaching the fundamentals. Students learn about the dynamics of face angle, club-head path, and angle of path. The instruction is practical and easy to understand. For example, the instructors drill in a preswing routine labeled with the acronym GASP: grip, aim, stance, and posture.

Unlike some schools, the emphasis here is on helping students correct bad habits while improving skills they already have. To this end, instructors practice a threefold strategy for strengthening their students' golf game: diagnosis, explanation, and correction. The school specializes in simple swing adjustments, introducing remedies that get quick results, particularly in dealing with the notorious slice, an affliction that plagues about 85 percent of the golfers who attend.

Hundreds of weekend, midweek, weekend, and commuter schools are scheduled throughout the year all over the country. The sessions are held at fine resorts offering all the pleasantries that turn a week of school into a luxurious vacation. Sessions are currently scheduled in Alabama, Arizona, California, Colorado, Florida, Hawaii, Michigan, Missouri, Nevada, New Jersey, New York, Oklahoma, Texas, Wisconsin, and Wyoming.

Classes, which make use of facilities including a driving range, putting green, chipping green, and practice traps, run from 9:00 A.M. to 3:00 P.M. After that, you can play free golf until the sun sets, use of carts included. As part of the school package, each student also receives a high-tech video swing analysis, a copy of the *John Jacobs' Instructional Manual,* and free club storage and cleaning.

Beyond the basic course, John Jacobs' offers a variety of special options. "The Playing Schools" combine daily instruction with an eighteen-hole playing lesson each day. With a 3:1 student-to-teacher ratio, there's ample opportunity for personalized on-course instruction. "Mental Golf" is a two-day traveling seminar that helps you understand your own game and the psychological factors that affect it. The focus is on identifying problem areas, breaking old habits, and learning to visualize your game creatively. The course begins at home, where you fill out a written questionnaire that is then evaluated via a personalized report. The report is reviewed during the seminar sessions as you explore new ways to improve and maintain your mental grip on the game.

COST: The fee for a one-week golf school package at a desert resort in Litchfield, Arizona, ranges from $1,250 to $1,395 per person from January to May. Package includes five days of golf instruction and amenities as described above, six nights' accommodation, and most meals. The fee for a standard golf school package at a country resort in Park City, Utah, is $845 per person. The package includes four days of golf instruction and amenities as described above, five nights' accommodation, and most meals. Commuter schools (tuition only) start as low as $245.

Sailing

SEA SAFARI SAILING SCHOOL

12060 Carver Ave.
New Port Richey, Florida 34654
(813) 856-0157, (800) 497-2508

Founded in 1990 by Laurel Winans, grandmother of four, Sea Safari Sailing is one of the only programs in the country specializing in multihull instruction. The school, based on the central west coast of Florida, prides itself on helping timid would-be sailors replace their fears with a burgeoning sense of self-confidence and competence. Known for their stability, multihulls don't heel over dramatically the way monohulls do. In the past three years, the school has taught 400–500 people to sail, well over half of them first-timers. As co-owner Georgia Hotton observes, with a multihull "people realize they don't have to hang on for dear life. It makes the entry-level cruiser just a lot more comfortable."

Sea Safari offers courses for women, for couples, and for families. Students sign on for two, three, five, or seven days of instruction covering terminology, points of sail, sail trim, chart reading, navigation, rules of the road, mooring lines, docking, knots, emergency procedures, ships' systems, VHF radio, electronic navigation, weather, seamanship, anchoring, and how to check out and provision a charter boat.

Instruction usually takes place aboard the twenty-eight-foot catamaran *Inanna*. During the course, students live aboard the boat and help out with cooking, deck swabbing, and other chores. During a typical cruise, the captain spends the first half of the first day familiarizing students with the boat while it is still lashed to the dock. On-the-water experience incorporates both offshore and coastal cruising. Time is also built in for snorkeling, swimming, shelling, dolphin watching, and dining at waterside seafood restaurants.

For advanced students, the school offers an instructional cruise to the Dry Tortugas, a tropical group of uninhabited islands just seventy miles west of Key West. As an added incentive, accomplished Sea Safari graduates are given the opportunity to participate, at no cost, as crew members on major yacht deliveries.

All groups are kept small, reflecting the school's commitment to customizing the training to complement each student's level of understanding. Instructors are chosen for their patience and teaching abilities as well as their superior boat-handling skills. As Captain Winans puts it, "We don't bark out commands or make anyone feel inferior. Our approach is to build up confidence and knowledge from a positive standpoint."

COST: The standard fee is $295 for two days, $445 for three days, $695 for five days, and $895 for seven days. All prices include on-board accommodations, meals, sailing instruction, and personal reference manual and study guide.

OFFSHORE SAILING SCHOOL

16731 McGregor Boulevard
Fort Myers, Florida 33908
(813) 454-1191

Founded in 1964 by Americas Cup and Olympic sailor Steve Colgate, Offshore Sailing School offers three- to seven-day courses covering all levels of sailing. Throughout the years, the school has taught over seventy thousand adults to sail. It is the only sailing school recognized for college credit by the American Council on Education.

Called "Learn to Sail," the core course is an intensive comprehensive program intended for beginning and intermediate sailors. The following areas are covered: nautical terminology; types of boats; rigging and sails; getting underway; proper winching techniques; finding wind direction; points of sailing; tacking and jibing; mechanics of wind and sail; tight maneuvering; slot effect; heeling and stability; wind shifts and apparent wind; wing and wing; stopping a sailboat; man-overboard recovery; sailing backwards; rudderless sailing; sail trim and sail shape; boat balance; hull speed; mooring, docking, and anchoring; knots; right-of-way rules; reefing techniques; grounding situations; heavy weather; steering with a compass; current sailing; weather and lee helm; introduction to navigation; and spinnaker techniques.

The course is taught over either two consecutive weekends, a three-day weekend, or three consecutive weekdays. Instruction takes place on a twenty-seven-foot Olympic-class Soling, an easy-to-sail, responsive, and safe training boat. Each day begins with an informative classroom session, after which you set sail to apply what you have learned. At the end of the program, together with your fellow crew members, you chart a course and set sail without your instructor, a testimony to your ability to now handle a boat on your own with confidence.

Experienced sailors can sign on for "Advanced Sailing," which covers all you need to know to sail a medium-sized boat. Some of the topics covered include advanced sail trim, practical navigation, extensive spinnaker work, cruising seamanship, and emergency situations. Instruction takes place aboard a twenty-eight-foot cruiser–racer.

The school also offers racing symposiums for sailors with good boat-handling skills who have little or no racing experience. A season's worth of experience—drills, spinnaker sets and douses, starts, and short races—is packed into four intensive days of instruction aboard the twenty-seven-foot Olympic

Solings. The course includes a three-hour practice sail on the final afternoon. Other courses prepare sailors for bareboat chartering. The school also offers "Women Offshore," a course option for those women who prefer to learn to sail with all-women crews and instructors.

The maximum number of students per boat is four, three in the racing courses, to ensure safety and personal attention. Upon receiving your registration, the school will send you a copy of the course textbook to study in advance.

Based in Fort Myers, Offshore Sailing School continues to operate at its original City Island location, just outside of New York City. In addition, courses are offered in Port Washington, New York, just thirty-five minutes from Manhattan. The school also has branches at resorts on Cape Cod in Massachusetts, on Florida's Captiva Island, and in the Caribbean. Making the basic courses even more accessible, the National Learn-to-Sail Tour takes the program on the road by bringing an instructor, a twenty-seven-foot Olympic-class Soling, and a complete classroom to locations in the following states: Alabama, Connecticut, Florida, Georgia, Illinois, Indiana, Iowa, Kentucky, Maine, Minnesota, Missouri, New Hampshire, New Jersey, New York, North Carolina, Ohio, Rhode Island, South Carolina, Tennessee, and Wisconsin. Send for a schedule.

COST: Tuition for "Learn to Sail" at City Island, New York, is $395–$435, depending upon the dates chosen; "Advanced Sailing" is $425–$435. Tuition for the "National Learn-to-Sail" course is $595 at all locations. The fee for resort courses (Cape Cod, Captiva, Caribbean locations) depends upon the particular package chosen.

COASTLINE SAILING SCHOOL & YACHT CHARTERS

Eldridge Yard
Marsh Road
Noank, Connecticut 06340
(203) 536-2689

Headquartered at the mouth of the Mystic River, offering easy access to the protected waters of Fisher's Island Sound, Coastline Sailing School offers instruction for sailors of all levels. An official training center for the American Sailing Association (ASA), Coastline provides programs in basic sailing, coastal cruising, and coastal navigation. All course fees include an official ASA textbook, *Sailing Fundamentals* or *Chartering Fundamentals*, personal ASA logbook, ASA certification upon successful completion, and all meals.

The school also offers one- and two-day classroom courses centering on topics ranging from practical navigation to diesel engines to a bareboat refresher seminar (the perfect chance for the experienced but out-of-practice sailor to fine-tune skills). Novices can get started by enrolling in "Basic Sailing," which is offered every weekend from April through June and in September. The course consists of two six-hour sessions of water instruction on a 27–30-foot keel boat. Instruction focuses on sailing terminology, boat handling, rules of the road, and sail control. Successful completion is rewarded with ASA Basic Sailing Certification, which qualifies you to enroll in a coastal cruising program.

During the three-day coastal cruising program, you'll learn to skipper a sailing vessel over thirty feet. Instruction centers on navigation, boat handling under power, sail handling, communicating on the ship's radio, anchoring, cooking aboard, and other seamanship skills. The ASA Basic Cruising Certificate is awarded on successful completion of the course, qualifying you to continue to move up the ASA ladder by participating in longer instructional cruises, eventually earning Bareboat

Chartering Certification and ASA Advanced Coastal Cruising Certification. Those who wish to hone their sailing skills during the winter months can head to the Caribbean, where Coastline Sailing School establishes operations at Red Hook, Saint Thomas. All of the ASA instructional programs are offered and there are more than a dozen yachts available for bareboat charter.

COST: The fee for the weekend-long "Basic Sailing" course is $245. For the "Three-Day Coastal Cruising Getaway," the fee is $575.

BANANA BAY SAILING SCHOOL

Banana Bay Resort and Marina
4590 Overseas Highway
Marathon, Florida 33050
(800) 448-6636, (305) 743-3500

Learn to sail in the warm, shallow, turquoise waters of the Gulf of Mexico. A lush resort secluded in a ten-acre tropical setting halfway down the Florida Keys, Banana Bay has its own sailing school featuring a five-day learn-to-sail package that combines classroom instruction with on-the-water sailing practice. Designed specifically for beginning sailors, the course includes an introduction to the fundamentals of sailing, terminology, seamanship, chart reading and sail theory, sail trim and points of sail, basic rules of the road, anchoring and mooring, safety, and knots. The week begins with a Sunday evening orientation session. Monday and Tuesday are devoted to both classroom and on-board instruction. Wednesday is given over to a group sail complete with picnic and snorkeling. On Thursday, the schedule calls for review, practice, and a sunset sail followed by a graduation dinner.

The lessons conclude early in the afternoon, leaving the rest of the day free to enjoy the resort's other features. In addition to course materials and instruction, the package includes tennis-court time and use of equipment, use of bikes, and use of the pool, spa, and beach and snorkeling area. A weekend program is also available.

COST: The fee for the five-day learn-to-sail package is $799 for one person, $1,199 for two (double-occupancy room) during the low season, and $1,199 for one person and $1,899 for two during the high season. This covers the sailing program, five nights' lodging, poolside continental breakfast, airport transfers, and use of resort amenities as described above.

PACIFIC YACHTING

333 Lake Ave.
Santa Cruz, California 95062
(408) 476-2370

Pacific Yachting features a "Six-Day Live-Aboard Instruction Vacation," a course designed to teach you everything you need to know to skipper a vessel up to thirty-three feet long, even if you've never even sailed before. Days are spent on the waters of Monterey Bay in the company of otters, seals, sea lions, and seabirds. Each night is spent tied up at the dock in Santa Cruz Harbor, with restaurants and grocery stores within easy walking distance.

If you master all the skills taught in the course, you will receive a certificate from Pacific Yachting stating that the company considers you qualified to sail a boat and recommends you to bareboat-charter companies around the world. That means you can go out and rent a 30–34-foot wheel-steered yacht and cruise on your own, a very different (and less costly and much more private) experience than chartering a boat with captain and crew. (Do be aware, however, that many bareboat companies will ask you to sail with one of their instructors for an hour or two before deciding to rent you a boat, a practice Pacific Yachting often follows when renting to unfamiliar sailors.)

For those interested in a less intensive training experience, the company offers a series of two-day courses involving twelve to fourteen hours of on-board instruction. "Basic Sailing and Seamanship" focuses on the fundamentals of sailing and boat handling. On completion of on-board instruction, you will be ready to take the test for the American Sailing Association (ASA) Basic Sailing Certification on tiller-steering boats. Those already familiar with the basics can opt for the "Intermediate Bareboat Sailing Course." Taught aboard a 32–34-foot yacht, completion of this course prepares you for the ASA Intermediate Coastal Cruising and Bareboat Charter qualifications. "Advanced Coastal Cruising" is taught on board 32–38-foot yachts. Skills covered include basic navigation with charts, Loran navigation, sailing with reduced visibility, running fixes, and much more.

Other programs include a five-hour classroom course in "Coastal Navigation and Piloting," a ten-hour "Celestial Navigation Course," and "Performance Sailing and Spinnaker Handling," a two-day class taught aboard the school's racing yachts.

The company maintains a fleet of eighteen meticulously maintained sailing yachts, including racers and cruisers ranging in length from twenty-five to forty-three feet. The variety ensures that each level of the training program is conducted on an appropriate vessel.

COST: The fee for the "Six-Day Live-Aboard Instruction Vacation" is $690 per student for a class of two and $621 per student for a class of 3–4. If you cannot arrange to spend six consecutive days aboard, you can divide the course up over three weekends or two long weekends for a somewhat higher tuition. The fees for the two-day courses run as follows: two students, $275 per student; three students, $225 per student; 4–5 students, $200 per student.

Canoeing, Kayaking, and Rafting

SUNDANCE EXPEDITIONS

14894 Galice Road
Merlin, Oregon 97532
(503) 479-8508

Sundance Expeditions has been in the business of teaching kayaking skills and leading trips on the Rogue River for the past twenty years. If you want a truly comprehensive introduction to white-water kayaking, this is the place to get it. The "Nine-Day Basic Kayak School" teams five days of on-water instruction and practice with a four-day river trip. The program is designed for adults with no previous kayaking experience. Video reviews, chalk talks, lectures, and slide shows supplement the hands-on learning.

On the first day, you will get an introduction to the boat and the gear. You will be outfitted with a kayak appropriate for your height and weight, along with top-quality equipment of the proper size and fit, including helmet, paddle, life jacket, spray skirt (to keep water out of the cockpit), paddling jacket, and paddling sweater. The first lessons focus on getting in and out of the boat while it's right side up, as well as how to get out when it's wrong side up. As the days pass you will learn, often working one-on-one with an instructor, the logistics of the Eskimo roll, the eddy turn, and the ferry, practicing on increasingly turbulent water as you become more competent and confident. The nights are spent in comfortable guest rooms at Sundance Riverhouse, where there's even an outdoor hot tub.

Days six through nine are devoted to a forty-mile wilderness river trip, pulling together all those new skills as you negotiate class II and III white water on the Rogue, running some rapids in formation and getting out to scout a drop from time to time. Evenings are spent camping by the river, enjoying excellent camp cooking courtesy of your guides, the same folks who accompany you down the river, rowing support rafts laden with all the necessary camping equipment and supplies.

Novices also have the option of taking just the first five days of the school, the intensive instructional component. Experienced paddlers can sign on for the last day of the instruction and the river trip. Classes in the kayak school average ten to twelve students, ranging in age from fourteen to fifty-five.

Sundance Expeditions also offers intermediate and advanced programs. Intermediate instruction focuses on the development of increasingly precise paddling skills, with an emphasis on bracing, off-side rolling, catching and leaving tight eddies, and using river dynamics for efficient maneuvering on class III and IV waters. Advanced programs provide the chance to run class IV and V water with support and guidance from the staff.

COST: The fee for the "Nine-Day Basic Kayak School" is $1,260, which includes use of equipment (wetsuit rental is extra), lodging, and meals. The fee for half the school (either the first five days or the last five days) is $700.

MAINE ISLAND KAYAK COMPANY

70 Luther St.
Peaks Island, Maine 04108
(207) 766-2373

Maine Island Kayak Company (MIKC) specializes in arranging custom sea-kayaking trips for groups of three to six. They cater to families with children seeking a little adventure and the chance to learn new skills, as well as to conditioned athletes capable of paddling up to thirty-five miles per day. Many of their trips require no previous experience and most guests have never been in a sea kayak before. Some of the trips are labeled "all invited," while others carry designations like "for stronger types" and "for strong and adventurous types."

MIKC organizes kayaking/camping trips of one to ten days, covering the entire Maine Island Trail, a network of seventy-four public and privately owned islands scattered along 325 miles of coastline extending from Casco Bay to Machias Bay.

All trips include guidance in the use and care of kayaks and gear, low-impact island use, safety procedures, navigation essentials, and forecasting weather and water conditions. "We're dedicated to developing the complete coastal kayaker," observes company owner/guide Tom Bergh. "It's a hell of a lot more than how the paddle goes in the water. We want people to learn about wind and waves, tides and current, chart and compass, wilderness medicine, group dynamics, route selection, and basic paddling skills including rough-water rescue."

For those who wish to enroll in an instructional program before embarking on an overnight trip, MIKC offers a one-day basic course for beginners that covers boat design and fitting, safety equipment, basic strokes, bracing and sculling, and wet exits and assisted rescues. There is also a one-day course devoted to self- and group rescue techniques. A two-day in-depth ocean touring course provides paddlers with the skills and knowledge they need to exercise good judgment on the ocean, covering weather analysis, wind and waves, tides and currents, route selection, group dynamics, island ethics, and trip planning. Courses are also offered in navigation, marine medicine, boat repair, and related subjects.

MIKC maintains a varied fleet of thirty fully outfitted, expedition-equipped single and double kayaks. In addition to matching you with the right kayak, they provide all group camping equipment, all safety gear, comprehensive safety backup and first aid, including radio communication, and all food. All you need to bring is your personal gear and a sleeping bag and pad. If you prefer more comfort, MIKC can arrange trips that include accommodations in Maine's coastal inns and seaside cottages.

COST: The fee for the one-day basic instructional course is $95. The fee for the two-day ocean touring course is $160. A four-day exploration of the waters and uninhabited islands of Muscongus Bay costs $450, plus $35 for membership in the Maine Island Trail Association.

OTTER BAR LODGE

Box 210
Forks of Salmon, California 96031
(916) 462-4772

Otter Bar Lodge represents one man's dream. Peter Sturges has built himself the ultimate wilderness lodge near Forks of Salmon, an isolated river hamlet about fifty miles south of the Oregon border. A three-quarter-mile stretch of the emerald-green (California) Salmon River crosses the forty-acre lodge property (you can hear the water from the veranda), which is surrounded by pristine swimming holes, stream-fed ponds, and private beaches. Otter Bar Lodge specializes in mountain biking and kayaking, and calls itself the only such facility in the country to offer deluxe lodgings and gourmet cuisine.

You don't need any previous experience to enroll in a week-long Otter Bar kayaking school. The instructors are well-known experts, the equipment first class, and the location, on one of the few undammed rivers in the country, is no less than perfect. The schools identify boaters as fitting into four categories. The "Beginner School" is for those who know nothing about kayaking but have a desire to learn. After being outiftted with all the necessary gear, including a life jacket, spray skirt, paddling sweater, paddling jacket, and boat, students spend two days learning and practicing safety procedures, stroke techniques, the "roll," and bracing techniques on a pond next to the lodge. Days three, four, and five are spent on the river, practicing skills and learning about eddy turns, ferrying, and bow draws. The last two days are devoted to an overnight trip, an opportunity to put together all the skills you've acquired.

For those who have previous kayaking experience, Otter Bar offers the "Basic Intermediate School," the "Intermediate School," and the "Advanced School." Throughout these programs, the emphasis is on improving skills while navigating increasingly difficult white water, culminating in the biggest challenges the California Salmon has to offer. Kayaking schools are offered from April into September. Whichever school you choose, you can be assured of optimum individual attention.

During August and September, Otter Bar offers a week-long mountain-bike program. The first day begins with a discussion on the basics of bike care and bike fit, followed by a bike-handling lesson on a nearly two mile single-track loop adjoining the lodge. Each morning from then on you will be presented with a choice of rides of varying difficulty, traveling to mountain lakes, high peaks, and to the edge of the river where rafts await to give you an afternoon of white-water excitement.

You will be supplied with a top-notch mountain bike and experienced instructors will teach you how to ride it on all types of terrain. Bike maintenance seminars are provided, too. The highlight of the week is an overnight ride to a cozy cabin at the top of a six-thousand-foot ridge.

In addition to the programs described above, in the fall the lodge offers a fly-fishing program complete with organized classes and an outdoor photography seminar in which student work is developed daily and critiqued by an instructor.

Small and personable, Otter Bar Lodge can accommodate up to ten visitors in its comfortable rooms, each with its own deck. At the end of a day of vigorous activity, guests can relax in the wood-fired sauna and the outdoor hot tub.

COST: The fee for the seven-day kayaking schools is $1,090. This covers equipment for the beginning and basic intermediate classes, instruction, lodging (double occupancy), and all meals. The fee for the seven-day mountain-biking school is $1,050. This covers use of bikes, guided outings, maintenance seminars, river rafting, introduction to kayaking, lodging (double occupancy), and all meals.

AQUA ADVENTURES KAYAK SCHOOL

7985 Dunbrook Road, Suite H
San Diego, California 92126
(619) 695-1500

The mission of Aqua Adventures Kayak School is to provide comprehensive, quality kayaking instruction for people at all levels of experience. All of the introductory clinics and trips make use of open-cockpit kayaks, which get beginners started quickly. For intermediate-level river and kayak surfing programs, students choose between a variety of boats.

The best way to get started is to sign up for a "Comprehensive Weekend." This program is designed for those who have never been in a kayak before. After completing the four 2½-hour-long instructional sessions, which can be taken individually or grouped together in one weekend, you will discover that you have become a safe and competent paddler prepared to encounter a variety of ocean and bay conditions.

The first lesson is an overview of kayaks and how to use them. The second lesson refines the paddling skills taught in the first class and introduces some of the basics of sea kayaking (the aquatic version of backpacking), such as trip planning and packing gear. The third class begins with instruction in how to launch and land the kayak in different surf conditions, and then continues with an opportunity to sample coastal exploration. During the fourth lesson, you will learn the basics of kayak surfing and then take some time to refine techniques introduced in the previous classes. The program is offered at locations in Los Angeles, San Francisco, San Simeon, and Santa Cruz.

Other course options include "Introduction to River Kayaking," a class for people with little or no previous kayaking experience. Instruction takes place on an easy stretch of river and focuses on the use of the boat, strokes and techniques, reading white water, hole playing, wave surfing, and safety measures. More experienced paddlers can sign on for the "Intermediate River Clinic," which includes the opportunity to improve your skills in reading and running rapids, eventually getting down to some serious wave surfing.

The school also offers a variety of guided trips in the western United States, Hawaii, and Baja California, many of which include kayak surfing clinics and other instructional elements. The most popular week-long trip, "Bahia de Los Angeles," takes you to a chain of uninhabited islands in the heart of the Gulf of California. In addition to honing your skills under the eye of your instructor/guide, activities include hiking, snorkeling with sea lions, fishing, and a volcano climb.

One of the most demanding and unusual trips is "Seafood Survival," a kayak outing that teaches you to live off of the sea. During the first three days, you will learn how to shelter yourself, how to catch and gather seafood, and how to cook it over an open fire. An optional solo follows, twenty-four hours to test what you have learned.

COST: The fee for the "Comprehensive Weekend" is $160 for the four classes ($45 each if taken separately). The fee for "Introduction to River Kayaking" is $149. Intermediate-level river trips cost $150 (two days) and $295 (five days). "Bahia de Los Angeles" costs $345. "Seafood Survival" costs $345.

MAINE SPORT OUTFITTERS

P.O. Box 956
Rockport, Maine 04856
(800) 722-0826, (800) 244-8799

In addition to running a wide variety of guided tours and offering an extensive rental service (bikes, fishing equipment, camping gear, and boats), Maine Sport Outfitters has its own outdoor school, which provides instruction in sea kayaking and canoeing, seascape photography, and island ecology. Courses are offered both to those who want to tackle a new sport and to those who want to fine-tune existing skills.

The company offers half-day, full-day, three-day, and five-day options. Kids' Kayak Clinics are available, too. During a full-day session, you begin on the school's pond, where you become familiar with the gear and equipment used and learn safe paddling essentials so that you feel at ease in the boat. In the afternoon, you take a harbor tour. During the longer sessions, you will learn how to land in the surf and navigate with chart and compass. Low-impact camping techniques and trip planning are also taught. All of the courses put heavy emphasis on safety and cover rescue techniques, how to use safety equipment, and how to read the weather.

Novice kayakers are also welcome to join two specialty schools. In "Seascape Photography" (a four-day/three-night course) you will have the opportunity to photograph at dawn and sunset, paddling and problem solving under a guest instructor who also happens to be an expert with a camera. Students return to comfortable lodgings ashore each evening, complete with a substantial down-east dinner. Your sea kayak becomes a floating classroom when you enroll in "Maine Island Ecology." Participants spend three days visiting islands and learning about the natural and interactive patterns of Muscongus Bay from an experienced naturalist/sea kayaker. You will sleep at an island campsite and feast on wilderness meals.

The school also offers instruction in canoeing and river reading. For beginners, there are full- and half-day canoe clinics on a pond or lake. You will learn paddling strokes and styles, entry and exit methods, plus safety and rescue tips. Experienced canoeists can sign on for a "Canoe Poling Weekend," an opportunity to learn the fine art of poling up- and downstream, a great technique for when it's too shallow or rocky to paddle and you don't want to portage.

Maine Sport Outfitters also offers a selection of specialty youth day camps focusing on either sea kayaking, canoeing, backpacking, or traditional campcraft. The week-long sessions are geared to kids nine to thirteen years old.

COST: The fee for the "Full-Day Sea-Kayak Course" is $75. For "Seascape Photography," the price is $535, which covers three nights' shared lodging, all meals, sea-kayak equipment, instruction, guide, and shuttle service. The "Maine Island Ecology" program costs $345, which covers all meals, camp and kayak equipment, guide, and shuttle service. Canoe clinics cost $45 (half-day) and $70 (full day), which includes instruction and the use of all necessary equipment. The fee for the "Canoe Poling Weekend" (introductory or advanced) is $160, which covers camping gear, meals, shuttle service, instruction, and poles; bring your own canoe or rent one for $35.

CANOE COUNTRY ESCAPES

194 South Franklin St.
Denver, Colorado 80209
(303) 722-6482

Learn to canoe in the magnificent Boundary Waters Canoe Area Wilderness of northeastern Minnesota and south-western Ontario. You'll have plenty of opportunity to fish and swim and you might well see moose and bald eagles as you travel the same lakes and portages used by the French-Canadian fur traders and, before them, the Ojibway Indians. Canoe Country Escapes offers a variety of five- to eleven-day packages, with special options for families with young children and for people over fifty years of age.

You don't have to have any prior paddling experience and you don't have to rough it much to participate in one of these canoe trips. "Lodge-to-Lodge" itineraries combine four nights of accommodations at comfortable lodges with several nights spent at preset campsites, where all the equipment has been portaged in advance. When you paddle ashore, you'll be wel-comed with dinner cooking over an open fire, tents set up, and sleeping bags rolled out.

There are other choices for those who want to experience less luxury and more camping. Again, prior experience is not necessary. "The 'Wilderness Medley' and 'Family Trips' include full immersion into all camping and navigation skills required for a wilderness canoe trip," explains Canoe Country Escapes founder Eric Durland.

All trips are led by experienced guides. Each package includes round-trip transportation covering the 150 miles between the Duluth Airport and the trip base, complete light-weight outfitting (tents, sleeping bags, canoes, etc.), a canoe instruction and practice session the night before setting out, and dinner, bunkhouse accommodations, and breakfast at the Gunflint Lodge the nights before and after the trip. There are also opportunities to hike with a naturalist or fish with an experienced fishing guide.

COST: The six-day, seven-night "Lodge-to-Lodge" package is $845 and the six-day, seven-night "Wilderness Medley" package is $595. A five-day, six-night "Family Trip" is $535 for adults, $360 for kids twelve and under.

NANTAHALA OUTDOOR CENTER

41 U.S. Highway 19 West
Bryson City, North Carolina 28713
(704) 488-2175

Located near the heart of the Great Smoky Mountains, Nantahala Outdoor Center (NOC) is a full-service outdoor education and recreation facility. Taking a course here is convenient as well as fun. NOC's main location on the Nantahala River offers lodgings ranging from vacation houses to motel rooms to bunkhouses. Other facilities include an outfitter's store, three restaurants, and a licensed day-care center.

A full slate of open canoe and kayak courses, varying in length from two to seven days, is offered from March through October. The NOC catalog includes a skill-level assessment list, making it easy to place yourself appropriately. Each course begins with a get-together the evening before instruction begins. You will have the opportunity to meet the others in your group and to discuss your goals for the course. Instruction usually begins with some flat-water time. In beginning classes, participants learn the basic strokes required to control the boat. Intermediate and advanced paddlers have the opportunity to fine-tune their paddling techniques and kayakers can work on their off-side and hand rolls. Then it's on to the river (four different ones are used, depending on water levels) to practice reading water, river strategies, and playing on the waves and in holes. Throughout, the emphasis is on personal and group safety. In the evening students gather with their instructors to watch films, to discuss the day's videotaping session, or to review material covered on the river.

For beginning and intermediate rock climbers, NOC offers weekend, three- and five-day programs, designed to lead you from the basics of equipment and rope handling to the principles and practices of lead climbing.

The center also offers some intriguing special courses. Those who have tried kayaking before and found it frightening can enroll in "The Tentative Kayaker," a four-day course designed to allay your fears. Patient instructors will help you work on the Eskimo roll and other fundamentals, easing anxiety with breathing and relaxation techniques. For well-conditioned confident sorts in a hurry to master the skills, there are "Seven-Day Fast-Track Kayak Courses." Parents and children sixty pounds and heavier (no age requirement) can learn together in the "Family Canoe Course," while kids ten to fifteen years old can sign up for a special three- or four-day course just for them.

For those who want to get a taste of a sport, NOC offers one-day "Samplers," introductory mini-courses in canoeing, kayaking, and rock climbing.

COST: The fee for the standard canoeing and kayaking courses, including instruction, equipment, local transportation, lodging, and meals, is $285 per weekend, $415 for three days, $535 for four days, $665 for five days, $790 for six days, and $915 for seven days. Discounts are available for those who wish to provide their own boat, lodging, or meals. Fees for "Rock-Climbing Courses" are $260 for a weekend, $370 for three days, and $580 for five days, all of which cover meals, lodging, camping fees, and local transportation. "The Tentative Kayaker" costs $535, which covers instruction, meals, lodging, and river equipment.

NORTHWEST OUTDOOR CENTER

2100 Westlake Ave. North
Seattle, Washington 98109
(206) 281-9694

Founded by five paddling entrepreneurs in 1980, Northwest Outdoor Center (NWOC) aims to provide safe, high-quality boating instruction. Located right on Lake Union, NWOC offers classes and rentals and sells kayaks and related gear. If you want to learn sea kayaking or white-water kayaking in the Pacific Northwest, this is the place to do it. The student-to-instructor ratio ranges from 2:1 to 6:1 depending on the class.

"Introduction to Sea Touring" is an economical way to learn what the sport of sea kayaking is all about. The two-session course combines a classroom seminar focusing on boat design, equipment, chart reading, safety destinations, and the local marine environment with a three-hour session on the lake. Kayaks and accessories are provided. "Fundamentals of Sea Kayaking," another option for beginners, takes place over the course of four days, combining lectures with both lake and saltwater outings. You will learn how to rescue yourself and others and how to prevent capsizing by using bracing strokes. The emphasis is on the development of both paddling skills and good sea sense.

If you want to learn sea kayaking quickly and comprehensively, you can opt for "The Total Immersion School of Sea Kayaking," a comprehensive five-day program that provides experiences that run the gamut from learning to hold a paddle properly to negotiating fast currents, to coming in and setting out through surf. Instruction begins on Lake Union and then continues at saltwater locations. The class camps out together throughout the course. For experienced sea kayakers there are programs centering on navigation and trip planning, bracing and rescue techniques, and surf techniques.

The basic beginner white-water class is "White-Water

Fever," an introductory course with sessions in the classroom, on the lake, in a warm swimming pool, and on the river. "The Total Immersion School of White Water" is a six-day course designed to help the beginner quickly develop confidence and competence. Instruction begins with a lecture and pool session in Seattle and quickly moves to area rivers for five days of work learning and fine-tuning basic white-water skills.

NWOC also offers a good selection of one-day and multi-day guided kayaking trips, with options suitable for beginners as well as more accomplished paddlers.

COST: The fee for "Introduction to Sea Touring" is $40, which covers instruction and use of kayak and related equipment. The fee for "Fundamentals of Kayaking" is $95 (kayak rental is $50 additional; wetsuit rental is $15). The "Total Immersion School of Sea Kayaking" is $475 ($375 with your boat and equipment); this covers instruction, transportation, equipment, and all meals and camping fees. The fee for "White-Water Fever" is $115 (kayak rental is $45 additional; drysuit rental is $20). The fee for "The Total Immersion School of White Water" is $495, which covers meals, lodging, instruction, boats, gear, and camping fees.

BIG BEND RIVER TOURS

P.O. Box 317
Lajitas, Texas 79852
(800) 545-4240

One of the best ways to experience the dramatic gorges and canyons of the Rio Grande, which forms the border between Texas and Mexico, is by float trip. Big Bend River Tours conducts river trips, with the emphasis on learning about the area's geology, natural history, and native folklore. Many of the guides are also talented naturalists, musicians, artists, and photographers, ready to share their skills with you as you explore the canyons in the Big Bend area together. Typical of these itineraries is the two-day, twenty-five-mile "Colorado Canyon Trip," rated "easy to intermediate." The route covers a section of the Rio Grande that affords intriguing views of volcanic rock canyons, opportunities to explore old Spanish and Indian ruins, and some fast rapids. Swimming and body floating are popular activities on the calm stretches between rapids. The trip allows ample time for nature study and side-canyon exploration.

Big Bend River Tours are nondemanding, with some itineraries suitable for families with young children as well as for senior citizens seeking adventure (Elderhostel works with Big Bend River Tours to offer short academic courses that involve a river trip). Guides row the rafts, but they also provide instruction for those guests who want to learn paddle a raft or canoe on their own.

The company also organizes river specialty trips. "Sketching the Rio Grande" is a three-day combination river trip and sketching seminar, with opportunities to draw in an old silver-mining town, in Boquillas Canyon, and at an old ranch. Conducted several times each year, the trip is led by a former college art instructor (also an accomplished guide) and is open to anyone who likes to draw. "Landscapes and Cloudscapes" is a combined three-day river trip and photography seminar. An accomplished photographer/guide will help you catch Big Bend's vistas on film as you explore Mariscal Canyon. Other river trips focus on astronomy and on the field study of the fifty-plus varieties of cacti and succulents that grow in the Big Bend area.

COST: The fee for the two-day Colorado Canyon trip is $205. "Sketching the Rio Grande" and "Landscapes and Cloudscapes" each cost $335. Fees cover all meals and the use of all necessary equipment.

SILVER CLOUD EXPEDITIONS

Jerry and Terry Myers
Box 1006
Salmon, Idaho 83467
(208) 756-6215

Silver Cloud owner/operators Jerry and Terry Myers have professionally guided on the Salmon River for the past seventeen years. They specialize in four- and five-day white-water rafting trips with an emphasis on interpretive learning. Folks from six to eighty are welcome on the trips, which travel through the River of No Return Wilderness Area, where eighty miles of class III rapids combine with sandy beaches, abundant wildlife, and a rich history to make Salmon River Canyon one of the most unique wild places in the country.

Silver Cloud provides a challenge for rafters of all ages and experience levels, from the first-timer to the experienced paddler. To meet the diverse needs of its clientele, the company uses a variety of top-quality equipment. The more adventuresome and adept can experience the river close up in self-bailing paddle rafts and inflatable kayaks. Other participants prefer the more comfortable passage available in the larger oar rafts. Your days on the river are filled with opportunities to learn not only how to navigate the water but to observe wildlife and Indian pictographs, soak in hot springs, and explore historic sites. Camp is set up each afternoon on a sandy beach, leaving time for fishing, hiking, gold panning, snorkeling, swimming, photography, and beach games. Evening programs, conducted around a cozy campfire, focus on natural history, fly fishing, gold panning, and other topics. You'll enjoy excellent dutch-oven meals cooked right by the river and when evening falls, you'll bed down in a roomy tent. At the conclusion of your trip, you will fly back to Boise or Salmon, enjoying a spectacular view of the river.

COST: The fee for a four-day, four-night rafting trip originating and terminating in Salmon is $725. This covers all rafting and camping equipment (except sleeping bag), tents, meals, expert guide service, and return by air charter.

UNICORN RAFTING EXPEDITIONS

P.O. Box T
Brunswick, Maine 04011
(207) 725-2255

In addition to organizing rafting trips on more than half a dozen rivers in Maine, Massachusetts, and New York, Unicorn Rafting Expeditions offers a series of kayak workshops throughout the summer months. The two-day introductory session covers paddling, river safety, and developing enough of a familiarity with river characteristics to successfully navigate class II rapids. If you have had some previous experience, you can enroll in the three-day beginner program, where the focus is on mastering ferry angles, eddy turns, and self-rescue techniques, as well as increasing your knowledge of white-water flow. In the three-day intermediate workshop, techniques covered include hole surfing, technical scouting, paddling accuracy, racing strokes, and rolling, in preparation for class II–IV river running. Both the beginner and intermediate workshops are also offered in five-day versions for those who want to become competent, confident kayakers more quickly.

No matter which workshop you choose, your day will begin at about 8:00 A.M. with some stretching exercises. Then you travel to the river by shuttle bus and set off for a full day of fun and instruction, with a break for a riverside lunch. After a couple more hours on the river, you will be transported back to Unicorn's base, where breakfast and dinner are served and where you will camp for the night (equipment available for rental or bring your own).

The kayaking workshops are suitable for anyone in good physical shape who is of average weight. The outfitter supplies all necessary equipment, including four-meter plastic kayaks, paddle, helmet, and life jacket.

COST: The fee for the kayak workshops is $175 per two-day session, $265 per three-day session, and $445 per five-day session. This includes instruction, campsite, and meals from lunch the first day to lunch the last day. Cabins are available at additional cost.

Hiking

WALKING THE WORLD, INC.

P.O. Box 1186
Fort Collins, Colorado 80522
(303) 225-0500

This unusual organization offers a year-round schedule of outdoor adventures in the United States and abroad specifically designed for people fifty and over. Carefully planned to create a balance between activity, rest, and personal time, the trip itineraries appeal to a diverse group of people. Some participants have often thought about going backpacking or hiking but have been hesitant about doing so independently. Others want to learn the basics of camping and hiking so they can later strike out on their own. Still others are attracted by the camaraderie and sharing of skills that group travel affords.

The programs provide instruction in the following areas: map and compass/route finding, backpacking techniques, trail techniques, expedition behavior and planning, stream-crossing techniques, back-country cooking, hazard evaluation, and back-country first aid/emergency procedures. Instruction also covers a variety of low-impact camping topics, including proper sanitation methods, fires, shelters, and campsite selection.

The trips are open to everyone fifty years old and up in good health, with no maximum age limit. All courses are graded according to ability, but sustained physical activity is a part of every program. Some trips require that you carry a light backpack but many require only a day pack containing lunch, water bottle, and raingear. Groups range from twelve to eighteen participants, accompanied by two instructor/guides. Walking the World supplies all group gear and meals. You need only bring personal clothing, boots, and a day pack or backpack.

U.S. trips usually range from one to two weeks. The "Arches/Canyonlands National Parks" tour in Utah is a ten-day trek originating in Grand Junction, Colorado. Hiking out of a base camp established in each park, you will have the opportunity to see ancient Anasazi dwellings, artifacts, and drawings. You will hike canyons, streambeds, and sandstone ridges, exploring some of the country's wildest and most remote canyons, arches, and natural bridges. Activities also include a one-day rafting trip on the Colorado River. This tour requires moderate walking at low and medium elevations and is usually scheduled in the spring and fall.

COST: The fee for the "Arches/Canyonlands National Parks" tour is $995.

KNAPSACK TOURS

5961 Zinn Drive
Oakland, California 94611-2655
(510) 339-0160

If you are a budget-minded outdoor enthusiast with an interest in invigorating moderate hikes and a willingness to pitch in with chores, take some time to explore the options offered by this unusual outfit. Knapsack Tours specializes in organizing inexpensive hiking tours free of the responsibility and duress of carrying a heavy backpack. The trips, which are scheduled from late May into September, combine comfortable lodgings with forays into magnificent natural settings. Participants include both couples and singles twenty years of age and above. They share a reverence for the environment and a healthy lifestyle (no smoking). To keep the pricetag down and the sense of camaraderie up, participants share some cooperative housekeeping responsibilities as well as a flexible attitude and a willingness to travel lightly. If you want to expand your hiking options in the company of knowledge-able guides but without the demands involved in carrying a heavy pack, Knapsack Tours offers an excellent alternative.

Typical of the tours is a five-day exploration of the Olympic Peninsula. The group is limited to twenty-eight people. Each morning you split up into small groups for the day's hike. On the trail, you'll learn about flora, fauna, and Indian lore as you explore an alpine environment, wild beaches, lush valleys, and a rainforest, accompanied by instructors from the Olympic Park Institute. After each day of hiking, you will return to a historic inn on the edge of a glacial lake, where breakfast and dinner are served family style. In the evening, instructors present nature-oriented lectures and programs.

COST: The fee for the Olympic Peninsula tour is $345, which includes lodgings (cabin or dorm), meals, guides, and transportation to trail heads.

THE APPALACHIAN MOUNTAIN CLUB

5 Joy St.
Boston, Massachusetts 02108
(617) 523-0636

Committed to helping people enjoy the mountains, trails, and rivers of the Northeast, the Appalachian Mountain Club (AMC) couples outdoor recreation with an obligation to protect the beauty of the natural environment. The AMC maintains over fourteen hundred miles of trails as well as a network of alpine huts, mountain lodges, and trail shelters designed to serve the needs of the outdoors lover with minimum impact on the environment. There are many ways to become part of the club's activities.

The AMC outdoor-learning headquarters is located in a spacious lodge in Pinkham Notch in the White Mountains of New Hampshire. Workshops are also held at AMC facilities in the Berkshires of western Massachusetts, Acadia National Park in Maine, and the Catskills in New York. Programs run year-round, last from one day to over a week, and are devoted to many different aspects of natural history and outdoor recreation. Designed to accommodate a wide variety of skill levels, some of the workshops are just right for families with small children, while others are intended for the experienced outdoorsman looking to hone a specific skill or get some wilderness emergency training.

Many of the New Hampshire programs involve use of the AMC hut system, a string of eight alpine huts accessible only on foot and located a day's hike from one another. Meals are served family style and sleeping quarters vary from large coed bunk rooms to smaller rooms accommodating two to eight hikers. Blankets and pillows are provided.

AMC guided hikes offer a great way to get familiar with the huts and to get involved in hiking in the company of an experienced trip leader knowledgeable about equipment, safety concerns, and natural history. Nearly two dozen White Mountain itineraries are offered, divided into three skill levels: easier, moderate, and challenging. Hikes range from one to eight nights with accommodations in the hut system. You can also choose from a variety of workshops centering on hiking and backpacking (including cross-country ski expeditions), as well as those devoted to other outdoor skills, including fly fishing, map and compass skills, llama trekking, rock climbing, mountain biking, caving, and wilderness first aid.

Natural history workshops focus on birdwatching, geology, flowering plants, and wild foods and herbs. Still other workshops focus on photography and the arts, including sessions that combine music and hiking. The AMC also offers canoeing and kayaking workshops.

The AMC also offers family-oriented "Environmental Day Programs." In the winter, you might learn the basics of snowshoeing or tracking animals in the snow under the guidance of a trained naturalist. Come spring, learn all about maple sugaring, trail cooking, or butterflies, or sign on for an evening owl prowl or learn to build a bat or bluebird house. Guided hikes to waterfalls and mountain peaks and ponds are offered, too.

COST: The fee for a two-day introductory kayaking trip, including meals, lodging, and equipment rental, is $170. Fees for "Environmental Day Programs" run from $10 to $30. You need not be a member of the AMC to participate in programs or to use the hut system; however, AMC members receive substantial discounts.

AMERICAN HIKING SOCIETY VOLUNTEER VACATIONS

P.O. Box 86
North Scituate, Massachusetts 02060
(617) 545-7019

If you are an experienced hiker in good physical shape, consider spending ten days giving back something to the land that has given you such great pleasure. Sign on with American Hiking Society Volunteer Vacations and help make some of the country's most spectacular recreation areas safer and more accessible. Learn how to build and maintain trails, contributing existing skills and developing new ones. Previous experience is not required. The work is accomplished by volunteer teams, working under the supervision of the National Park Service, the U.S. Forest Service, and state park personnel. To qualify for participation on a team, volunteers must be in good health and good physical condition, able to live outdoors and do hard manual work for ten days. Participants also must be experienced backpackers who can easily walk five to ten miles a day. Many of the projects involve working in remote, rugged terrain at high altitude.

Each team consists of 6–15 volunteers, ranging in age from sixteen to seventy. Volunteer Vacation groups work primarily in national parks, national forests, and state parks. Teams are also sent to sites in Alaska, Arizona, Arkansas, California, Colorado, Florida, Idaho, Maine, Michigan, Montana, New Hampshire, Vermont, Virginia, Washington, and Wyoming.

Last year the program sent approximately 250 volunteers to work at 29 different sites. While most projects take place during the summer months, there are also several fall, winter, and spring opportunities.

COST: Volunteers supply their own camping equipment and pay for their own transportation to and from the project area. Government agencies and outside donors supply hardhats, tools, and food. Upon acceptance to a team, participants pay a $40 registration fee. This fee, along with all personal expenses such as travel to and from the site, is tax deductible.

AMC VOLUNTEER TRAILS CONSERVATION CORPS

P.O. Box 298
Gorham, New Hampshire 03581
(603) 466-2721

Last year more than eight hundred volunteers logged in over ten thousand hours of public service conservation work, maintaining and building shelters and trails throughout the Northeast as participants in the AMC's Volunteer Trails Conservation Corps. Joining in is an excellent way of supporting the future of the nation's parks and forests while enjoying a wilderness vacation. You might spend a spring weekend helping to construct a new section of Appalachian Trail in western Massachusetts, learning trail-building skills from experienced leaders. Or perhaps you're ready to commit yourself to an autumn week of trail projects in Maine's Acadia National Park, after the summer crowds have departed. As a club bulletin observes, "The work is important and rewarding, the people are great, and the scenery is spectacular!"

Volunteer opportunities run from one day to a weekend to a week or considerably longer. More ambitious programs include the ten-day service projects (some prior backpacking experience required) based at parks and forests around the United States. Crews of ten to twelve members live in backcountry tent camps and work under the guidance of a leader as they maintain trails and construct new routes. Six days of work are complemented by a weekend's worth of free time for fishing and hiking.

You don't need to have any prior trail work experience to help out on most of the volunteer programs, but the jobs can be strenuous, so good health is a must. Tools and instruction are provided.

Many additional opportunities to contribute are offered by the eleven AMC chapters in the Northeast, running from Washington, D.C., north to Maine. The best way to learn about these is to join the AMC and become active with your local chapter.

Note: Average age for most volunteers is 18–40, with a range from 10–65+. Minimum age for trips of a week or longer is sixteen, although younger volunteers may be accepted if accompanied by an adult.

COST: For programs lasting a week or longer, there is a modest program fee (approximately $25–$60 per week); meals and lodgings are provided without charge.

Biking

PEAK PERFORMANCE CONSULTANTS, INC.

P.O. Box 14714
Gainesville, Florida 32604-4714
(904) 378-2479

Bicyclists Betsy King and Anna Schwartz set a new twenty-four-hour marathon tandem world record of 435 miles in 1991. Together they run peak performance cycling camps and tours. Their programs offer cyclists of all ages and ability levels the opportunity to train with pros who have coached many national and world-class athletes.

In February and March, Peak Performance offers week-long performance camps in Arizona and Florida. Structured to provide individualized coaching and a high coach-to-rider ratio, the camps can meet the needs of serious recreational riders, triathletes, and racers. The program begins with a Sunday organizational meeting. Coaching begins Monday and continues through Friday. During a typical day, rides are alternated with classroom sessions covering bike position, strategy, training methods, aerodynamics, sprinting, team work, climbing techniques, time trialing, mental preparation, and interval techniques. Each camp is limited to twenty participants, who are accommodated in fully equipped two-bedroom condominiums with swimming pools and exercise equipment. The terrain at both locations is flat to rolling.

During May, Peak Performance offers a series of week-long climbing camps based in the Blue Ridge Mountains of Virginia. Structured around rides individualized to each participant's ability level and the degree of climbing you choose to undertake, the program is designed to teach cyclists to climb faster and better. The emphasis is on training techniques that will improve all aspects of your riding and racing. Coaching and discussion sessions focus on the following areas: climbing seated, climbing out of the saddle, descending, training on limited time, applications to racing, nutrition, injury prevention and care, and interval methods. Each session is limited to twelve participants, who are lodged in cottages with kitchens.

COST: The fee for a week of performance camp, including lodgings, is $435. The fee for a week of climbing camp, including lodgings, is $465.

MAMMOTH ADVENTURE CONNECTION

P.O. Box 653
Mammoth Lakes, California 93546
(619) 934-0606, (800) 228-4947

Learn to mountain bike in the Sierra Nevada with the help of Mammoth Adventure Connection. Based at the Mammoth Mountain Inn, part of a ski-resort complex, the company offers mountain-bike rentals and specializes in instructional clinics and guided tours. The bike program is flexible enough to meet the needs of cyclists of all abilities, from beginner on up.

Once you've learned the basics, you can sign on for a guided trip through some magnificent country. Your guide will lead you on a two-hour, half-day, or full-day trip, exploring mountain lakes, waterfalls, natural springs, national parks, even historic ghost towns. The particular route will be determined to complement your cycling experience and abilities. The guides, who offer expert advice on riding techniques and bicycle maintenance, are also knowledgeable about the natural history of the area.

A mountain-bike lift ticket entitles you to unlimited access to the park's extensive trail system, using the park's gondola to carry you and your bike to the 9,600-foot mid-chalet and the 11,053-foot summit. Single-track trails and roads originate from both points, providing access to over fifty miles of trails, with options for both the advanced beginner and the expert rider. The trail network includes opportunities for riders who want to cruise the flats as well as for those who seek the physical challenge of an uphill climb and crave the thrill of a downhill run. In addition to the trails, facilities include a Bicycle Motor Cross-style course just for kids, a timed slalom race course (face off against a friend or race the clock), and an obstacle arena. The park is open to cyclists from June into September.

Note: In cooperation with Kittredge Sports, Mammoth

Adventure Connection also offers fly-fishing schools. See page 179 for additional listing.

COST: The fee for a two-hour guided bike tour is $30 for one person, $15 each for 2–5 persons, and $10 each for 6–10 persons. For a full-day guided tour, fees are $80 for one person, $40 each for 2–5 persons, and $35 each for 6–10 persons. A daily all-facilities pass to Mammoth Mountain Bike Park is $15. Bike rentals are available at additional cost.

BACKROADS

1516 5th St.
Berkeley, California 94710-1740
(510) 527-1555

Backroads offers inn and camping biking trips to sixty-four destinations in the United States and abroad. Itineraries currently focus on nineteen states: Alaska, Arizona, California, Colorado, Florida, Hawaii, Idaho, Louisiana, Maine, Minnesota, Mississippi, Montana, New Mexico, North Carolina, Oregon, Utah, Vermont, Virginia, and Washington.

The trips are designed for flexibility and most are suitable for beginning, intermediate, and advanced riders. Some itineraries offer short, easy mileage, while others cover more challenging terrain. Instead of traveling in a pack, you ride at your own pace, choosing from route options of varying difficulty. There are direct routes for beginners and challenging side trips for the more energetic. On most trips, the distance between each night's lodging can be covered in three to five hours.

Backroads produces a handsome catalog packed with informative trip descriptions, each of which includes specific details on terrain difficulty and mileage. Whichever route you choose, you need only ride as far as you want. Each trip is accompanied by a van shuttle that is always ready for guests who want a break. A customized trailer transports luggage, spare parts, food, beverages, guest purchases, and bicycles. One leader covers the route in the van while another cycles at the rear of the group, ready to lend support and tend to any mechanical problems that develop.

Backroads maintains an extensive fleet of custom-designed twenty-one-speed rental touring bicycles and mountain bikes. If you choose to rent, your bike will be waiting for you when you arrive. Throughout your trip, your leaders will check the bike daily. They'll teach you to ride it safely and efficiently and answer any questions you may have about shifting, braking, or other concerns. Bikes are also available for purchase, or you can bring along your own.

A six-day inn trip through Mississippi and Louisiana features gently rolling and level terrain and is designated as appropriate for beginning and intermediate cyclists. Route options vary from sixteen to sixty-one miles. A five-day inn or camping trip in the San Juan Mountains of Colorado is appropriate for energetic beginners (will need occasional van shuttles) and intermediate and advanced cyclists. The terrain includes mostly gradual grades, three mountain passes, and one longer grade. Daily route options vary from nineteen to ninety-seven miles.

Backroads also offers a number of specialty trips. For those who prefer to travel with birds of a feather, there are trip dates specifically designated for singles, for families, and for adults aged fifty-five and over.

Other trips cater to specific interests. The health and fitness trip winds through the California wine country and includes organized runs, hikes, swims, and stretch classes in addition to the bicycling. It also incorporates a rest day at a premier spa/fitness resort. The art lovers' inn trip explores the backroads of the Sonoma and Napa valleys, combining bicycling with visits to two or three of the region's finest artists each day, including sculptors, ceramicists, painters, a landscape designer, and a blacksmith.

If you want to learn how to cross-country ski, sign on for a cross-country ski vacation headed up by professional leaders certified in Nordic ski instruction. The five-day packages, offered in the Sierra of California, the Northeast Kingdom of Vermont, and the Canadian Rockies, include lodgings and gourmet meals at fine country inns. For your convenience, Backroads offers top-of-the-line ski equipment rentals.

Trips last two to sixteen days and are offered year-round. The average group, guided by two to four professional leaders, consists of fourteen to twenty-six guests.

COST: The fee for the Mississippi/Louisiana trip is $998. The fee for the San Juan Mountains Colorado trip is $1,155 (inns) or $598 (camping). Prices include accommodations, most meals, pretrip materials, detailed maps and directions, leader services, daily van support and luggage transfers, attraction and park entry fees, gratuities, taxes, and service charges.

VERMONT BICYCLE TOURING

Box 711
Bristol, Vermont 05443
(802) 453-4811

Vermont Bicycle Touring (VBT) pioneered country inn-to-inn cycling vacations twenty years ago. Today the company offers thirty-five different tours in the United States and abroad with four hundred different departure dates. Tours last from two to nineteen days and are designed to accommodate beginning, intermediate, and advanced cyclists. Most of the domestic tours originate in Vermont, with other options offered in Maine, Massachusetts, Virginia, California, and Hawaii. All tours include overnight stays and fine dining at comfortable, often elegant country inns.

VBT rents lightweight twelve-speed touring bikes that are

equipped with special low gears that make them easier to pedal than most bikes. If you don't know how to use a twelve-speed, VBT staffers will teach you how. Your tour leader will continue to offer advice and instruction during the tour and by the end of the trip you will know a lot more about bicycling than you can imagine.

On all tours, you are given your choice of two or more routes to ride. This enables each person to choose the distance and pace that feels right, with the whole group reuniting at the next inn for dinner. Weekend getaways and midweek mini-tours are divided into "roundabouts" and "rambles," making it even easier to further personalize your tour. Roundabouts are designed for beginning through intermediate-level cyclists; participants choose either an easy, leisurely 10–20-mile ride or an easy-to-moderate 20–30-mile ride. Rambles are designed for athletic beginner, intermediate, and advanced cyclists; each day involves three or more choices ranging from an easy-to-moderate 20–35 miles, a moderate 35–45 miles, or a challenging 45–75 miles. Five-day tours are divided into "wanderers" and "vagabonds," reflecting the same sorts of choices as those described for the weekend getaways.

The "Okemo Roundabout," a typical weekend getaway, combines cycling with a stay in a lovely Victorian inn, swimming in pools formed at the base of a waterfall, and stops at historic sites. The "Northeast Kingdom Wanderer" is a five-day exploration of Vermont's most rural region. You will ride along bucolic back roads with spectacular views. The panorama embraces glacial lakes, mountain peaks, and river valleys that shelter pristine farms and small villages. There is an opportunitiy to swim every day. Evenings are spent at three different inns.

COST: The fee for the "Okemo Roundabout" is $249 from May to early June and $279 from mid-June through early October. The fee for the "Northeast Kingdom Wanderer" is $599 in May and $699 during the summer and fall. Tour prices cover lodgings, breakfast, dinners, and leader services. A support van accompanies each inn-to-inn tour, transporting luggage and providing assistance when necessary.

WESTERN SPIRIT CYCLING

P.O. Box 411
Moab, Utah 84532
(800) 845-2453, (801) 259-8732

Bicycle skills and environmental education are integral parts of the mountain-bike tours offered by Western Spirit Cycling. Trips are planned to accommodate riders of all abilities, with an eye to improving skills while enjoying outdoor adventure. Staff members are more than tour-group leaders. Skilled naturalists, bicycle instructors, mechanics, and back-country chefs, they share their knowledge of geology, flora and fauna, mountain and desert ecology, proper trail etiquette, and low-impact travel and camping techniques.

Trips run from one to six days with itineraries that explore back-country routes in Utah's canyon lands, Colorado, and Idaho. Some are camping trips, while others make use of inns.

Typical of the trips is "Trail of the Ancients," which begins in Moab and covers 75–115 miles. Nine major mountain ranges are visible during the tour, which includes a visit to spectacular Anasazi Indian ruins. The "Back-Country Hot Springs Tour" begins in Sun Valley, Idaho. Winding through the foothills of the Sawtooth Mountains, the route visits eight different natural hot springs (plenty of opportunity to plunge in) and an authentic ghost town. Both of these tours are camping trips and both run five days and four nights.

Western Spirit Cycling calls its trips "Civilized Tours in Uncivilized Terrain," and they mean it. Great pride is taken in the quality of the meals. Each group is served by a support vehicle equipped with a full kitchen, bicycle repair tools, solar showers, and chaise longues, all of which make for comfortable camping. The van also provides rides for weary cyclists. Tour-group sizes are limited to fifteen riders, with a minimum of five.

Physically fit riders of all ages and abilities are encouraged to join the tours. If you are new to mountain biking or if you want to fine-tune your skills, consider enrolling in the two-day, two-night "Bicycle Skills Seminar," scheduled throughout the spring and fall seasons. The staff has developed an instructional program designed to illuminate both the obvious and subtle aspects of the sport. Geared toward riders of all abilities, the seminar features in-depth personalized instruction. Topics covered begin with stretching before and after riding, correct bike fit, proper use of safety equipment, and a preflight check, during which you will get some basic maintenance tips and learn how to determine if your bike is road-worthy. After an introduction to basic riding principles, the group takes to the road. During the ride, instruction focuses on shifting, uphill and downhill techniques, braking, cornering, and trail etiquette. Riders are divided into small groups to home in on specific skills. On the second day, the program continues with reinforcement of biking principles as well as instruction centering on weight shifting, special considerations for different riding conditions, and how to negotiate obstacles. The instructors are also willing to work on any specific problem you may wish to address.

Western Spirit Cycling rents "state-of-the-art" handbuilt American twenty-one-speed front-suspended bikes, as well as high-quality camping gear, including tents, sleeping bags, and pads.

COST: The fee for "Trail of the Ancients" is $595 and the fee for the "Back-Country Hot Springs Tour" is $625. The fee for the "Bicycle Skills Seminar," which includes two nights' inn lodgings, all meals, and use of a high-performance bike, is $275 for double occupancy. For use on tours, bike rental is $25 per day and the camping equipment package is $15 per day.

ROADS LESS TRAVELED

P.O. Box 8187
Longmont, Colorado 80501
(303) 678-8750

Learn about the geology, history, and vegetation of Colorado, New Mexico, and Utah while you explore unpaved roads and trails well off the beaten track with Roads Less Traveled. This hiking and biking adventure travel company sticks to territory its staff knows best, the Rockies and the canyon lands. Several weeks before you embark on your biking/hiking adventure you will receive in the mail a chunky booklet compiled specifically for your trip. It contains background information specific to the region you will visit, along with maps detailing the routes you will follow.

The company builds plenty of free time and flexibility into its biking tours, combining days of cycling with days of hiking, along with opportunities for rafting, sailing, horseback riding, exploring ancient Indian cliff dwellings, and soaking in natural hot springs. Each group is limited to thirteen riders, making it possible to take advantage of small, family-style inns that can't accommodate larger crowds.

Biking tours are rated according to four categories: beginner, athletic beginner, intermediate, and advanced. A support vehicle accompanies each tour, carrying all baggage and supplies, dispensing drinks and snacks throughout the ride, and giving tired cyclists a lift. In addition to the driver, a second guide cycles with the group, assisting with any repairs or mechanical adjustments that arise and providing insight into the areas visited.

The hiking segments of the tours are geared for the average adult. A typical day on the trail covers a distance of six to eight miles and involves elevation gains of about six hundred feet. Each hiking expedition includes a lesson on map and compass navigation and tours involving camping include instruction on low-impact back-country travel skills.

For beginning hikers and first-time bikers, the five-day

"Rocky Mountain National Park Bike 'n' Hike," conducted June through September, is a good choice. Time is divided between exploring the park's valleys, lakes, and wide-open spaces on foot, driving the Trail Ridge Road (at twelve thousand feet, America's highest road) to observe herds of elk, and two days of cycling in Winter Park, home of Colorado's largest trail network. Each cycling day includes instruction in bike handling and technique. Evenings are spent in comfortable inns.

If you don't have your own mountain bike, you can rent a high-quality, well-equipped model from Roads Less Traveled. Camping gear is also available for rental. All trips include double-occupancy accommodations, all meals, national park fees, guide and support vehicle services, and some special activities.

COST: The fee for the "Rocky Mountain National Park Bike 'n' Hike" is $765.

Climbing

AMERICAN ALPINE INSTITUTE, LTD.

1212 24th St.
Bellingham, Washington 98225
(206) 671-1505

The most comprehensive guide service, training, and expedition center for climbing and skiing in North America, the American Alpine Institute (AAI) is based in the North Cascades of Washington, where the climbing season stretches from mid-May through early October. Easy mountain access combined with the immensity of the glaciers and widely varied snow, ice, and rock conditions make this a perfect training ground for all alpinists. Serving novice climbers who seek their first mountain experience as well as seasoned rock and ice climbers who want to improve their skills, AAI offers courses at basic, intermediate, and advanced levels.

AAI guides are among the world's most accomplished climbers and skiers. They are also insightful mountain educators. Beyond their ability to help clients acquire the specific skills required for successful rock, snow, and ice climbing, they understand the importance of confidence building and of teaching aspiring climbers to accept responsibility for their own decisions. In addition to their mountaineering credentials, all guides hold at least one academic degree in a discipline related to the physical or cultural aspects of the environment in which they work. They contend that "rock climbing is like a puzzle, the key to which lies in the proper application of both mental and physical skills."

Backpacking experience is the only prerequisite required for enrollment in the introductory six-day alpine mountaineering session, which is held throughout the climbing season. Groups of three to five students are paired with one instructor, while groups of six to ten travel with two instructors. The program aims to make mountain enthusiasts with little or no previous experience capable of safe access to trailless wilderness alpine areas. The curriculum is designed to make them proficient in basic rock, snow, and ice mountaineering skills and to help them develop an understanding of the fragile alpine environment.

The first day is spent learning about personal equipment needs and usage, rope handling, protective systems, and basic free-climbing technique in an easily accessible rock-climbing area. On the afternoon of the second day, participants reach their first alpine camp, where the snow-climbing instruction begins. As the week unfolds, a complete repertoire of alpine skills is introduced and practiced, first on gentle ground and then on steeper terrain. After additional training in glacier travel, crevasse rescue, and route finding, participants draw together all the skills they have learned during the week in an individual and team effort to reach the summit of Mount

Baker. Upon completion of the program, each participant should be capable of safely ascending alpine routes of intermediate difficulty as a technically competent rope-team member.

COST: Tuition for the six-day introductory alpine mountaineering program is $650, which also covers the use of all technical gear and group climbing equipment. Personal equipment, such as packs and sleeping bags, is available for rental.

INTERNATIONAL MOUNTAIN CLIMBING SCHOOL

Box 1666
North Conway, New Hampshire 03860
(603) 356-7064, (603) 356-6316

One of the largest year-round climbing schools in the United States, the International Mountain Climbing School (IMCS) is headquartered in North Conway, New Hampshire, a vibrant mountain resort community with plenty of lodgings to choose from and a rich selection of activities to happily occupy traveling companions who will not be climbing. The school offers both group and private lessons daily year-round for climbers of all abilities, including the bona fide beginner.

The emphasis at IMCS is on teaching you to climb safely while helping you to acquire the skills needed to reach your maximum potential. "Rock climbing is a risky sport," a school brochure explains, "and we at IMCS recognize that many people want to learn to identify and deal properly with these risks. In our courses we attempt to empower you with the knowledge to choose and evaluate future partners, select appropriate routes, and increase awareness of dangerous situations."

Preparation for a successful experience begins in advance. Plan to arrive in North Conway well rested and in good physical condition, supplied with the appropriate food, clothing, and equipment as indicated on the instruction sheet you'll receive before you leave home. IMCS provides all necessary technical equipment, but you are welcome to bring any gear you already own and wish to use.

The "Four-Day Basic Rock Course" is a flexible program of instruction that can be completed either in four consecutive days or spread out over two, three, or four weekends. The maximum group size for the course is three students to each instructor, assuring plenty of individualized attention. Day one begins with a lesson on the theory and use of the technical climbing system. Basic knots and belaying methods are taught and risk management is discussed. In the afternoon, participants embark on a short climb, taking into account each student's level of ability.

Each of the three additional days is devoted to a multipitch climb, during which the instructor will teach a variety of skills, including jamming, face climbing, and rappelling. Rope management and safety procedures are consistently reviewed. If you want to try climbing but aren't ready or able to commit yourself to a four-day course, you can sign on a for a single-day class.

In addition to the basic course, the school offers a "Three-Day Advanced Rock Course." Guided climbs on Cannon Mountain and Mount Washington can be arranged, too. There's also an offering called "Women on the Rock," a weekend-long climbing instruction course offered several times each season that is designed for women of all abilities who want to learn to climb in the company of other women. Rock-climbing courses are offered from the end of April through the end of October.

During the winter and spring months, IMCS offers a "Three-Day Mountaineering Course" that combines an opportunity to develop competence in lightweight camping skills under arctic conditions with instruction in efficiently climbing moderate-angled snow and ice.

Other winter programs include a "Four-Day Basic Ice Course" (an introduction to technical climbing in the winter), and a "Four-Day Presidential Traverse" for experienced winter climbers ready to take on one of the East Coast's most difficult mountaineering challenges. As in the summer, daily classes and guided one-day climbs are also available.

COST: The "Basic Rock Four-Day Course" or "Basic Ice Four-Day Course" is $415; the "Advanced Rock Three-Day Course" is $310; the "Three-Day Mountaineering Course" is $300; and a daily class (rock or ice) is $110. Discounts are available to two or three people booking the same course together.

VERTICAL ADVENTURES

P.O. Box 7548
Newport Beach, California 92658
(714) 854-6250

Vertical Adventures teaches rock climbing year-round. From October to May, classes are held at Joshua Tree National Monument in the high desert north of Palm Springs. From June to September, they are taught at Tahquitz and Suicide Rocks in the San Jacinto Mountains.

If you have never climbed before or if you need a refresher, "Basic Rock Climbing" is the place to start. The one-day course covers equipment, terminology, knots, anchoring, belaying, climbing techniques, communication signals, rappelling, and climbing ethics. The emphasis is on having fun while learning the essentials of safely climbing steep rock. Instruction takes place on low-angle, moderate rock. The sequence of one-day courses continues with "Intermediate One," "Intermediate Two," and "Intermediate Three," all essential steps in the process of becoming capable of climbing on your own.

For more experienced and able climbers, the "Advanced Seminar" provides a two-day individualized program customized to focus on technique, route selection, state-of-the-art equipment, training methods, and workout routines. Another option is the "Big-Wall Seminar," a two-day course useful to aspiring climbers who want to learn the secrets of big-wall climbing.

Vertical Adventures also offers five- to seven-day climbing camps for experienced climbers. Guided climbing (private or semiprivate sessions designed to meet your personal goals and scheduled at your convenience) is available to individuals and small groups at all ability levels.

COST: The fee for "Basic Rock Climbing" is $65. The fee for "Intermediate One" is $70. "Intermediate Two" and "Intermediate Three" cost $75 each. For the "Advanced Seminar," "Big-Wall Seminar," and guided climbing, fees run $145 per day for one person, $90 each for two people, and $80 each for three. The school provides all technical rock-climbing equipment except for rock-climbing shoes, which are available for rental.

HIGH ANGLE ADVENTURES, INC.

5 River Road
New Paltz, New York 12561
(800) 777-CLIMB, (914) 658-9811

The Shawangunk Cliffs, just a ninety-minute drive from New York City, offer high-quality climbing opportunities for beginner, intermediate, and advanced rock climbers. If this is your maiden climbing foray, you will spend your first day taking an in-depth look at some of the sport's crucial safety procedures, including knots, anchors, and belays. Then your instructor will set up a short, moderate climb to see how you take to the sensation of operating in a vertical environment. The climb gives the staff the opportunity to evaluate the kind of natural aptitude you bring to climbing. That assessment gives them the information they need to develop a teaching plan based on the rate at which you are likely to best assimilate new techniques and procedures. Highly individualized, this method successfully accommodates both those who progress quickly and those who require a bit more time.

For intermediate and advanced climbers the approach continues to be personalized. After evaluating your skills, your instructor will present you with an increasingly challenging set of problems. You will be introduced to the demands of multipitch climbs and you will have the opportunity to make decisions based on all the information and skills you've accumulated. For advanced climbers, the company provides guided climbs as well as exposure to specialized techniques that allow you to explore in relative safety the possibility of learning to lead.

Classes are limited to no more than three students per instructor. For beginners, instruction is offered every weekend from April through November. The company supplies all the necessary equipment, even climbing shoes. All you bring is a light lunch, lots of water, and perhaps insect repellent and sunscreen.

High Angle Adventures also offers programs just for women that are taught by women instructors.

COST: Prices are $150 per day for a private session; $125 each for a semi-private session for two; and $100 per person per day for groups of three.

ADIRONDACK ROCK & RIVER GUIDE SERVICE, INC.

P.O. Box 219
Keene, New York 12942
(518) 576-2041

Located in the heart of the Adirondack Mountains, Adirondack Rock & River Guide Service is well organized to serve guests who seek instruction in rock climbing, ice climbing, mountaineering, and kayaking, as well as those outdoor enthusiasts who simply want an unstructured mountain vacation. Rock & River prides itself on its knowledgeable group of guides, all of whom share a deep affection and respect for the history and traditions of the Adirondacks as evidenced by their decision to settle permanently in the region. Most are over thirty, many are teachers by profession, and all are accomplished, experienced climbers.

The company is based in an 1800s homestead in a serene mountain valley bordered by park wilderness (Adirondack Park is the largest state or national park in the continental United States.) Facilities include campsites, a streamside lean-to, a farmhouse, and two comfortable lodges.

During the winter months Rock & River features ice-climbing and mountaineering opportunities, including two-day courses in rock and ice climbing, a four-day course called "Beginning Mountaineering" (requires previous winter camping experience and some basic ice-climbing experience), and two two-day advanced workshops, "Intro to Leading Ice" and "Winter Self-Rescue." For a good introduction to climbing, enroll in "Rock and Ice." The first day is spent climbing the indoor rock wall, learning about fundamental climbing concepts. On the second day, you'll visit a frozen waterfall for a top-roped ice-climbing session. As with all the other climbing courses, necessary gear is provided except for double plastic boots, which are available for rental.

Rock-climbing instruction is offered spring, summer, and fall. The courses are organized in a flexible course progression designed to promote continual skill development along with reinforcement of the fundamentals. Two-day courses are offered in beginning, novice, and intermediate rock. Advanced workshops are also offered. "Beginning Rock" is the right choice for someone just starting out and wanting to learn the basics of climbing.

Spring, summer, and fall are also devoted to kayaking instruction. Choose from two- and three-day courses in white-water or flat-water paddling. During the two-day "Beginning Paddling" course, you will spend one day on a nearby lake learning and practicing basics such as entry, exit, stroke technique, and the Eskimo roll. A short river session is incorporated into the second day of the program. Rock & River provide all necessary equipment except for wetsuits, which are available for rental.

If you prefer to learn at a pace of your own choosing, you can take advantage of Rock & River's private guiding service. One-on-one instruction is offered at all levels in any discipline the company normally teaches. Flexibility is the name of the game. This service is also available at reduced cost to two people registering together, including parent/child teams. Rock & River also offers combination courses affording the opportunity to experience an introduction to two different skills back to back.

COST: The fee for "Rock and Ice" or "Beginning Rock" is $130, including lunch. The fee for "Beginning Paddling" is $140. Lunch is included for all three courses. Private guiding rates run $125 per weekend day for one person, $160 for a parent/child duo. Accommodations are available as follows: campsite is $10 per day for one person, $15 for two people; bunk is $25 per person with breakfast; private room with bath is $40 per day for one peron, $60 for two people, breakfast included.

JACKSON HOLE MOUNTAIN GUIDES CLIMBING SCHOOL

P.O. Box 7477
165 N. Glenwood
Jackson, Wyoming 83001
(307) 733-4979

The Tetons' only year-round climbing school and guide service, Jackson Hole Mountain Guides Climbing School (JHMG) offers first-rate instruction for climbers at all levels, including beginners. The school's guides are highly accomplished and committed climbers, capable of leading any level climb, whether rock or ski mountaineering. If you have a sense of adventure and the motivation to climb, this is the right place to get started.

Introductory programs provide vital practical training and instruction. Groups are limited to 3–5 students for the beginning courses and just two for the advanced ones. The school provides the necessary climbing gear and group gear.

For summer expeditions, completion of the full-day basic and intermediate classes is usually sufficient preparation for joining a guided climb. In the "Basic Class" you learn how a rope team works as a unit for safe climbing. Instruction covers belaying, rappelling, rope handling, knots, and climbing signals. This is a fun, nonthreatening yet challenging day, appropriate for people of all ages who want to find out what climbing is all about. The "Intermediate Class" is structured as a day of multipitch climbing and instruction. The goals of the session are to prepare you to be part of a climbing team and to give the guides an opportunity to determine which climbs would be most appropriate for you. Both of these classes are taught in groups of three to five participants.

Other one-day summer options include an "Advancing Class," which is geared to meet the needs of the experienced climber who wishes to work on a specific skill, and "Summer Snow School," designed to teach mountain hikers, skiers, and climbers how to safely contend with hard, steep snow while savoring a day on summer snow on a peak near Jackson. All of the day classes convene at the school's office in downtown Jackson.

During the winter season, the school offers one-day ski tours appropriate for beginners (bring your own gear or rent it locally). Experienced skiers can sign on for "Ski Mountaineering," a day in the back country with time devoted to skill development and avalanche awareness instruction, including the use of avalanche transceivers (supplied by JHMG). Beginners as well as more experienced climbers can also elect "Rock Climbing," a full day of instruction delivered on cliffs overlooking the Jackson Hole Refuge, home of ten thousand elk, bison, deer, and antelope. One- to four-day ice-climbing courses are also offered.

During the winter months, the school offers "Overnight Ski Hut with Guided Back-Country Skiing and Instruction." The Mount Glory Ski Hut is located at the top of Teton Pass, about an hour's ski from the road. Complete with wood stove, kitchen, and sleeping arrangements, the hut provides easy access to back-country skiing, from introductory trips to demanding mountain crossings. In the fall and spring months, three-, four-, and seven-day climbing courses are offered in the desert parks of Nevada, California, Utah, South Dakota, and in Devil's Tower, Wyoming.

COST: Fees for classes run as follows: basic, $50; intermediate or "Snow School," $65; "Advancing," $90 per person for two people or $160 per day for one; one-day ski tours, $80 for one person and $35 for each extra person; one-day mountaineering, rock climbing, or ice climbing, $180 for one person and $75 for each additional person; "Overnight Ski Hut with Guided Back-Country Skiing and Instruction," $200 for one person and $75 for each additional person.

ENVISION EXPEDITIONS

Box 22724
Santa Fe, New Mexico 87502-2724
(800) 488-4402

Envision Expeditions conducts a series of eight-day mountaineering and canyoneering courses from May through mid-November. Planned to accommodate healthy adults eighteen and older with little or no previous wilderness experience, the itineraries are geared to those who enjoy exercise, teamwork, and the opportunity to experience dramatic weather and pristine natural settings. The goal of each expedition is to encourage participants to learn about themselves—their physical, emotional, and social strengths and abilities. All Envision instructors are well experienced in wilderness travel, group facilitation, and outdoor and experiential education.

As an expedition member, you will face many different types of challenges. You will develop skills in mountaineering, rock climbing, rappelling, and canyoneering. You will learn about route finding, map and compass use, campcraft, wilderness safety, and first aid. You will also have opportunities to face challenges that test your personal and social skills as they relate to teamwork, leadership, decision making, cooperation, and the ability to communicate clearly.

Canyoneering expeditions take place at Grand Canyon National Park in Arizona and Canyonlands National Park in Utah. Mountaineering courses explore the San Juan Mountains and Collegiate Peaks in Colorado.

During the summer months, Envision offers seven- and ten-day wilderness trips specifically designed for eleven- to fifteen-year-olds.

COST: The fee for the mountaineering and canyoneering courses is $680. This covers transportation from the point of origin (nearest city with a major airport), food, equipment, and instruction.

Skiing and Dogsledding

KEYSTONE SKI SCHOOL

Box 38
Keystone, Colorado 80435
(800) 255-3715

Located just seventy-five miles west of Denver in the Rocky Mountains, Keystone Resort encompasses four mountain peaks, each with a different personality. The resort is the home of a comprehensive ski school with an excellent reputation. Instructional programs are coded according to eight ability levels, ranging from level 1 ("people who have never skied before") to level 8 ("expert skiers who can ski all terrain in strong, stable, parallel"). Structured to meet specific objectives, the 2½-hour-long adult classes are held daily and each one is limited to eight participants. Skiers fifty years and older can enroll in a special weekly "Seniors' Day" program, which is taught from 10:30 A.M. to 3:30 P.M. from mid-January through mid-March. A similar "Ladies' Day" program is also offered for those who want a day of skiing taught by women instructors. Snowboarding instruction is available, too.

The Children's Ski School is divided into "Mini-Minor's Camp" for three- and four-year-olds (two to four hours of skiing, lunch, and indoor activities), "Minors' Camp" for five- to twelve-year-olds (four to five hours of skiing in class), and "Teen Ski" for thirteen- to seventeen-year-olds (up to four hours of instruction in groups formed by age and ability).

For those seeking the dramatic improvement that comes with several consecutive days of consistent instruction, Keystone offers two additional options. The resort is the home of the Mahre Training Center, which features an instructional program based on the special training techniques used by Olympic medalists Phil and Steve Mahre. The program serves skiers of all ages and abilities, from beginners who have never skied before to advanced racers.

Three- and five-day sessions are offered from the end of November through February, and a spring session is offered in May (testimony to the great spring snow conditions). The five-day sessions include five days' lift tickets, six hours of daily coaching using the Mahre methodology, video with coaches' analysis, evening discussions and films, fun races, and several social events. The three-day sessions cover the same material as the five-day sessions, but in a more concentrated form.

For a somewhat less intense instructional experience, the Keystone Ski School offers "The Keystone Ski Week," a five-day package that includes a five-day lift pass, three hours a day of coaching in groups of no more than seven students, video-taping with coaches' analysis, evening discussions, and films. Skiers are grouped according to ability. Balance exercises are used to develop a natural stance and improved control. Specific instruction paves the way to moguls, steeper terrain, and powder.

For cross-country skiing enthusiasts, the Keystone Cross Country Skiing and Touring Center has its own school, directed by former U.S. Olympic team member Jana Hlavaty. Group instruction includes beginner, step-up, skating, and beginning telemark lessons. You can also opt for a "Family Class," a 1½-hour session for parents and children who want to learn together. One-hour mini-lessons are available for children from six to twelve years of age. Also offered are "Women's Cross-Country Seminars," weekend programs consisting of two days of instruction held a week apart from each other. The first day is devoted to track skiing and the second to improving your downhill technique on cross-country skis.

COST: The 2½-hour adult classes cost $50–$52, which includes full-day ski rental and beginner's lift ticket (for levels 1–3) or an "all" lifts ticket (levels 4–8). The fee for "Seniors' Day" and "Ladies' Day" is $42 for the lesson alone or $62 for lesson and "all" lifts ticket.

The fee for the "Mini-Minor's Camp" and the "Minor's Camp" is $60 for full day, $50 for half-day, which includes ski rental, lessons, and lift ticket. "Teen Ski" costs $67 for full day or $57 for half-day, including "all" lifts and ski rental. Lunch is included for all full-day programs.

Tuition for the "Keystone Ski Week" is $260. Tuition for the Mahre Training Center program is $575 per five-day session, $355 per three-day session. A group cross-country ski lesson costs $25; full-day cross-country package including lesson, rentals, and trail fee is $35. The "Women's Cross-Country Seminars" cost $66 for both days.

ASPEN SKIING COMPANY

P.O. Box 1248
Aspen, Colorado 81612
(800) 525-6200, (303) 925-1220

Together Snowmass, Aspen, and Tiehack/Buttermilk encompass over three thousand acres of skiing. The Aspen Skiing Company Ski Schools offer programs at all three mountains and, like the mountains themselves, each school has a different personality.

Snowmass is one of the largest ski mountains in the country and is considered an excellent family facility. The Children's Ski School offers "Snow Cubs Snowplay and Ski School," which caters to those eighteen months to three years of age. The toddlers enjoy lots of indoor activities as well as time to play in the snow. The three-year-olds get a fun introduction to skiing, learning on a slope especially contoured for kids; skis are provided. Four- and five-year-olds join "Big Burn Bears," spending more time on the slopes, divided into small groups according to experience. Rental equipment is available for this group. Both programs run from 8:30 A.M. to 4:00 P.M. Beepers are available for rental for parents who feel more comfortable being reachable.

Both Snowmass and Tiehack/Buttermilk run Children's Ski School classes for kids from first grade up to twelve years old. Children are grouped according to age and ability. Half- and full-day options are available. For young adults, Tiehack/Buttermilk offers its Teens' Ski School, which is structured around groups based on age and ability and incorporates races, mountain picnics, and evening activities like pizza parties and ice skating. Group and private snowboarding lessons are also available at Tiehack/Buttermilk.

For beginning adults, "never-ever" skiers are well served by the three-day "Learn to Ski" program, also based at Tiehack/Buttermilk. Most students are able to ski the mountain top-to-base by the end of the third day, but if you're not one of them you get a free fourth day of instruction.

Experienced adult skiers can choose from several specialty classes offered at Snowmass and Aspen Mountain. There are two- and three-hour-long group lessons focusing on style, moguls, and powder. Strong intermediate skiers can learn the fundamentals of racing by enrolling in the regularly scheduled race program. The "Disabled Skier Program" provides free instruction and use of equipment to the physically challenged, including blind skiers. The Aspen Skiing Company also offers "Women's Ski Seminars," taught by women instructors. Participants set personal goals and progress at their own pace in a supportive environment.

Skiers of all abilities can enroll in the Vic Braden Ski College, an intensive program that focuses on analyzing your existing skills, figuring out what you need to do to progress to the next level, and then working with you to get there. The program is directed by licensed psychologist Vic Braden, an experienced teacher who has spent over thirty years as a sports researcher, using computer technology to improve performance in a number of sports for both amateurs and professionals. The four-day ski college begins with a Sunday afternoon orientation meeting, followed by full ski days from Monday through Thursday.

The Ramer Adventure Skiing Program is geared to intermediate to expert skiers who want to get off the groomed trails and experience the back country. During the four-hour "Introductory Course," your instructor will provide an overview of adventure skiing while teaching you how to downhill ski on Ramer alpine skiing gear. Instruction covers techniques for skiing variable snow conditions, ski climbing, touring, and avalanche rescue techniques. The "Basic Course" begins with the introductory overview and continues on with an afternoon guided tour from the top of Aspen Mountain, skiing down one thousand vertical feet of untracked powder, attaching climbing skins, and then heading back up the mountain to do it again. The use of all necessary equipment (including skis, bindings, boots, and poles) is part of the package.

If you would prefer to concentrate on cross-country skiing, head for the Snowmass Club Touring Center, which connects with one of the most extensive free trail networks in the country, spanning sixty kilometers and crossing three valleys. The center's "Beginner I" lesson provides an introduction to the diagonal stride and the basics of skiing flat terrain and gentle slopes. "Beginner II" introduces uphill, downhill, and flat-track techniques. Each lesson lasts 1 ½ hours. Private instruction is also available. The center also conducts guided tours, some of which include instruction.

COST: The fee for "Snow Cubs Snowplay and Ski School" and "Big Burn Bears" is $40 for half-day, $60 for full day, $280 for five days. Children's Ski School classes and Teens' Ski School classes cost $40 for half-day, $48 for one day, $135 for three days, $200 for five days. Snowboarding group instruction is $48 per day. The fee for the three-day "Learn to Ski" program is $99. The "Women's Ski Seminars" cost $260 (lift tickets additional). Tuition for the Vic Braden Ski College, including four days of instruction and lift tickets, is $595.

Tuition for the Ramer Adventure Skiing Program is $60 for the "Introductory Course," $90 for the "Basic Course"; prices are based on a minimum of three people. "Beginner I" and "Beginner II" cross-country lessons cost $20 apiece.

BOUNDARY COUNTRY TREKKING

590 Gunflint Trail
Grand Marais, Minnesota 55604
(800) 322-8327, (218) 388-4487

Boundary Country Trekking organizes dogsled adventure trips and yurt-to-yurt cross-country skiing trips through the Boundary Waters Canoe Area of northern Minnesota, a million acres of pristine wilderness blessed by reliable snow conditions well into April.

Professional dogsled racer Arleigh Jorgenson, who has competed in most of the country's leading dogsled races, oversees Boundary Country Trekking's dogsledding program. Under his guidance and that of his associates, you will learn to keep tight the gangline that holds the dogs in line, because if it gets slack the animals think the sled will run them over. Five to seven dogs, each weighing 35–55 pounds and bred for speed and endurance, are harnessed to each sled. The challenge is to get them to function smoothly together as a team, which means paying attention to each one's position and unique personality.

Your dogsledding adventure begins with an orientation session that focuses on harnessing a team (a procedure that takes about an hour), caring for the dogs, sledding safety precautions, what to expect on the trail, and details of the trip itinerary. From then on, it's learn by doing. Together with your instructor/guide, you will experience the thrill of mastering a dog team as it pulls you through the woods and across frozen lakes. Keep an eye alert for moose and other wildlife while standing firmly on the runners behind your team, learning to feel like a musher. New mushers are often astounded at how quiet dogsledding is. Sure, there's barking from time to time, but for long stretches all you will hear is the crunch of paws running through the snow.

The typical trip is a three-day, three-night adventure offered from December through March. Two people normally share a sled. You will mush twenty to twenty-five miles each day, spending the nights in a rustic cabin, a yurt (more about these below), and a remote cabin with modern conveniences located a kilometer from the nearest plowed road. Substantial, delicious meals are part of the package. Shorter and longer mushing adventures are available, too.

If you would prefer to explore the Minnesota wilderness on skis, you can opt for a yurt-to-yurt ski adventure. These trips are not guided, but each yurt is staffed by an experienced outdoorsman ready both to cook excellent meals and to give you the advice you need to make the most of your days on the trail, whether you are a novice, intermediate, or expert cross-country skier. Most ski itineraries follow the twenty-seven-kilometer Banadad Ski Trail, the longest groomed and tracked trail in the area and the backbone of the 187-kilometer system known as the Gunflint Nordic Ski Trails. You will ski the Banadad encumbered only by a day pack. Your gear and all necessary supplies are transported from one yurt to another by Boundary Country Trekking's able staff, which also arranges for your car to be waiting at the end of the trail.

For the most part, lodgings take the form of three yurts, round canvas-covered dwellings used for centuries by the people occupying the Mongolian plateau. The yurts are warm and cozy, each one outfitted with wood stove, bunk beds, dining area, and nearby outhouse. The basic trip is a two-night "Yurt-to-Yurt Ski Adventure," complete with Mongolian firepot dinner.

COST: The fee for a three-day, three-night "Mush Your Own Team Adventure" is $660 per person. This covers lodgings, guide/instructor, all meals, dogs, sled, and sled equipment. The fee for a two-night "Yurt-to-Yurt Ski Adventure" is $310 for one person and $220 per person for 2–3 people traveling together, with additional discounts for larger groups. This covers lodging, all meals, and car shuttles.

WINTERGREEN DOGSLEDDING LODGE

Ring Rock Road
Ely, Minnesota 55731
(800) 584-9425, (218) 365-6022

Here in the north woods area of Minnesota, the country's foremost recreational dogsledding center, Wintergreen Dogsledding Lodge director Paul Schurke and his staff can teach you everything there is to know about being comfortable and enjoying the winter wilderness. Programs revolve around dogsledding, relying on the energies of Canadian Eskimo freight dogs, who range in size from sixty to ninety pounds. All programs originate at the lodge, which offers bunk room, meeting room, kitchen, heated outhouse, and a wood-heated sauna.

Wintergreen offers two types of trips. The three-, four-, and five-night "Lodge-to-Lodge Dog-Sled Tours" are open to people of all ages, including children, and require no prior winter experience or special physical fitness. Accompanied by expert staff mushers, you mush your own team of Eskimo dogs along the Kawishiwi trail corridor, which extends from Snowbank Lake to White Iron Lake. Each of the trips includes an evening arctic program with Paul Schurke, who in 1989 led a Soviet–American team on a dogsled trek from Siberia to Alaska. You will also have the opportunity to try snowshoeing, ice fishing, and cross-country skiing. All equipment is provided. Evenings are spent in wilderness cabins with facilities ranging from full service to rustic.

If you want to learn all the tricks and techniques of winter wilderness travel, including camping skills, consider the lodge's "Dog-Sled and Ski Camping Programs." You will spend the first two nights at Wintergreen Lodge. The day in between is devoted to comprehensive skills instruction, focusing on all aspects of low-impact winter camping and travel: mushing and dog handling, back-country skiing, snowshoeing, winter ecology, use of map and compass, dressing for cold weather, ice safety, snow shelters, and fire building. After that, you head out into the wilderness to apply those new skills during three days of dogsled camping. The next two evenings are spent tent camping and listening to informative talks by Schurke and other staff members, delivered around the campfire. Your last night is spent back at Wintergreen Lodge. The standard five-night program, "Wintergreen Classic," is open to anyone who is physically fit and ready to spend the entire day outdoors and active. Prior experience is not required. Wintergreen provides all necessary equipment.

If you have previous winter camping experience, consider the challenge offered by one of Wintergreen's advanced programs. Five-, seven-, and fourteen-night combination dog-sledding/skiing expeditions are offered. Good fitness is absolutely essential.

COST: The per-person fee for "Lodge-to-Lodge Dog-Sled Tours" is $390 for the three-night program, $490 for the four-night program, and $590 for the five-night program. The fee for the five-night "Wintergreen Classic" is $475. Advanced programs cost $525 for the five-night expedition, $675 for seven nights, and $975 for fourteen nights. Meals are included in all of these programs.

TAG-A-LONG EXPEDITIONS

452 North Main St.
Moab, Utah 84532
(800) 453-3292, (801) 259-8946

Just east of Moab, Utah's La Sal Mountains stretch high into the sky, capturing winter snow and transforming it into a deep powder that blankets the landscape from November to April. Tag-A-Long Expeditions has offered a variety of guided trips throughout this area, which includes the Colorado River, Arches National Park, and Canyonlands National Park, since 1964. Working closely with the U.S. Forest Service, the company now offers a high-quality backcountry winter cross-country skiing experience.

The La Sal Mountain Hut system consists of three huts located within a day's skiing distance of one another. Each location was chosen because of the variety of skiing opportunities available, including gentle trails for the beginner, intermediate routes, and challenging telemark slopes that ascend up to twelve thousand feet. The huts accommodate ten to twenty-four visitors in bunk rooms and small cabins. Each hut offers heating, lighting, cooking and sanitary facilties, kitchen supplies, and mattresses and pillows. Tag-A-Long Expeditions provides trained guides knowledgeable about back-country trail routes, hut operations, and safety issues like avalanche awareness, first aid, emergency rescue, and map and compass reading. The guides also provide skiing instruction. The company offers a good selection of package tours that complement a range of skiing levels. Three-, four-, and five-day hut-to-hut trips are the mainstay. The packages combine hut lodgings, all meals, transportation to and from the trail head, professional guiding and ski instruction, Snowcat gear shuttle to and from the huts, and the use of sleeping bags appropriate to the climate.

COST: The fee for a four-day hut-to-hut expedition is $395 (with discounts for groups of five or more persons).

NORTH RIVER RIM NORDIC CENTER

Canyoneers, Inc.
P.O. Box 2997
Flagstaff, Arizona 86003
(602) 526-0924, (800) 525-0924

Situated just south of the Utah–Arizona border at the outer reaches of Grand Canyon National Park, the Kaibab Plateau is a fifteen-hundred-square-mile "island in the sky," towering about a vertical mile above the surrounding red-rock desert. Kaibab Lodge, home of the North River Rim Nordic Center, sits at the center of the plateau. The parkway that leads to the lodge is closed by heavy snow in the winter. But while cars can't make the trip, the North Rim Nordic Center can get you there in heated SnowVans that carry twelve to fifteen passengers. The trip from Jacob Lake takes about two hours, depending on the weather. A helicopter connection is also available.

The North River Rim Nordic Center uses sophisticated tracking and trail-grooming machinery to groom up to forty kilometers of trails around the lodge, including set diagonal tracks and ski-skating lanes for beginning, intermediate, and advanced cross-country skiers. Expert skiers can break their own trails, enjoying plenty of untracked back-country skiing. Staffed by fully certified ski instructors, the center offers beginner through advanced classic ski lessons along with skating and telemark lessons. Informal evening programs focus on ski technique, winter clothing, and winter survival, as well as Grand Canyon geology and photography.

Two- and three-night package plans are offered, with accommodations in a private cabin or in a less expensive group yurt (a type of canvas shelter long used by Mongolian herdsmen to ward off the cold). In addition to lodgings, all of the packages include round-trip SnowVan transportation from Jacob Lake, unlimited use of trail system, daily group lessons, daily guided ski tours, use of hot tub and main lodge facilities, and free breakfast on day of departure. Equipment rentals are available at the lodge at additional cost.

COST: Fees for the packages described above run as follows: three days, three nights with private cabin, $225 per person double occupancy; three days, three nights with group yurt, $165; two days, two nights with private cabin, $180 per person double occupancy; two days, two nights with group yurt, $140.

Fishing

THE JOAN & LEE WULFF FISHING SCHOOL

Beaverkill Road
Lew Beach, New York 12758
(914) 439-4060

Under the direction of Joan Wulff, who has run the school since the death of her husband in 1991, the Joan & Lee Wulff Fishing School is headquartered on the Beaverkill, the Catskill Mountains' best known river and the birthplace of dry fly fishing in America. The only woman ever to have won a national distance-casting championship against all-male competition, Joan Wulff also holds the International Woman's Fishing Association records for brook trout and Atlantic salmon. She also writes a fly-casting column for *Fly Rod and Reel* magazine and is the author of two authoritative books, *Fly Casting Techniques* and *Joan Wulff's Fly Fishing: Expert Advice from a Woman's Perspective*, which are used as course textbooks.

The Wulff School offers intensive weekend trout-fishing seminars throughout May and June. Suitable for both beginners and experienced trout fishermen, each program begins with an overview of the trout's habitat and then moves on to cover the theory and practice of casting on ponds and river;

stream entomology; fishing knots; reading water; tackle know-how; fly selection, approach, and presentation; and wading, playing, landing, and releasing fish.

Joan Wulff is personally involved in each session. The weekend begins with a Friday night demonstration of the special casting techniques she has developed, along with a showing of films designed to help you learn to think like a trout. On Saturday, students move back and forth between classroom lectures and outdoor practice sessions at the casting ponds. Techniques introduced include the roll cast, the basic cast, false casting, and shooting line. Each student is videotaped in action and the tapes are analyzed. Lectures on stream entomology are also presented. Instruction continues well into the night with postdinner lecture and films focusing on fly selection and tying. The indoor/outdoor schedule continues through Sunday, highlighted by a wading and casting session on the river, with each student working a separate stretch of water.

The school maintains an instructor-to-student ratio of 1:4 and caters to men and women, young and old. Your fellow students are likely to include singles, couples, friends who enroll together, and even parent/child combinations.

Unlike many fishing schools, the Wulff School is not associated with a particular tackle company. The school provides all necessary tackle, pulling together products from a dozen different suppliers. Of course, you are also welcome to use your own.

COST: The fee for the weekend school is $400 per person (instruction only) or $470 (instruction plus three meals at the Beaverkill Valley Inn). Participants arrange for their own accommodations.

SWEETWATER FISHING EXPEDITIONS

P.O. Box 612
Crowheart, Wyoming 82512
(307) 486-2266

George and Paula Hunker both worked as instructors for the National Outdoor Leadership School in Wyoming before forming their own business, Sweetwater Fishing Expeditions, in the mid-1970s. They've been leading backpack fly-fishing trips into the Wind River Range ever since. A rugged Rocky Mountain range inhabited by a formidable herd of bighorn sheep, the Winds contain thousands of glacier-carved lakes. These lakes provide a home for a wealth of cutthroat and brook trout, along with less predominant species like golden, lake, rainbow, and splake.

The goal of Sweetwater Fishing is simple: to arrange for guests to camp in solitude in a magnificent wilderness setting where the trout are plentiful. Each trip is individually planned, taking into account the physical capabilities, fishing experience, time limitations, and goals of your party. Lake fishing is done "New Zealand style," spotting and stalking individual trout, and instruction is woven into the experience according to need. As George and Paula explain, these trips are "for everyone: eight-year-old children, football stars, young mothers, middle-aged executives, housewives, grandmothers and grandfathers. These types of people have all been with us."

The Hunkers aim to maximize your fishing time. That means the cooking and dishwashing are taken care of for you. And while Sweetwater trips involve backpacking to the fishing site, the amount you carry depends on your preference. Horses can be used to pack in your gear if you wish.

Sweetwater provides all food and cooking and eating utensils, while participants are expected to provide their own personal gear. However, some sleeping bags, tents, packs, and rods are available for loan if you don't have your own.

COST: The fee for a one-day fishing trip is $185 for one person, $235 for two people. A five-day expedition is $1,700 for one or two people, and $750 for each additional person. Longer expeditions can also be arranged. An additional fee is charged if horses are required.

ROCKY MOUNTAIN ANGLERS

P.O. Box 6306
Navajo Dam, New Mexico 87419
(505) 632-0445

Rocky Mountain Anglers provides on-stream instructional trips and fly-fishing guide service on the San Juan River in northwestern New Mexico. A favorite with fishermen because of the consistency of its water temperature and its many large pools, the San Juan offers a great fishing experience year-round. The water is loaded with trophy-sized rainbow, Snake River cutthroat, and brown trout.

Co-owners Rick Hooley and Paul Faust grew up in the area and have been fishing the San Juan since they were kids. They will teach you the basics of fly fishing for trout in a situation that also gives you the opportunity to catch and release a good-sized rainbow trout. "We also cover stream ecology, local flora and fauna, and wading techniques," writes Hooley.

Depending upon your interest and abilities, you can schedule a walk-in wade trip or a float trip. The current in the river is swift and the water temperature (hovering near forty degrees Fahrenheit) makes chest waders a must (insulated waders are highly recommended). The float fishing trips take a less strenuous approach than the wade-in trips. The sixteen-foot fiberglass McKenzie-style river boats are equipped with straight-backed swivel seats and level casting platforms from which to fly fish.

COST: The fee per day for a walk-in wade trip with

instruction is $200 for one or two people, and $50 additional for a third person. The fee per day for a float trip is $210 for one person, $225 for two people, and $275 for three people. All fees include lunch.

PARADE REST RANCH

7979 Grayling Creek Road
West Yellowstone, Montana 59758
(406) 646-7217, (800) 753-5934

From November 15 to April 15:
Walt and Shirley Butcher
P.O. Box 4135-85278
Apache Junction, Arizona 85278
(602) 983-2653, (800) 753-5934

An original homestead on the Old Banock Indian Trail, Parade Rest Ranch is nestled between the foothills of the Gallatin Range of the Rocky Mountains and the rushing waters of Grayling Creek. Located ten miles northeast of West Yellowstone (elevation 6,666 feet), snuggled up close to the west side of Yellowstone National Park, the ranch sits in the heart of some of the finest fly-fishing country in the world.

Under the direction of Jim Danskins, a widely published fishing writer with forty-five years of experience as an outfitter, guide, and instructor, the ranch offers a three-day-long fly-fishing school from mid-May through mid-September. Here beginners learn the basics of fly fishing while intermediates improve their technique. Instruction, 90 percent of which takes place on the stream, focuses on choice and use of equipment, basic casting techniques, line control, accuracy, knots, basic entomology, reading the water, and wading. Classes are restricted to a minimum of two and a maximum of four students, allowing plenty of personal attention.

Family members who do not enroll in the fishing school will also find plenty to do at the ranch. Horseback riding is a big draw, with easy morning, afternoon, and sunset rides scheduled for novices, and more challenging full-day excursions to higher elevations organized for experienced riders. Other activities include western-style cookouts, outdoor hot tub/whirlpool, volleyball, horseshoes, badminton, and hiking. The community lodge contains a library and room for socializing and watching television.

Up to forty-eight guests can be accommodated in cozy log cabins complete with modern bathrooms, most of them heated by wood-burning stoves. Breakfast and dinner are served buffet style in the dining room, and guests receive a packed lunch to take along on their day's activities.

COST: The fee for the fly-fishing school, which covers three days' meals and lodging, two days of instruction, and one day of guided fishing is $650, including all equipment except waders. Other visitors pay $95 per person per day, which covers meals, lodgings, and horseback riding; single occupancy add $10 per day. Children 6–9 pay $73; rates for younger children are negotiable. Guests who wish to fish but are not enrolled in the fishing school must bring their own equipment.

KITTREDGE SPORTS

Mammoth Adventure Connection
P.O. Box 353
Mammoth Lakes, California 93546
(619) 934-0606, (800) 228-4947

Kittredge Sports, Mammoth's foremost fly-fishing guide service with over twenty-seven years of experience fishing High Sierra lakes and streams, offers a four-day fly-fishing school monthly from May through October. In cooperation with Mammoth Adventure Connection, students purchase a package that combines accommodations at the luxurious Mammoth Mountain Inn with a hearty dose of on-water instruction. Geared for beginners, the curriculum covers all the basic information and skills required to get started. Working with a small group of four to six students, your instructor will use lectures, slide shows, and demonstrations to supplement on-water practice.

School begins with an opening night welcome reception and orientation session. The second day is divided between a morning session focusing on equipment, leaders, and knots, a casting lesson with video analysis, and a lecture on stream-reading tactics. The third day is spent at Hot Creek, practicing casting skills and learning about water reading and stream entomology. A late afternoon lecture on fly-pattern selection and an evening awards dinner round out the day. On the fourth day, students spend the morning pulling all their new skills together, fishing Hot Creek.

If you have less time to spare or if you cannot coordinate your schedule to attend a fly-fishing school, you can opt for a guide trip. An expert guide will share his knowledge of the streams and lakes while teaching beginners proper technique as well as sharing a few secrets useful in the pursuit of the elusive trout. Experienced anglers can fine-tune their skills while becoming familiar with the variety of fishing opportunities afforded by the Mammoth area.

COST: The fee for the fishing school is $422 per person double occupancy; this covers all instruction, three nights' lodgings, daily box lunches, welcome reception and awards dinner, and use of a Fenwick fly rod and reel and an assortment of fly patterns. The fee for a guide trip is $166 per person double occupancy, which covers two nights' lodging, one day/eight hours' guide service, and one box lunch.

MONTANA TROUTFITTERS
ORVIS SHOP

1716 West Main St.
Bozeman, Montana 59715
(406) 587-4707

Montana Troutfitters Orvis Shop (MTOS) offers the only fly-fishing schools in the state endorsed by the Orvis Company of Manchester, Vermont, the granddaddy of fine fly-fishing instruction. Under the direction of proprietor David Kumlien, the four-day-long Orvis Fly Fishing Schools are geared to meet the needs of beginning fly fishermen. The curriculum covers the basics of casting, knot tying, fishing strategies, and equipment.

MTOS schools are based at the historic Gallatin Gateway Inn about ten miles west of Bozeman, within walking distance of the Gallatin River. One of the grand railroad hotels of the 1920s and 1930s, the recently refurbished inn is listed on the National Register of Historic Places. Schools, which begin on Wednesday morning and end on Saturday evening, are scheduled for July, August, and September. Each student is given an Orvis rod-and-reel outfit to use during the school. Wading gear is required; bring your own or rent it from MTOS.

Classroom sessions feature intensive work on knots, leaders, lines, equipment, basic entomology, and fly selection. Students receive concentrated fly-casting instruction, supplemented by daily videotape critiques, at the inn's custom-built fly-casting pond. Friday afternoon is devoted to an on-stream session at the Gallatin River, with the emphasis on casting and line control, wading safety, entomology, and basic fishing with nymphs, dry flies, and streamers. On Saturday students go on a guided float fishing trip on the Madison or Yellowstone rivers. Assigned two per guide, you test your new skills against the browns and rainbow trout.

MTOS also offers an annual Orvis Advanced Fly Fishing School, a three-day program designed for the serious fly fisherman. Instruction and fishing take place on a variety of area rivers and one day is spent float tubing on a private lake. The curriculum covers advanced techniques for casting, knot tying, reading the water, and nymph, streamer, and dry-fly fishing. Students can try out a variety of Orvis fly rods during the school.

For those who are unable to participate in a school, MTOS offers individual instruction for groups of one to three. Full guiding services are also available, including float trips, walk trips, and float-tube trips.

COST: Tuition for the Orvis Fly-Fishing School is $575. A complete package, including tuition, four nights' accommodations, and meals at the Gallatin Gateway Inn, is $915 for double occupancy, $1,065 for single occupancy. Tuition for the Orvis Advanced Fly Fishing School is $500. A complete package, including three nights' accommodations and meals at the Gallatin Gateway Inn, is $805 for double occupancy, $905 for single occupancy. Individual instruction is also available at $50 per hour (three-hour minimum) for a group of one to three fishermen.

ELKTROUT

Box 614
1853 County Road 33
Kremmling, Colorado 80459
(303) 724-3343

Located two hours west of Denver, Elktrout aims to provide the highest quality experience to anyone who loves to fly fish or wants to learn. The lodge offers access to ten miles of completely private trout waters open only to guests, including stretches of the Colorado River and the Blue River, along with ten ponds and lakes. Here you can wade and cast at will, mile after mile, without ever encountering another fisherman. The combination of Elktrout's catch-and-release policy and the private water means big fish. Two-pound rainbows and browns are common in the rivers, while the ponds regularly produce four-pounders and up.

The variety of water caters to every skill level. The most experienced angler is ensured a challenge, yet because of Elktrout's guided fishing program even the novice will feel competent. Guides serve as instructors and escorts. They do not fish.

Elktrout's fishing season runs from May through mid-October. Three- and six-day fly-fishing schools for both seasoned anglers and novices are scheduled in May and July. Instruction begins in the classroom but soon moves outdoors, where students fish a variety of streams and also experience the opportunity to fish to rising trout from float tubes on the ponds and lakes. Throughout the season, the lodge's guides provide beginning to advanced casting instruction and "on-the-water" service.

Elktrout can accommodate twenty visitors at a time and boasts an "atmosphere of casual elegance." Guests are accommodated in twin-bedded rooms with private baths and the high-quality cuisine is served in a turn-of-the-century dining tent complete with crystal chandeliers and wood-burning stoves.

COST: The cost of the six-day fly-fishing school, including lodging, meals, instruction, and guide service, is $1,512–$1,879 per person (depending upon single or double accommodations). For the three-day school, the cost is $850–$1,057. Nonfishing spouses are billed $150 per night for lodging and meals.

CRAIG FELLIN'S BIG HOLE RIVER OUTFITTERS

Box 156
Wise River, Montana 59762
(406) 832-3252

Big Hole River Outfitters is located in wilderness surroundings where it is not unusual to sight moose, elk, deer, and mountain goats. A small operation with the emphasis on personalized service, this outfitter provides one guide for every two guests. Guests are welcomed by the week. During your stay, you will fish for brown trout, brookies, rainbow trout, cutthroats, and grayling on a variety of water including the Beaverhead, a small, narrow river that, according to local biologists, has more trout measuring over twenty inches than any other stream in Montana. Under the direction of your guide, you will practice both long-reaching casts and small-stream tactics. Chest waders are recommended for the smaller bodies of water. On the larger expanses of water, fishing is conducted by floating with Avon rafts.

During your stay, you will live in a comfortable cabin located steps away from the Wise River and just a few minutes from the Big Hole River. Breakfast and dinner are served in the main lodge, where guests gather in the early evening to discuss the day's adventures. Lunch is usually served streamside to maximize fishing time. Big Hole River Outfitters accepts up to twelve guests at a time. The season runs from June through early October.

COST: The rate for a six-night stay with five full days of fishing is $1,470 per person based on double occupancy. This covers round-trip transfer from Butte, accommodations, meals, complimentary beer and wine, and the services of a guide/instructor.

GEORGE ANDERSON'S YELLOWSTONE ANGLER

Highway 89 South
P.O. Box 660
Livingston, Montana 59047
(406) 222-7130

Several of the finest small trout streams in the world, spring creeks that flow into the Yellowstone River, are located just eight miles south of Livingston. The spring creeks, home of large wild trout, are located on private ranches that limit access, charge a daily fee, and operate strictly on a catch-and-release basis.

George Anderson's Yellowstone Angler is a fly shop located on the way to the spring creeks and the Yellowstone River. The shop specializes in flies and tackle suited to the spring creeks and other local waters. It also serves as a valuable and generous source of information. All staff members are accomplished fishermen, ready to supply up-to-the-minute observations on stream conditions and hatches. The staff can arrange guided trips on the creeks (but you must reserve well in advance), as well as float trips and wade trips on many other area waters.

Each summer George Anderson (who writes for *Fly Fisherman*), Brant Oswald (former director of the Orvis West Coast Fly Fishing Schools), and some of the guides teach a number of Yellowstone Angler Fly Fishing Schools, with options for all fly fishermen. Beginners benefit from a good start and experts learn some new tricks. Casting is an important focus of the schools, and casting skills taught extend from the basics of a good casting stroke to the intricacies of the double haul. Students learn how to use different presentation casts to adapt to various fishing situations.

During seminars, conducted in a comfortable classroom in the shop, you will learn how to tie knots and listen to discussions centering on tackle, lines, and leader formulas. You will also learn about angling entomology, stream strategy, conservation, stream etiquette, and different fishing methods, including how to fish nymphs, emergers, drys, midges, and streamers.

Classes are small and the teachers are some of the best in the business. Casting practice takes place on the large lawn beside the shop. Students also have the chance to put all of their skills together on one of the spring creeks. With your instructor beside you, you will have the opportunity to apply the knowledge garnered in the classroom and on the lawn. In an ideal situation, you will decide to combine the school with a day or two of guided fishing. The guides serve as on-site instructors who can continue teaching technique as conditions require.

Instead of offering schoools on preset dates, Yellowstone Angler customizes the schedule to meet the client's needs. In effect, you put together your own school—either for yourself alone or for you and another angling enthusiast or two.

COST: The rate for fly-fishing instruction is $210 per day for one person and $235 for two. For larger groups, the rate is $100 per person per day. These fees do not cover meals or the rod fees charged to fish private waters.

TROUT & GROUSE

300 Happ Road
Northfield, Illinois 60093
(708) 501-3111

A fly-fishing and upland hunting shop less than an hour from Chicago, Trout & Grouse caters to both beginning and experienced anglers. Manager Peter Sykes produces a newsletter several times a year detailing the classes, seminars, and guided trips offered by the outfitter.

Trout & Grouse has been teaching folks to fly fish for sixteen years, taking an approach that makes learning the skill easy and fun. One-day fly-fishing schools are offered in April, May, June, and July. The sessions are conducted right at the shop and include outdoor casting instruction. Students are taught basic knots needed for changing flies and tippets. Equipment, fly selection, stream strategy, and choosing a fishing spot are among the other topics covered.

One-day fly-tying classes for beginners and intermediates are offered in the fall, winter, and spring.

COST: The fee for the fly-fishing schools is $150, continental breakfast and lunch included. The fee for the fly-tying class is $70, which includes all necessary materials.

KAUFMANN'S FLY FISHING EXPEDITIONS, INC.

P.O. Box 23032
Portland, Oregon 97223
(800) 442-4359

Kaufmann's Fly Fishing Expeditions offers fly-fishing, fly-tying, and steelhead schools. All programs are based in a modern air-conditioned three-story riverside house in Maupin. Three-day fly-fishing schools are conducted from May through early October. You will fish along the banks of Oregon's Deschutes River under the guidance of expert instructors. Each group is limited to eight students with an instructor-to-student ratio of 1:4, so there is plenty of opportunity for individualized attention. That makes the schools valuable both to beginning fishermen, who will save themselves years of unnecessary struggle by learning proper techniques from the start, and to advanced anglers who want to refine their technique. The course takes the form of a relaxed, flexible, on-the-water fly-fishing experience, conspicuous both for its lack of regimentation and for the large amount of fishing time offered.

Participants receive hands-on instruction appropriate to their skill level, covering all aspects of fly fishing, including tackle, knots, leaders, casting, surface and subsurface fly presentation, line control, reading the water, entomology, food sources of trout, fly patterns, fly tying, trout behavior, and fishing strategy.

In late August Kaufmann's runs a four-day Steelhead School. The program is limited to six anglers, with an instructor-to-student ratio of 1:3. Instruction covers steelhead tackle, leaders, fly patterns, fly tying, and casting and presentation techniques, with lots of fishing time and the opportunity to learn how to land and release these magnificent and very aggressive fish.

If you choose to attend a Fly-Tying School, offered several times a year, expect to join a small, informal group including both beginning and advanced tyers. Participants spend about six hours a day at the tying bench and all necessary gear is provided. There is also ample time for fishing. You will learn the tricks involved in tying perfectly proportioned dry flies, nymphs, streamers, steelhead, hair wing, and specialty flies.

Upon receipt of your deposit and registration, Kaufmann's will forward you an equipment and information sheet. Kaufmann's also runs schools and seminars at its locations in Washington. If you are interested in finding out more about these opportunities, call (206) 448-0601 in Seattle or (206) 643-2246 in Bellevue.

COST: The fee for the Fly-Tying Schools is $395. The fee for the Steelhead School is $795. All fees cover food, lodging, and instruction.

HUNTER'S ANGLING SUPPLIES

Central Square, Box 300
New Boston, New Hampshire 03070
(800) 331-8558, (603) 487-3388

From the end of May and continuing throughout June, a period coinciding with prime insect activity in the area, Hunter's Angling Supplies offers beginning, intermediate, and big-water fly-fishing classes. Classes, which begin Friday evening and end Sunday afternoon, are based in North Conway with instruction on the Saco and Ellis rivers.

The beginner's class hones in on three basic issues: how to cast, where to cast, and what fly to use. Students are also introduced to basic knot tying, wading technique, angling etiquette, and other aspects of the sport. Those who have fly fished for a couple of years can enroll in the intermediate class, which covers advanced casting and mending, entomology, nymphing techniques, and fly selection. There is also a "big-water" class, where students learn about sinking and sink-tip line techniques and how to "read" a big river. Included is an opportunity to drift the Androscoggin River in a McKenzie river boat under the supervision of an accomplished guide and teacher.

Hunter's Angling also offers a series of weekend seminars on various aspects of fly fishing. Each course provides a hands-on experience. Instruction takes place from 9:00 A.M. to 4:00 P.M. with a break for lunch. For beginners, "Fundamentals of Fly Fishing" provides a comprehensive introduction to the basics of tying trout flies, starting with the selection of proper materials. More experienced tyers can choose from seminars focusing on saltwater flies, Atlantic salmon fly tying, building bass bugs, and other aspects of fly tying. Students bring their own tools (or you can purchase a basic fly-tying tool set at the store, where the sessions are held).

COST: The fee for the fly-fishing classes is $325, which covers all instruction and two nights' lodging, based on double occupancy. The fee for the weekend seminars, which covers instruction, class materials, and lunch, ranges from $115 to $145.

Horseback Riding and Ranch Life

VISTA VERDE GUEST & SKI TOURING RANCH

P.O. Box 465
Steamboat Springs, Colorado 80477
(303) 879-3858, (800) 526-7433

Vista Verde, a six-hundred-acre spread posed at an elevation of seventy-eight hundred feet, is a working ranch with its own cattle and herd of horses as well as plenty of other farm animals. Guests participate in a variety of learning experiences, making this an ideal place to conveniently introduce yourself to several new skills. During the summer months, the emphasis is on horseback riding. The riding program includes in-depth arena instruction for riders of all levels, as well as guided trail rides on the ranch and in the adjoining national forest. More than fifty horses are stabled at Vista Verde.

If you plan your visit for the first week in June or for the middle of September, you can take part in an authentic cattle drive. Because the winter and summer grazing areas are fairly near to one another, the drive itself takes only one day. Participants arrive on Sunday and spend Monday through Thursday getting prepared. Mornings are spent learning to care for your horse, roping, riding, and repairing fences. In the afternoon, there are arena sessions to help you get to know your horse better. On Friday, you'll herd the cows between Elk

River Valley and the Vista Verde, returning to the ranch by sundown.

In addition to the riding activities, a one-week package at the ranch also includes a half-day introductory rock-climbing trip. Professional instruction is provided along with all the necessary equipment needed to experience climbing and rappelling.

The package also covers participation in a well-organized hiking program. Ranch guides lead full- and half-day treks in the Rockies, matched to your abilities and interests. Explore turn-of-the-century mining artifacts on the Gilpin Mine tour. Discover hidden waterfalls and visit beaver ponds, always keeping alert for deer, elk, coyote, beaver, ermine, and many species of birds. Enjoy walks and talks that focus on subjects ranging from fitness to stargazing to the habits of hummingbirds.

During the winter season, from the holidays through mid-March, the emphasis shifts to skiing. Vista Verde averages 350 inches of dry snow a year. Certified instructors provide introductory and in-depth instruction on both the ranch's twenty-kilometer network of groomed ski tracks and on forty kilometers of marked, ungroomed trails in the adjoining national forest. A special six-day, five-night instructional package, "Vista Verde NordiClass," is offered once in January and once in March. Under the guidance of certified instructors, skiers from novice to expert experience all types of Nordic skiing—traditional, skating, back-country, and telemark.

The ranch accommodates up to thirty guests (twenty during the winter season) in its eight comfortable private log cabins, each one equipped with a wood-burning stove, full kitchen, open living room, and a porch from which to ponder the spectacular view. Guests feast on gourmet meals, often served outdoors in the summer and in front of the fireplace in the winter.

COST: The rate for a one-week summer stay, including lodging, all meals, horseback riding, and the other activities described above, is $1,275–$1,375 for adults, $875–$975 for children under twelve. Shorter stays (minimum of three days) are sometimes possible. The rate for the "NordiClass" package is $750 per person, which covers lodging, all meals, instruction, and use of equipment. Shorter winter stays (two-day minimum) cost $120–$150 per day for adults, $75–$95 for children under twelve.

LATIGO RANCH

P.O. Box 237
Kremmling, Colorado 80459
(303) 724-9008

Latigo Ranch sits at nine thousand feet high in the heart of the Colorado Rockies. The ranch specializes in horse-back riding and maintains a string of fifty horses. Guests are free to ride as often or as little as they like.

Each guest is assigned to a horse for the week, with horse and rider carefully matched according to ability, physical requirements, and temperament. Individual instruction is available nearly every day in the spacious riding arena, enabling those who wish to hone their skills to progress rapidly. Guided trail rides, divided according to ability, take place twice each day. The rides last from 1½ to 2½ hours. An overnight pack trip is available at no additional cost.

Other activities include swimming in the heated swimming pool, hiking, square dancing, hay rides, and guided nature walks/talks that focus on the area's vegetation, wildlife, geology, and history. There is a good fishing stream and fishermen should bring their own fly-fishing equipment and waders. Some rental poles are available for kids to use in the ranch's stocked pond. Other recreational facilities include an indoor hot tub, Foosball, volleyball, ping-pong, pool table, and western ballroom for dancing.

The ranch also runs a supervised children's program, allowing families lots of flexibility. Children ages 3–5 learn about mountain animals, plants, and rocks and hear stories about horses and Indians. They work at crafts projects in the "sheriff's office" and the tipi, go on nature walks, take pony rides, learn educational games, sing songs, and feed ranch pets. Kids 6–13 years old take riding lessons and participate in fun riding activities. They participate in all ranch activities and may eat meals either with their families or at a separate table with their peers and counselors.

Two weeks a season, the activity focus shifts to photography. The "Wildflower Photography Workshop" is held at the end of June, timed to coincide with the peak of the wildflower season, when over one hundred species of flowers blossom at the ranch. Subjects covered include developing an understanding of the limitations of equipment, film, and lighting; understanding color (how lighting affects it and how it can best be communicated); and the best uses of close-up work.

In mid-September, the ranch offers its "Cattle Roundup Photography Workshop," scheduled to coincide with the annual fall cattle roundup, when cowboys herd hundreds of head of cattle from the high-mountain pastures down to winter pastures. Topics covered include action photography, capturing color, landscape photography, portraiture, and the photo essay.

Up to thirty-five guests can be accommodated in the ranch's modern log cabins, each of which has a sitting room and either one or three bedrooms.

COST: From late June through Labor Day, the weekly rate is $1,075 for adults, $715 for children 6–13 years old, $525 for those 3–5 years old, and free for infants two and under. Rates are discounted substantially from mid-May to mid-June and from Labor Day through mid-October. Shorter stays (minimum three days) are accepted during the discount periods.

The rates cover meals, lodging, horseback riding, overnight pack trip, and all recreational activities. The fee for the "Wildflower Photography Workshop" is $975 and the fee for the "Cattle Roundup Photography Workshop" is $845; both include instruction, lodging, meals, and the use of all recreational facilities.

THE HOME RANCH

P.O. Box 822
Clark, Colorado 80428
(800) 223-7094, (303) 879-1780

The Home Ranch in the Elk River Valley offers comfortable lodgings, gourmet western-style meals, and a full plate of outdoor adventure. In summer, the emphasis is on horseback riding with lessons provided for guests, from novices to experienced riders eager to try their luck at roping and barrel racing. Fishing instruction is also provided, along with guided day hikes into the wilderness.

In the winter, the ranch offers cross-country skiing lessons. Ski guides are provided for everyone from the beginner to the experienced telemarker, and there is plenty of country to explore as you glide over forty kilometers of tracked trails throughout the valley, all around the ranch, and even down to the local store.

A stay at the ranch combines rigorous activity with luxurious creature comforts. After a day of skiing or riding, swim in the lap pool, enjoy the sauna, and get to know the other guests in the recreation hall and around the large fireplace in the main house, which also contains guest rooms. In addition, there are seven private guest cabins, furnished with antiques, down comforters, Indian rugs, and a jacuzzi on each porch.

COST: Rates, which cover all meals, airport transfers,

horseback riding and lessons, guided hikes, and fishing instruction, are per couple and vary according to accommodations chosen. The nightly rate in a lodge room is $310–$375; $375 in a one-bedroom/living room private cabin. Children receive reduced rates.

HIGH ISLAND GUEST RANCH

Box 71
Hamilton Dome, Wyoming 82427
(307) 862-2374

Learn ranching skills firsthand by heading for the Rocky Mountains and becoming a cowboy for a week. At High Island Guest Ranch there are no tennis courts, television sets, or swimming pools, and even the plumbing is sparse. This is an authentic working ranch, not a resort, where guests pitch in as little or as much as they choose. Unlike most dude ranches, you can also ride as much as you like. Each guest is assigned a horse on arrival, and from then on you're free to strike out and explore the range to your heart's content.

The ranch welcomes visitors from May through September. Guests sign on for a week's stay—called a "Roundup Week"—that begins as a two-day wagon-train trip traveling from the lower lodge (elevation four thousand feet) to the mountain lodge (nine thousand feet) overlooking Rock Creek. You can ride your horse or travel in a wagon, experiencing the countryside as the pioneers did. The remainder of the week is spent exploring the Owl Creek Mountain Range—visiting an ancient tipi site, learning about native plants and animals, including the abundant elk population, and fishing for cutthroat trout in Rock Creek. There's plenty of opportunity to work with the cowboys, packing salt and minerals, fixing fences, riding the range, and rounding up stray cattle. During "Branding Week," held in early May, guests are also involved in branding and doctoring cows.

In the spring and fall, three weeks are designated as "Cattle Drives." Visitors join ranch wranglers on a thirty-five-mile drive, escorting the cattle to seasonal grazing grounds, moving them from their summer range in the mountains to their winter pastures near the lower ranch or the other way around, depending on the season. After a talk on cattle drives and a basic orientation to horsemanship, guests set out with the herd, learning on the job about western lore, spending nights under the stars and eating meals cooked over a campfire.

Informal, informative talks on wildlife, geology, and anthropology are a regular part of a stay at the ranch, where every week wraps up with a western-style barbecue and dance.

COST: Fees, which include all meals, lodging, horses, and tack, run as follows: "Cattle Drives," $1,100; "Roundup Weeks" and "Branding Week," $950 for adults, $750 for children 12–15.

EQUITOUR

P.O. Box 807
Dubois, Wyoming 82513
(800) 545-0019, (307) 455-3363

Equitour offers worldwide riding holidays, including many options within the United States. Trips are designated A (advanced rider), B (strong intermediate), and C (intermediate). For most trips, riders should have a good knowledge of the basics as well as some experience riding cross country at a gallop. If most of your riding has taken place in a ring or arena, you might consider spending a week at Bitterroot Ranch, Equitour's home base. Friendly and informal, the atmosphere is closer to that of a family farm than a guest ranch. Visitors are welcome from June through September.

The last ranch in a remote valley, Bitterroot borders the Shoshone National Forest, home of elk, bear, deer, bighorn sheep, moose, and coyote. From the ranch, mounted groups head out in all directions, experiencing a varied terrain encompassing sagebrush plains, grassy meadows, rocky gorges, forested mountains, and alpine clearings.

The ranch keeps over a hundred riding horses, assuring mounts suitable for all skill levels. Because there are usually about twenty-five guests at a time, each person can ride several horses. A week-long stay runs from Sunday to Sunday, with six days of riding. The usual routine includes two rides a day, each averaging 2–3 hours, with a full-day picnic ride on Saturday. Small groups mean that riders of similar ability travel together.

Both western and English instruction are available for those who want it, with videotaped lessons offered at no extra charge on Tuesday and Thursday. All in all, a stay at the ranch is an excellent opportunity for beginning and intermediate riders to strengthen their skills. Advanced riders will enjoy the jumping course.

Several intensive week-long clinics are also offered. These combine morning instructional sessions with afternoon trail rides and are best suited to intermediate and advanced riders who want to perfect their riding skills.

Equitour offers organized rides in California, Kentucky, Arizona, Vermont, New Hampshire, Virginia, and Wyoming. Most last from a weekend to a full week. They combine riding through magnificent and often remote countryside with opportunities to meet local people or learn about the area's history and culture.

Accommodations vary from comfortable campsites to classic inns. The "Navajo Ride" takes place in Arizona's Monument Valley, characterized by wind-shaped canyons, shifting sand dunes, and free-standing red-stone mesas that rise straight up from the desert floor. Traveling through ancient tribal lands, the journey is steeped in Navajo culture. You will see ruins and petroglyphs dating back hundred of years and you will meet modern Navajos who frequently join the group for meals. Guitar playing and singing often fill the evening hours at the comfortable base camp.

During the Wyoming "Pony Express Ride" you will spend six days covering a stretch of the nineteen-hundred-mile route the Pony Express riders traveled from Saint Joseph, Missouri, to Sacramento, California, in the mid-nineteenth century. The pace averages about six hours of riding a day and it is quite common to see wild horses and antelope. You will also see well-known historical sites and landmarks.

Both of these week-long rides are rated BC, appropriate for intermediates and strong intermediates.

COST: The price of the "Navajo Ride" is $1,200, which covers horses, meals, lodgings, and transfers. The price of the "Pony Express Ride" is $1,050, which covers meals, tents, two motel nights, and horses.

CHEROKEE PARK RANCH

P.O. Box 97
Livermore, Colorado 80536
(303) 493-6522, (800) 628-0949

During the 1880s, Cherokee Park Ranch, one of the earliest guest ranches in Colorado, served as a stagecoach stop on the route between Fort Collins and Laramie. Today that history of hospitality continues.

Like most dude ranches, horseback riding is the main attraction. Realizing that many guests have had virtually no previous riding experience, the wranglers do all they can to make you feel confident in the saddle. Riding instruction is handled on both a group and individual basis in the ranch's arena, where you can also try your hand at riding games like barrel racing and pole bending. A variety of guided trail rides is available every day, ranging from gentle, scenic hour-long forays to all-day outings and overnight pack trips perfect for the well-seasoned rider.

The ranch offers introductory fly-fishing instruction for beginners of all ages, with the necessary equipment provided. The ranch has a heavily stocked pond, perfect for kids and beginners, or you can fish in the Poudre River, which runs through the property and boasts a healthy population of brown trout. Experienced anglers can take a half- or full-day guided trip on the river, its tributaries, and several lakes.

The ranch extends a warm welcome to families. Counselors care for children three years and older, entertaining them with activities including riding, swimming, hiking, fishing, nature studies, and crafts. Kids six and up can go on trail rides, while younger children will be given pony rides by the counselors. Baby-sitting can be arranged or you can bring along your own baby-sitter at no extra charge if they share a room with your kids.

Although the historic ranch buildings have been thoroughly modernized, many of the furnishings in the lodge and the cabins date back to the nineteenth century. The lodge has both individual rooms and suites, and cabins vary from one to four bedrooms. All units have private bathrooms. Family-style meals, many of them cooked and served outdoors, feature hearty fare such as steaks, ribs, and pork chops, "all you can eat."

The ranch welcomes guests for week-long (Saturday to Saturday) stays from May through October.

COST: The basic rate for a week-long stay including lodging, meals, horseback riding, and all other activities is $850 for adults, $550 for children 6–12, $400 for children 3–5; infants are free. Additional charges for overnight pack trips and river-rafting trips.

THE ALISAL

1054 Alisal Road
Solvang, California 93463
(805) 688-6411

One of the potential problems with learning vacations is that while everyone involved may be eager to tackle a new skill or work on an existing one, they may not all share the same interest. At the Alisal, there are distinct choices. An eleven-thousand-acre working cattle ranch, the Alisal has welcomed guests for over forty years and has built a superb reputation as a family resort. Today the ranch can accommodate two hundred guests in its magnificent and remote setting of rolling hills, oaks, and sycamores just three hours from Los Angeles. Unlike many guest ranches, the emphasis here is equally as much on tennis and golf as on horseback riding.

For horse fans, expert wrangler guides lead two-hour morning and afternoon trail rides each day. Riders are divided into groups according to ability (slow or walking, intermediate, loping or fast) and each group travels a different trail. Private lessons are available, too.

For golfers, the Alisal has its own par 72 championship golf course. Head pro John Hardy oversees a variety of golfing programs, catering to beginners as well as to the most advanced players and including a popular option for junior players. Relying on state-of-the-art technology to enhance instruction, he employs a split-screen technique, using two cameras with instant-replay ability. This technique enables students to view their performance from two distinct angles. Paired with an accompanying audio portion documenting individual instruction, the film provides a permanent record to refer to back home.

For tennis players, the ranch offers seven courts and an extensive program overseen by tennis director Walter Seeman. Pee-wee, teenage, and adult clinics cater to players of diverse ages and abilities. Mixed doubles and round robins are also arranged, as are private lessons.

If you want to learn to sail or windsurf, head for private ninety-six-acre Alisal Lake, where lessons are offered. Here you can also go rowing or paddle boating. For fishing enthusiasts, the lake is well stocked with largemouth bass and bluegill. Tackle and boats are available for rental. Scheduled shuttle vans depart for the lake throughout the day.

Accommodations are modern and comfortable; you won't find a television or telephone in your room, but you will find a fireplace stocked with wood. Room rates are modified American plan, which includes sumptuous breakfasts and dinners. You will be assigned to a table, which remains yours throughout your stay.

COST: Depending upon the accommodations chosen (ranging from studio room to two-room suite), the nightly rate for two people varies from $255 to $330. The Alisal requires a two-night minimum stay.

WHITE TAIL RANCH OUTFITTERS, INC.

Ovando, Montana 59854
(406) 793-5666

White Tail Ranch has specialized in organizing wilderness pack trips since 1940. Surrounded by the soaring peaks of the Rockies, the ranch occupies a fourteen-hundred-acre spread in the Blackfoot Valley, sixty miles east of Missoula. Trips traverse different parts of the Bob Marshall, Scapegoat, and Great Bear Wilderness Areas, affording the opportunity to see abundant wildlife, including deer, elk, mountain goat, coyote, moose, mountain sheep, porcupine, and golden eagle.

If you want to learn about and experience the quiet, magnitude, and isolation of the wilderness, a White Ranch summer pack trip is an excellent way to do it. You can either join a scheduled trip or a trip can be arranged to focus on a specific interest such as photography or fishing for cutthroat and rainbow trout. Prior horseback-riding experience is not required for these trips, which are open to everyone from children to senior citizens. Trips are organized as small parties (two to eight people) or large parties (nine to fifteen).

Participants are asked to arrive at the ranch the evening before their pack trip commences. You will eat supper with other guests and the crew, gathering later in the lodge for an orientation to the coming adventure. After a substantial breakfast the next morning, you mount your horse (the ranch hands have already loaded your personal gear onto the pack mules) and head out, riding high along the twisting mountain trails, "switchbacking in dead earnest," until you emerge into a high alpine pass. On a typical day, the ride is broken up by lots of stops to loosen up, take pictures, and enjoy lunch alongside a stream. You reach the campsite in midafternoon and have the rest of the day to fish and explore before chowing down a hearty dinner, sharing stories around the glow of the campfire, and settling into the guest tents.

In the course of a White Tail Ranch pack trip, you will learn to identify wildflowers and wildlife and you will become knowledgeable about the area's geological history. You will get the hang of feeling at home on a horse and you will have the opportunity to learn about primitive fire building, low-impact camping, and nature preservation.

The ranch also runs a special program called "Cross Roads," a pack trip designed for women who are experiencing the physical, mental, and spiritual changes that accompany settling into middle age. The trip provides the time and space for the reflection and relaxation that can help ease the way through changes in family, relationship, or career. If you are in good physical condition and have a sense of humor and a strong desire to make your life better, this might be just the experience you are looking for. You will learn how to care for and relate to your horse, even if you are a new rider. You will learn about the wilderness and you will learn the ancient art of making a fire with a bow and drill.

Each day you will also have the opportunity to sort out your feelings in a group discussion led by a qualified counselor. While "Cross Roads" is appropriate for any woman who needs time to think and chart new directions for herself, it is particularly helpful for those who have experienced divorce, the loss of a loved one, abuse, or problems with their children.

COST: The rate for a ranch stay, including cabin accommodations and three meals a day, is $70 per day per person. For room and meals plus the use of a horse, the rate is $100 per day. Participation on a pack trip of five or more days is $162 per person per day; the rate is $173 per day on shorter trips. Children under twelve always receive a 10 percent discount.

Hang Gliding and Soaring

FREEFALL RANCH

P.O. Box 39
Warm Springs, Georgia 31830
(404) 672-1400

A member of the United States Parachute Association (USPA), Freefall Ranch offers all three of the types of first-jump programs recognized by the USPA: static line, accelerated free fall, and tandem. Training is provided by USPA-rated instructors and jump masters using up-to-date, well-maintained equipment. Classes are taught every Saturday and Sunday starting at 9:00 A.M., rain or shine. Appointments for first-jump classes and jumps can also be scheduled during the week. Facilities include retail sale and rigging loft, large grassy landing areas, a paved runway, and air-conditioned classrooms.

Static line is the traditional method of skydiving instruction. Students in the "Static-Line Program" participate in a six-hour video-supported ground school. You will be able to train and make your first jump in the same day. A minimum of five jumps (the last three complete with well-executed practice ripcord pulls) is required before you are cleared for free fall.

If you get hooked on skydiving, you can transfer into the "Accelerated Free-Fall Program," a more intensive and individualized training format. During the seven-level program, which includes an eight-hour video-supported ground school, dives are made from typical altitudes of 10,000–12,000 feet, allowing close to a minute of free-fall time on each jump. You receive one-on-one ground training and in-air instruction from your jump master. Statistically, this is the safest training method.

For those who are in a hurry, the "Tandem/AFF Program" enables you to skydive under the direct supervision of a highly skilled tandem pilot, using a dual-controlled main parachute. Because the instructor is there to handle emergencies, students are in the air for their first skydive after only about an hour of training.

COST: The fee for the "Static-Line Program" (first-jump course and first jump) is $150. The fee for the "Accelerated Free-Fall Program" (first-jump course and level I dive) is $275. The fee for the "Tandem/AFF Program" (tandem training and first tandem dive) is $175.

KITTY HAWK KITES

P.O. Box 1839
Nag's Head, North Carolina 27959
(800) 334-4777, (919) 441-4124

Kitty Hawk Kites, the world's largest hang-gliding school, is located on the Outer Banks of North Carolina just a few miles from the spot where the Wright brothers made their maiden flight in 1903. Here consistent ocean winds and soft sands combine to make Jockey's Ridge, the largest sand dune on the East Coast, a superb site for learning to hang glide. Well over 150,000 students ranging in age from eight to eighty-two and almost equally divided between men and women have received instruction at the school over the past twenty years.

There are many programs to choose from, accommodating those who want to devote a day, a weekend, a week, or more to learning to fly. The "Beginner Dune Lesson" is a three-hour package incorporating a training film with ground school and at least five flights on the sand dunes. Your first flights will carry you only a few feet off the ground, your instructor running alongside, and will last for only seconds.

The "Beginner Pilot Package" includes eight lessons and can be completed in less than a week. It enables most students to achieve the United States Hang Gliding Association (USHGA) beginner rating, which requires that a pilot launch unassisted, demonstrate the ability to consistently maintain correct air speed and make good landings, and pass a written test. Other packages are offered for those who are ready to learn the advanced skills necessary for flying at altitude.

If you would like to experience high-altitude flying right from the start, you can opt for a "Beginner Tandem Tow Lesson." With tandem towing, instructor and student are hooked into a glider together for a flight lasting about ten minutes. The craft is launched from a boat or truck and instruction takes place one thousand feet above the countryside.

Kitty Hawk Kites provides instruction seven days a week year-round. Five times each year the school offers a hang-gliding camp. Participants are housed together in the school's beach cottage. You will enjoy a full week of hang-gliding instruction, including daily lessons, two tandem tows, and evening seminars on aerodynamics and micrometeorology.

COST: The fee for the "Beginner Dune Lesson" or the "Beginner Tandem Tow Lesson" is $59. The fee for the "Beginner Pilot Package" is $395. The fee for the week-long camp, including housing, is $695. These fees cover the use of all necessary equipment.

LOOKOUT MOUNTAIN FLIGHT PARK AND TRAINING CENTER

Route 2, Box 215-H
Rising Fawn, Georgia 30738
(706) 398-3541

If you have always dreamed of flying like a bird, Lookout Mountain Flight Park and Training Center is a good place to turn your fantasy into reality. The park features a 1,340-foot-high ridge and a 25-acre landing field. Soaring conditions are so attractive that more pilots choose this location for their first mountain flight than any other mountain in the country. Intermediate pilots enjoy the twenty-five-mile round-trip soaring flight between Cloudland Canyon, Georgia, and Chattanooga, Tennessee, which boasts open fields within an easy glide the whole length of the thirteen-mile ridge.

All of the center's instructors are certified by the USHGA, and Lookout Mountain staff members wrote and published *Hang Gliding for Beginning Pilots*, the official USHGA flight training manual. Here you will learn at your own pace, following a step-by-step progression. Morning lessons are offered every day of the week year-round and afternoon lessons can also be arranged.

Instruction begins with a fifteen-minute introductory training film. After that, head for Beginning Ground School, conducted on flat ground. The grassy, gently sloping bunny hill serves as the site of your first flights, which will carry you just four or five feet above the ground. A padded harness and training wheels help assure comfort and security. The next step is the Turns Ground School, after which you will have the opportunity to hone more advanced skills on the novice hill. Once you've mastered the skills required to qualify for a USHGA novice rating, you'll be ready for Mountain Ground School and supervised mountain flights. Determined students who want to sign on for an intensive series of lessons are sometimes able to move from the beginner hill to their first mountain flight within a week.

Package plans are based on a specific number of flights, which you can schedule in a cluster or spread out over several weeks or even months. If you are simply curious, you can start off with the "Intro Lesson," which includes ground school and five training-hill flights, or the "Beginning Package," which offers fifteen hill flights and can be completed in one to three days, weather permitting. For the more committed, the "Mountain Package" is an excellent value. It includes three ground schools, fifty training-hill flights, and three supervised high-altitude flights from the Lookout Mountain launch site.

COST: Fees run as follows: "Intro Lesson," $89; "Beginning Package," $199; "Mountain Package," $499. All packages include the use of glider and all necessary training equipment.

WASATCH WINGS

2534 Murray Holladay Road
Holladay, Utah 84117
(801) 277-1042

People come from many parts of the world to learn to hang glide here at Point of the Mountain, where an ideal landscape combines with dependable winds, creating excellent flying conditions for both beginning and advanced pilots. Owner and lead instructor Gordon Pollock, who is certified through the USGHA as an instructor for students at all levels, has spent over twenty-five hundred hours aloft in a hang glider over the past eighteen years. Under his guidance, Wasatch Wings teaches new pilots how to fly as safely and quickly as possible. If you would like to experience the thrill of hang gliding before committing yourself to learning the skill, you can sign on for a tandem flight. Teamed up in the same glider with an experienced instructor who handles takeoff and landing, you will be permitted to pilot the glider while ridge soaring far above the ground.

To learn to fly by yourself, the only requirements are that you be able to run and that you weigh between 90 and 250 pounds. The most physically demanding part of hang-gliding lessons is pushing the glider back up the hill in preparation for the next flight.

Wasatch Wings offers a variety of instructional options. During an "Introductory Lesson," you will learn how to set up the glider and make a preflight check. To get a feel for proper nose angle, turning, takeoff, and landing, your instructor will teach you to run with the glider on flat ground. By the end of the four-hour session, fitted with harness and helmet, you will move to the hill to make your first flights.

The "Gliding Course" is a five-lesson (four hours each) package that includes the introductory lesson as well as a tandem flight. With plenty of opportunity to practice taking off, airspeed control, gentle turns, and landings, you will find yourself flying two hundred feet high by the time you have completed your lessons. A ten-lesson package, the "Soaring Course" offers students the opportunity to learn ridge soaring, a technique used to stay aloft for long periods of time. Many students complete their first hour-long solo flight by the time they have finished this course. For the truly dedicated, Wasatch offers the "Mountain Course," a fifteen-lesson package that includes the "Soaring Course" and then goes on to introduce students to thermal soaring, working at five-thousand-foot elevations.

Students are permitted to camp on the south side of Point of the Mountain. For those whose tastes are less primitive, a motel and campground are located ten minutes up the road.

COST: Fees run as follows: "Introductory Lesson," $75; "Gliding Course," $350; "Soaring Course," $600; "Mountain Course," $850; tandem flight, $125. These prices cover instruction and the use of all necessary equipment, including appropriate-sized harness, helmet, and glider.

SEQUATCHIE VALLEY SOARING SUPPLY

Route 2, Box 80
Dunlap, Tennessee 37327
(615) 949-2301

Rick Jacob, owner/manager of Sequatchie Valley Soaring Supply (SVS), a year-round United States Hang Gliding Association Certified School, describes hang gliding as "the flyingest kind of flying." If you want to find out more about what's involved before signing up, you can take advantage of the free SVS orientation ground school.

Today's gliders are sophisticated soaring machines outfitted with instruments, radios, and rocket-deployed parachutes. Relying on gravity and wind, they fly at speeds averaging twenty-five miles per hour. Beginners practice "ground-skimming" flights, just a few feet off terra firma, while accomplished pilots can soar aloft for hours at a time.

SVS offers a variety of instructional arrangements, with an emphasis on tandem instruction, pairing the student with a certified flight instructor copilot. For a taste of hang gliding you can take an introductory lesson, which includes a ground-school session and instruction in setup and breakdown procedures and launching and landing techniques. The highlight of the lesson is an introductory ten- to fifteen-minute tandem flight. Packages incorporating two and six lessons are also available for those more sure of their interest. As Leonard da Vinci expressed it, "Once you have tasted flight, you will walk the earth with your eyes turned skyward, for there you have been and there you long to return."

The school's most popular course is the "Learn to Fly" package, which includes a total of fifteen lessons (each lesson defined as either five flights down the hill or a tandem flight lasting seven to thirty minutes). Upon completion of the course, most students qualify for the United States Hang Gliding Association novice rating, the rating required for solo mountain flight.

COST: The fee for the introductory lesson is $69.95. The fee for the "Learn to Fly" package is $599.95.

BERMUDA HIGH SOARING SCHOOL

P.O. Box 1510
Thermal Trail
Lancaster, South Carolina 29721-1510
(803) 475-7627

The largest soaring operation east of the Mississippi, Bermuda High Soaring School is dedicated to promoting the sport of soaring. If you have never been soaring, you can sign on for a 20–30-minute introductory ride or an introductory instructional flight with a Federal Aviation Administration (FAA)-certified commercial pilot or flight instructor.

If you decide you seriously want to learn to soar, you can register for the "Beginner Training Course." Intended for those with little or no experience in flying a sailplane or a power plane, the course is taught on an individualized basis. It is designed to fulfill all of the FAA requirements for a private pilot glider certificate. On the average, a student is ready to solo after 30–35 dual flights, accompanied by an FAA-certified flight instructor. Flights are divided among eight lessons, each of which lasts about two hours. To qualify for the certificate, you must accumulate at least twenty solo flights and seven hours of solo flight time, in addition to satisfying other FAA requirements. The school has an FAA flight examiner on staff.

Camping facilities and limited overnight accommodations are available at the school, which is open Wednesday through Sunday year-round.

COST: The fee for the "Beginner Training Course" is $920 (approximately, instruction to the point of being ready to solo) and an additional $675 (approximately, instruction from solo to readiness to earn private sailplane rating). Books and materials run about $90. There is a fee of $200 for the recommendation flight and check ride required for certification.

CHANDELLE

6880 Sir Francis Drake Boulevard
P.O. Box 799
Forest Knolls, California 94933
(415) 488-4202

Learn to hang glide in the San Francisco Bay area with Chandelle, a retail shop that has offered the finest state-of-the-art hang-gliding equipment, technical service, and instruction for the past seventeen years. Lessons begin on gentle, sloping hills, where you first learn about the equipment. Soon you will be ready to experience the sensation of being lifted off the ground and into the air, traveling at first only two or three feet off the ground. As you learn to launch, land, and steer the glider and as your confidence develops, you will move higher up the hill. To help make your flying experience safe and rewarding, supplemental ground-school sessions reinforce the theory behind the skills you learn practicing with the glider.

Chandelle also offers paragliding instruction. The classic hang glider weighs between forty and ninety pounds and fits on top of a car. The paraglider, which weighs only about fifteen pounds, is a new addition to the hang-glider family, popular because of its ultralight weight, compact size, and low cost.

Whether you choose to learn hang gliding or paragliding, instructional options include a one-day introductory lesson, a five-day basic course, and a ten-day novice-level course (to be completed within a month). Additional options for hang-gliding students include a "Twenty-Day Ultimate Course," which comes with the guarantee that you will achieve your USHGA novice rating, and a one-day tandem lesson, which provides the opportunity to experience high-altitude flight accompanied by an experienced instructor. All classes are limited to five students per instructor.

COST: For both paragliding and hang-gliding classes, fees run as follows: one-day introductory lesson, $150; five-day basic course, $600; ten-day novice-level course, $1,000. The fee for the "Twenty-Day Ultimate Course" is $1,500 and the fee for a one-day tandem lesson is $200. Substantial discounts are available to students who arrange purchase of a paraglider or hang glider from Chandelle.

GOLDEN WINGS

1103 Washington Ave.
Golden, Colorado 80401
(303) 278-7181

A full-service hang-gliding facility, Golden Wings offers sales, service, and instruction. Under the direction of USHGA-certified instructors, students develop confidence in their own abilities and judgment.

If you want to know more about the sport before committing yourself, you can attend the free three-hour ground school offered each Thursday evening. Three hours of classroom instruction are supplemented by video materials and the use of a hang-gliding simulator. If you decide to continue, you can sign up for a single-day lesson, a tandem lesson (which allows the inexperienced student to fly side-by-side with a competent instructor at altitudes of one thousand feet or more), or a comprehensive package.

The "Basic Package" includes five full days of lessons on the hill, five ground-school sessions, temporary USHGA membership, textbook, T-shirt, and the use of all necessary equipment. The "Beginner/Novice Package" includes a minimum of nine full days on the hill, ten hours of classroom instruction, one day of tandem towing, and all the other features of the "Basic Package." Most students can attain a USHGA beginner rating in five days of instruction, and a novice rating in ten days.

COST: The fee for a single-day lesson is $85 ($150 for

private instruction). The "Basic Package" costs $375 and the "Beginner/Novice Package" costs $850.

HANG GLIDER EMPORIUM

613 North Milpas St.
Santa Barbara, California 93103
(805) 965-3733

Want to learn to fly an aircraft you can fit in a back-pack? As literature from the Hang Glider Emporium explains, "Paragliders combine the light weight and safety of sport para-chutes with the convenience, low cost, and soaring capability of hang gliders." Like hang gliders, paragliders are foot-launched and foot-landed. You lay out the canopy on the ground (it only weighs about fifteen pounds), put on the har-ness, and then launch by running down a gradual decline, gliding to the landing area below.

Lessons combine teacher demonstrations, opportunities to observe other students, hands-on experience, and ground classes. Skills are initially introduced on the flat. Your first few flights originate near the bottom of the training slope, carrying you only a few feet above the ground. As the lesson pro-gresses, you move further up the slope, enjoying higher, longer flights. You don't have to be particularly strong or ath-letic to learn to paraglide. In fact, the most physically demand-ing part of a training session is walking back up the hill to pre-pare for your next flight. Most students are competent enough to begin practicing on their own after about five to seven days of lessons. Instruction is offered year-round.

The Hang Glider Emporium also offers hang-gliding lessons. Using modern high-performance gliders, experienced instructors take you from total hang-gliding ignorance to the point of being able to fly in the Santa Barbara Mountains for hours at a time. The training area is located three hundred yards from the Pacific Ocean. Each training session lasts about six hours and classes average six students. One-, three-, five-, and ten-day courses are offered, along with the "Mountain Pilot Program," which involves twenty-plus days of instruction and comes with the guarantee that you will be able to fly unsupervised from a thirty-eight-hundred-foot intermediate site upon course completion.

COST: Fees for paragliding instruction runs as follows: introductory, $50; single lesson, $100; five-lesson package, $400; seven-lesson package, $490. All fees cover instruction and the use of harness, helmet, paraglider, and radio during the lessons. For hang gliding, fees are as follows: one-day course, $95; three-day course, $225; five-day course, $375; ten-day course, $700; "Mountain Pilot Program" (twenty-day minimum), $1,300. Prices cover instruction, equipment rental, and manual with flight log.

WESTERN HANG GLIDERS

P.O. Box 828
Highway 1 at Reservation Road
Marina, California 93933
(408) 384-2622

Western Hang Gliders is conveniently located right at its teaching site, Marina State Beach, where students learn to fly in the company of seabirds, soaring along the coastal cliffs and dunes. Everyone starts with the "Beginning Course," a half-day lesson that opens with a film and a ground-school session. Then you move outdoors to the gentle slope where you will have at least five flight opportunities, becoming familiar with the basics of hang gliding as you glide along the beach several feet off the ground. If you decide you want to learn more, working toward the sustained flights that are the real reward of hang gliding, the cost of this initial lesson can be applied toward a continuing package.

You can advance from one package to another, paying the balance of the next level's program and taking those lessons that were not included in your previous package. For example, let's say you enroll in the "Beginning Package," a three-lesson program with a fee of $215. If you decide you would like to continue, you can then enroll in the "Fledgling Package," a six-lesson program with a fee of $425. You pay an additional $210 and then enjoy the three advanced lessons and the advanced ground school, which are part of this package but were not included in the previous one.

Open year-round, Western Hang Gliders offers continuing education to pilots at all levels. Lessons are offered seven days a week, beginning at 10:00 A.M. and 2:00 P.M. Inquire about tandem training, instructor training, mountain clinics, group flying tours, and advanced skills seminars. In addition to the flight school, Western Hang Gliders maintains a fully equipped pro shop.

COST: The fee for the "Beginning Course" is $75 and the fee for the "Master Package" is $650. The fee for the "Eagle Program" is $1,150, with a $100 discount if you choose to enroll immediately following completion of the "Beginning Course."

Driving

JIM HALL KART RACING SCHOOL

1555-G Morse Ave.
Ventura, California 93003
(805) 654-1329

If you have visions of yourself as the next John Andretti or if you simply want to see what it feels like to race, sign on for one of the Jim Hall Kart Racing School programs. Driving a 145-pound sprint race "kart," you can learn racing strategies, braking techniques, passing, and more, traveling at speeds in the range of eighty-five miles per hour.

The Jim Hall racing programs are professional race instruction courses. World-class instructors introduce novices to the sport and help veteran drivers increase their skills. The most comprehensive course option is the "Two-Day Race School," which includes vehicle dynamics, safety procedures, braking drills, inside/outside racing lines, and a lead-and-follow session. Students learn about race procedures, practicing their skills on two different racetrack configurations. By the time the course is completed, you will have driven approximately 140 laps.

Other programs include "Introduction to Kart Racing," a half-day course for those who want to get a taste of what racing is all about. There are also half-day options for those who have completed the introductory session and want either more sophisticated racing instruction, advanced driving techniques, or supervised lap sessions to work on weak areas and get additional pre-race practice. If your skills are already in place, you might opt for the two-day "JHR Kart-Racing Series," the ideal situation for beginning your racing career. The weekend is divided into a practice day and a race day, with drivers competing in identically prepared karts.

Anyone five feet or taller is eligible to participate in the school's programs. The average student age is thirty-three years. The school provides the karts (which retail for approximately $3,200), jackets, helmets, helmet collars, and gloves. Programs are offered daily throughout the year.

COST: The fee for the "Two-Day Race School" is $550. The fee for half-day programs ranges from $125 to $175. Participation in the two-day "JHR Kart-Racing Series" is $400. There is also a five-day program, which includes the two-day race school, a half-day advanced lapping course, and a race weekend, all for $975.

JEAN-PAUL LUC WINTER DRIVING SCHOOL

P.O. Box 774167
Steamboat Springs, Colorado 80477
(303) 879-6104

The first school in America to specialize in teaching students to drive safely under winter conditions, the Jean-Paul Luc Winter Driving School mixes classroom instruction with the hands-on experience you need to learn how to avoid panic situations and how to drive with confidence on snow- and ice-covered roads. Emphasis is placed on the development of the good reflexes so essential for safe winter driving. By facing difficult situations in a safe, controlled environment, "drivers can develop their reflexes to the point that a response is a habit rather than something they have to think about when an emergency arises," explains manager Mark Cox.

Directed by former world-class French Rally driver Jean-Paul Luc, the school caters to a broad variety of students, including teenagers with brand-new driver's licenses, grandmothers, law enforcement officials, and members of the White House security staff. It is headquartered at the base of the

Steamboat ski area, surrounded by magnificent mountain scenery. Its prize facility is a one-mile, nine-turn driving circuit, surfaced with an ultraslippery combination of frozen water and snow. Equipped with snowbank guard rails that "pardon" any driver error, the course incorporates hill, valley, and straightaway. You'll face blind curves, steep grades, sharp turns, and even a slalom course as you get experience in handling a full range of winter driving challenges on packed snow and glare ice. The school provides the cars, and they come equipped with CB radios so that your instructor can tell you just what it was you did that led you to end up plugged into a snowbank.

Three course options are offered. "Ice-Driving Immersion" combines a one-hour classroom session with two hours of driving on the course. "Formula One" is a full-day course that begins with "Ice-Driving Immersion" in the morning and adds on a three-hour afternoon session incorporating ice-driving practice and an on-track videotape analysis. "Grand Prix" combines "Formula One" with a second day, three-hour ice-driving rally-racing session with a private instructor. Courses are taught seven days a week from Thanksgiving to early March.

COST: Fees run as follows: "Ice-Driving Immersion," $80; "Formula One," $170; "Grand Prix," $290.

SKIP BARBER RACING SCHOOL

Route 7
Canaan, Connecticut 06018
(203) 824-0771

Want to know what it feels like to hunker down into a racing car and go really fast? While many professional race-car drivers launch their careers at the Skip Barber Racing School, you don't need to be an aspiring champion to participate. Lots of people take the course simply because they are curious. They want to learn about the skills involved in racing and, in the process, to become better drivers on the road.

The largest school of its kind in the world, the Skip Barber Racing School offers classes at twenty-one different racetracks in California, Connecticut, Florida, Georgia, Hawaii, Illinois, Indiana, Kansas, Michigan, Nevada, New York, Ohio, Pennsylvania, Wisconsin, and Washington. No matter where you enroll, your "textbook" is a state-of-the-art Mondiale B-1 Formula Ford. Designed for comfort, safety, and speed, the Skip Barber Formula Fords can accelerate from zero to sixty miles per hour in five seconds.

To participate in a racing course, the only requirements are that you be at least sixteen years old and that you hold a valid driver's license. All you need to bring is a comfortable pair of shoes and the ability to drive a manual transmission. The school provides helmet, racing suit, the car, and even insurance.

If you've dreamed about seat time in a race car, enrollment in "Introduction to Racing" offers a relatively inexpensive way to turn that dream into a reality. For just a bit more than the expense of a speeding ticket, you will become familiar with the racing line, race-style downshifting, braking, and cornering. The half-day course combines ninety minutes of driving time with an hour of classroom instruction. The focus is on car control, safety, and precision driving, the same skills so vital to professional race-car drivers.

For a far more intense experience, you can elect the "Three-Day Competition Course." The main objective of this course is to teach you the skills needed to race successfully. Daily classroom sessions begin with a general introduction to racing and a description of the race cars and then continues on to cover specific driving techniques, rules, theories, and skills. First-day driving sessions include a slalom exercise, shifting practice, and full-course lapping sessions. On the second and third days, track work includes "threshold" braking exercises and a series of increasingly faster lapping sessions.

The "BMW/Skip Barber Advanced Driving School" is geared to the individual who wants to become a more competent, safer driver on the road. Taught by full-time professional drivers, the curriculum emphasizes driving technique, car control, and safety.

While many of the same skills taught in the racing school are introduced, the emphasis here is on improving overall driving ability and building confidence for everyday situations. The course is offered in one- and two-day versions. Both cover skids, slides and recoveries, threshold braking, and autocross skills. Both include classroom sessions focusing on vehicle dynamics. The two-day session allows extra practice time plus the chance to learn additional techniques like heel-and-toe downshifting, braking while turning, emergency lane changes, and evasion techniques.

The school also offers courses for advanced racing drivers who want to further improve their competitive skills.

COST: Tuition is $295 for "Introduction to Racing" and $1,995 for the "Three-Day Competition Course." The fee for the "BMW/Skip Barber Advanced Driving School" is $475 for the one-day program and $925 for the two-day version.

5

Natural History and Wilderness Challenges

Outdoor Skills/ Leadership Schools

NATIONAL OUTDOOR LEADERSHIP SCHOOL

Box AA
Lander, Wyoming 82520-0579
(307) 332-6973

The National Outdoor Leadership School (NOLS) is committed to providing the highest quality of instruction in wilderness skills and leadership, paying careful attention to the well-being of both participants and the environment. Forty different types of courses are offered at the school's sites in Wyoming, Arizona, Alaska, Mexico, Kenya, and Chile. As the director explains in the introduction to the catalog of courses, "Our purpose is to teach you what it takes to ensure that an expedition is safe, successful, and leaves no trace upon the land. Our classroom is the wilderness and much of what we teach is connected to the surrounding environment. We believe that information becomes knowledge only after you practice and experience what you have learned."

When you enroll in an NOLS course, you sign up to experience skills like rock climbing or ocean kayaking. But make no mistake about it, NOLS is not in the business of providing luxurious adventure travel tours. The role of the instructors is not to do it for you but to teach you how to do it—whether *it* is cooking a meal under arctic conditions or taking responsibility for the care of a pack animal on a wilderness horse-packing trip. To really benefit from a NOLS course, it's important to be in good physical shape and to arrive prepared for strenuous activity. Depending upon the course you choose, you might be expected to carry a backpack weighing fifty-five to eighty-five pounds at altitudes of fourteen thousand feet or higher. The people who prosper most from the experience are those motivated to learn new skills and to work cooperatively in challenging situations with people they've never met before. The demands are great; so too are the rewards.

Courses are divided into three major categories: wilderness, water, and mountaineering. Each course incorporates the NOLS core curriculum, which focuses on safety and judgment, leadership and teamwork, outdoor skills, and environmental studies. Each course takes the form of an expedition, lasting from ten days to three months. Traveling with two to four instructors, groups of eight to seventeen students hike, climb, kayak, and ski through remote wilderness areas. As the course progresses and their outdoor skills develop, students assume increasing responsibility for the day's activities and for each other.

Typical courses include a fourteen-day-long winter ski course in Absaroka, Teton, or other Wyoming mountain ranges and a similar-length white-water river expedition on the Green River in Colorado and Utah. Students range in age from their teens to their seventies, but the mean age is about twenty. There is a special course for fourteen- and fifteen-year-olds and there are courses specifically designated for those twenty-five years old and up.

COST: The tuition for most NOLS courses is $70–$80 per day, which covers instruction, food, equipment shared by the group, and transportation during the program.

RUSH'S LAKEVIEW GUEST RANCH

2905 Harrison Ave.
Butte, Montana 59701
Winter: (406) 494-2585, Summer: (406) 276-3300

If you love the outdoors and want to develop the skills and confidence necessary to cope effectively in a wilderness setting, take a look at the programs offered by Rush's Lakeview Guest Ranch. Remotely located, surrounded by Red Rocks Lakes Wilderness and National Wildlife Refuge, the ranch is the home of a professional guide and outfitter's school geared toward those who want to learn the skills required for a career in outfitting and guiding. The school also offers programs for those who want to become competent outdoorsmen, proficient in horsemanship, back-country safety, and packing. Classes run from June through September.

The "Guide and Outfitting School" is an intense thirty-day program involving at least twelve hours of work each day, a minimum of 360 hours during the month. The curriculum covers leadership, horsemanship, packing techniques, guiding, rafting, hunter safety and ethics, cooking, wilderness survival and emergency first aid, and business management. The skills learned range from learning how to make fast, accurate decisions in a variety of field situations to learning correct riding techniques and basic veterinary skills. You will also learn proper campsite selection, big-game tracking and field dressing of game, water safety regulations and rescue techniques, proper handling of firearms, proper kitchen arrangement and sanitation, recognizing plants as emergency food sources, compass and map reading, and how to obtain licenses and permits and manage an outfitting business. The course is open to anyone eighteen years of age or older who is in good health.

If your goal is to develop horsemanship and back-country skills with the aim of feeling more confident as you explore the wilderness on your own or with your family, consider enrolling in the ranch's "Horsemanship and Pack School," a fifteen-day course that teaches the same skills as those covered in the thirty-day course, but with less emphasis on guiding and hunting. Instruction combines five days at the ranch with ten days in the back country. Still another option is the "Wildlife Course," a ten-day back-country program for focusing on horsemanship, wildlife study, and camping skills. Most of the training occurs in the mountains on pack trips, reinforcing the school staff's belief in the concept of learning by doing. The minimum age for participation in the fifteen-day course is fifteen years. There is no minimum age for the ten-day course.

A multipurpose year-round operation, Rush's Lakeview Guest Ranch welcomes visitors of all ages. This is not the right place for those seeking luxury. It is instead just perfect for those looking for outdoor adventure in an informal, hospitable atmosphere. Guests are put up in rustic cabins or in bunkhouses and meals are served at long tables in the mess hall.

COST: Fees run $2,500 for the thirty-day "Guide and Outfitting School," $1,400 for the fifteen-day "Horsemanship and Pack School," and $875 for the ten-day "Wildlife Course." These fees cover all equipment, meals, lodgings, and instruction. You bring only personal gear and a sleeping bag.

ALASKA WOMEN OF THE WILDERNESS

Box 775226
Eagle River, Alaska 99577
(907) 688-2226

Alaska Women of the Wilderness (AWW) provides a safe, noncompetitive approach to wilderness adventure travel for women who want to get outdoors and develop both new skills and a new sense of confidence. The programs offer an excellent opportunity to try out new experiences in a supportive atmosphere, enjoying the company of other women who share your interests.

Programs are offered year-round and usually run from one to eight days. For most subjects, a series of workshops is offered, each session built on skills previously acquired. For example, if you would like to try your hand at fishing, you can register for a single-session evening workshop where you will be introduced to fly and reel fishing, learn to rig up your pole, and receive pointers on how to find a good fishing spot. After that, you will be ready for a full-day fishing clinic, where you will practice rigging up the equipment, casting, and, one would hope, catching a fish or two. More experienced anglers can sign on for a two-day expedition fishing the Russian River with instructors who teach the art of catching Alaska's salmon. There is also a mother–daughter fishing campout where girls and their moms can spend two days learning to fish, canoe, and camp together.

AWW offers an introductory course called "Experience Alaska's Glaciers," which combines two evening sessions focusing on glacier features, route finding, rope safety, and knot tying with a weekend on the glacier. The whole course takes place within a single week. There is also an introductory workshop on map and compass use and several classes in bicycling, including a session in basic repair and a two-day bike hike. There are sea-kayak workshops and expeditions as well as a series of day hikes in the Chugach Mountains designed for the whole family.

COST: The fee is $50 for a one-day fishing clinic and $30 for a one-day bike hike. A 2½-day sea-kayak workshop, including all food and equipment as well as instruction, is $375.

WILDERNESS HAWAII

P.O. Box 61692
Honolulu, Hawaii 96839
(808) 737-4697

An outdoor education and adventure program, Wilderness Hawaii offers wilderness experiences designed to enhance personal empowerment and self-esteem. The basic format is a backpacking expedition, during which participants receive training in wilderness skills and safety, communication, teamwork, and leadership. The courses are open to all who are willing to face new challenges and who have a taste for adventure. Previous wilderness experience is not required.

Wilderness Hawaii offers four-day expeditions for teenagers, for adults, and for women only. Designed for city folks hungry for the opportunity to hike, swim, explore, and fish without ever hearing a telephone, each trip begins with a rigorous seven-mile hike carrying full backpacks while descending three thousand feet. At the end of the day the group arrives at Halape, a remote beachfront campsite hidden at the base of a thousand-foot cliff, where you will camp for the next three nights. The following two days are devoted to swimming and snorkeling in the protected lagoon and learning to take underwater pictures in the freshwater pond. The group will also hike about a mile to see the petroglyphs in a lava tube at a Hawaiian archaeological site. On the fourth day, you break camp before dawn to beat the heat on the demanding hike out.

The expedition allows visitors to learn new skills while experiencing a part of Hawaii where only stars light the night.

A fourteen-day expedition is also available for teenagers.

COST: The fee for the four-day expedition is $275. This covers use of all camping and backpacking equipment and food.

AMERICAN WILDERNESS EXPERIENCE, INC.

P.O. Box 1486
Boulder, Colorado 80306
(303) 444-2622

If you know you want an outdoor adventure that involves physical exertion and learning new skills, but you don't know just what kind of activity to pursue, American Wilderness Experience (AWE) may be the answer. This organization pulls together a varied selection of package trips offered by dozens of different outfitters.

There are trips on horseback, white-water rafting adventures, fishing trips, and hiking and trekking expeditions. Other options include sailboat, sea-kayak, and canoe trips, mountain biking, wagon-train adventures, and cattle drives. Still other trips revolve around snowmobiling, dog sledding, and cross-country skiing. There are also special-interest and combination trips, for those who would like to experience more than one activity.

The "Mountain Sports Week Adventure" in Colorado includes basic rock-climbing instruction, detailed horsemanship lessons, a raft trip, and an overnight mountain-bike expedition. The "Dancing with Dolphins Wellness Workshop" is a one-week package highlighted by opportunities to learn about and to swim with dolphins in the wild and at the Dolphin Research Center in Grassy Key,

Florida. The program combines boat excursions, pool sessions, and snorkeling with sessions on marine biology, the art of training and communicating with dolphins, and how to maintain a healthy lifestyle.

Prior experience is seldom required for participation in an AWE trip. Participants must, however, be in good health and good physical condition. When you choose a trip, AWE will recommend an exercise and fitness program to help you condition those muscles before the commencement of your adventure. Instruction and guidance are essential components of each package. Your guide will teach you what you need to know in order to travel safely and comfortably.

COST: The fee for the "Mountain Sports Week Adventure" is $625 ($595 for those 10–16 and those 65 and over), which covers all instruction and activities, meals, and accommodations ranging from rustic ranch lodgings to tent to mountain condo. The fee for the dolphin workshop is $1,200, which covers all activities, six nights' lodging in Key West, and all meals.

OUTWARD BOUND USA

384 Field Point Road
Greenwich, Connecticut 06830
(203) 661-0797

The largest and oldest adventure-based program in the world, Outward Bound offers six hundred courses in the United States each year serving more than thirty thousand people from varied backgrounds. Students range in age from fourteen to seventy-five (there is no upper age limit) and about 40 percent of them are women. As explained in their catalog, "they learn to share, to lead and to follow, and to work together as a group." The programs are based on the belief that "overcoming difficult but surmountable challenges increases a student's self-esteem and self-confidence."

Courses range from three days to three months; the average adult course is about a week long. The activities involved are designed to be physically, mentally, and emotionally challenging. Yet while the courses are demanding, no prior experience is required. They are intended for people in average physical condition and instruction is provided at a beginner's level. Most students have never hoisted a backpack or sailed a boat. They come to learn, and in doing so, they not only learn how to live safely and comfortably in the wilderness but develop skills in leadership, problem solving, decision making, and communication.

The courses vary in terms of specific activities but all incorporate both individual and group challenges. Groups are composed of eight to twelve students and two instructors. Activities involving extensive technical instruction are used to expedite personal and interpersonal growth. Whatever the focus of the particular program chosen, students spend the early part of the course working on physical conditioning. They also learn technical skills and safety training, including wilderness first aid procedures, field food planning and preparation, map and compass use, route finding, and expedition planning. Rock climbing, ropes-course work, and rappelling are incorporated in many of the courses.

There are five Outward Bound wilderness schools in the United States and between them they offer programs in over twenty states as well as abroad. The Colorado Outward Bound School runs programs in Alaska, Arizona, California, Colorado, and Utah. Programs focus on alpine mountaineering, canyon trips, and white-water rafting. The Hurricane Island Outward Bound School (Maine) offers coastal sea-kayaking and sailing courses in Maine, Maryland, and Florida, as well as backpacking, rock climbing, canoeing, and cycling courses throughout New England. The North Carolina Outward Bound School runs multielement courses (which incorporate a wide range of activities in a single course) in North Carolina and winter canoeing and backpacking courses in the Florida Everglades.

Alpine mountaineering is at the heart of the experiences offered by the Pacific Crest Outward Bound School (Oregon), which offers glacier-climbing, backpacking, rock-climbing, and rafting courses in California, Oregon, and Washington. Based in Minnesota, the Voyageur Outward Bound School specializes in canoe expeditions among the interconnecting lakes, rivers, and pine forests along the Minnesota/Canada border and also offers courses in Illinois, Montana, and Texas.

The course offerings are divided into the following categories, based on the "primary" activity involved (those that receive the most emphasis): alpine mountaineering; sailing and sea kayaking; canoe expeditioning; desert backpacking and canyoneering; multielement courses; white-water rafting and sportyaking; mountain backpacking and horse trailing; cycling; dog sledding, skiing, and winter backpacking.

COST: Tuition varies widely depending upon the nature and length of the program chosen. By way of example, an eight-day sailing program in the Florida Keys costs $875; a nine-day sea-kayaking course along the Outer Banks of North Carolina costs $995; a fourteen-day alpine mountaineering course in Washington's Cascade Mountains costs $1,425; a twenty-two-day canoeing expedition in the Boundary Waters Canoe Area of Minnesota costs $1,600. Financial assistance is sometimes available.

Tuition covers all equipment, food, and most transportation costs during the course. Additional expenses include a $60 nonrefundable application fee, transportation to and from pickup locations, personal clothing, and a physical exam if you have not had one within a year of your course starting date.

WOODSWOMEN

**25 West Diamond Lake Road
Minneapolis, Minnesota 55419-1926
(800) 279-0555, (612) 822-3809**

The largest adventure travel organization in the world just for women, Woodswomen is based in Minneapolis, with affiliates in Seattle, Atlanta, and Berkeley, California. Woodswomen enables women to meet a variety of demanding challenges in the outdoors in the company of and under the guidance of other women. Over seventy different trips and activities are scheduled each year in the United States and abroad, affording opportunities for personal growth, learning new skills, developing one's own leadership style, and just plain having fun.

As a participant in a Woodswomen program, you will learn to enjoy outdoor recreation and close contact with nature while sharing in group decision-making and improving your judgment. Groups consist of fifteen or fewer women, often only six to eight. The guide-to-participant ratio ranges from 1:8 to 1:5. Participants range in age from twenty to over seventy, representing a full spectrum of fitness and experience levels.

Woodswomen offers bicycle touring, trekking, backpacking, flat-water canoeing, white-water canoeing, sea kayaking, white-water rafting, snorkeling, SCUBA diving, rock climbing, mountaineering, horse packing, and skiing. Most trip groups combine women of many ages, some with lots of previous experience and others with none.

Trips are divided into four categories. "Skills Trips" are specifically geared to serve women who are new to a particular activity or those who want to make a concentrated effort to improve their abilities in this area. "Adventure Vacations" provide a mix of activities, from challenging to relaxed, with accommodations in cabins, inns, cruise ships, or campgrounds. "Wilderness Journeys" are at the core of the Woodswomen experience. They involve camping and packing in all necessary supplies, whether traveling with backpack, canoe, or kayak. "Leadership and Professional Development Trips" are demanding courses meant for women who want to learn how to guide outdoor trips.

The majority of Woodswomen's trips and activities take place in Minnesota and the upper Midwest. Typical programs include "Dog Sledding in the Northland," a five-day winter program that features instruction in dog sledding, skiing, and snowshoeing; "Horse Packing in Wisconsin," a long-weekend summer trip that gives you a feel for horse packing; and the "Great Books Canoe Vacation," a week-long summer camping and canoeing expedition that features discussions of women's literature and poetry.

For those who want to share outdoor adventures with their children, Woodswomen offers an overnight camping trip as well as one-day women's and kid's trips centering on either fishing, canoeing, or rock climbing.

COST: Fees for the programs described above run as follows: "Dog Sledding in the Northland," $485; "Horse Packing in Wisconsin," $265; "Great Books Canoe Vacation," $545. Prices cover guide/instructor, food, permit and camping fees, group camping and safety equipment, canoes, and climbing equipment for beginning trips. Most of the one-day programs run between $15 and $50.

BOULDER OUTDOOR SURVIVAL SCHOOL (BOSS)

P.O. Box 3226
Flagstaff, Arizona 86003-3226
(602) 779-6000

If you are seriously interested in learning to live simply and in concert with nature, radically reducing dependence on modern contrivances, consider the educational opportunities offered by Boulder Outdoor Survival School (BOSS), based in the canyons and deserts of the Colorado Plateau in south-central Utah. Its mission statement reads as follows: "Boulder Outdoor Survival School is dedicated to the instruction and preservation of primitive survival arts and the development of people through experiences with the natural world and aboriginal tradition." Survival skills are taught by transporting students figuratively into the past, an approach rooted in the belief that in recognizing how much we can learn from primitive people, we learn a lot about ourselves in the process.

In solving the problems associated with food, shelter, heat, clothing, travel, and other survival needs, BOSS students make use of only the most simple technology. As a course participant, you will experience the diet of "Paleo-man," a healthy blend of simply processed grains, fresh meat, and plants. You will learn trail navigation skills, fiber production, open-hearth cooking, and much more. Learning to live with limited gear, you will discover yourself growing increasingly fit and aware as you become progressively more attuned to living in balance with nature.

In "Earth Skills," a week-long instructional workshop, you will learn the standard skills used on the trail, including how to make fires without matches, constructing primitive emergency shelters, trapping and fishing skills, techniques for navigation and cross-country travel, basic plant use and identification, and much more. You will camp in primitive shelters, cook on an open hearth, and eat many wild foods.

You can practice your skills further by enrolling in a "BOSS Walkabout," where you will have a chance to test yourself physically, mentally, and emotionally, and to experience real adventure in a safe environment. You will hike over rugged terrain, camp under primitive conditions, and face tasks and obstacles designed to teach you to live with nature on its terms. There are seven-day, fourteen-day, and twenty-seven-day walkabouts. Each begins with a day of orientation, equipment checks, and simple physical training and testing. The rest of the time is spent in deserts, canyons, and mountains, learning to live simply yet deliberately. The core curriculum covers fire making and shelter building from scratch, plant life, trapping and fishing, cooking, food preservation, water locating, ultralight desert and canyon travel, lithic arts, fiber arts, simple weapons and tools, and cross-country navigation.

BOSS maintains a teacher-to-student ratio of 1:4 for most courses. Skills courses are open to all, but they do require some hiking and a willingness to live under primitive conditions. The walkabouts are extremely rigorous and are intended only for those in good physical condition. The average group consists of twelve men and women from age sixteen to sixty. There is a special two-week-long "Stone Age Youth Adventure" program for teens thirteen to sixteen. Courses are offered from late May through August.

With over twenty years of desert experience, BOSS is the oldest, most intense, and most comprehensive of the current crop of wilderness survival skills schools. As explained in the course catalog, "BOSS is not just a skills school, but a process; an experience in living simply yet deliberately."

COST: Fees are as follows: seven-day "Earth Skills" course, $475; seven-day "Walkabout," $475.

COLORADO MOUNTAIN SCHOOL

P.O. Box 2062
Estes Park, Colorado 80517
(303) 586-5758

Based in the Rocky Mountains, the Colorado Mountain School offers small, individualized courses in winter climbing, ice climbing, and cross-country skiing. Get started in winter climbing by enrolling in "Winter I." In just five days you will have experienced an alpine summit climb and gained a familiarity with ice climbing, snow caves, ice ax, self-arrest, avalanche, and basic expedition skills. Course activities center on climbing Ptarmigan Ridge on the north ridge of 12,324-foot Flattop Mountain.

Day one is devoted to ice-climbing instruction. On day two, you will pack and climb to the tree line and dig a snow cave. Day three is spent training in the use of the ice ax and crampons, and learning self-arrest, avalanche, and alpine climbing techniques. Day four is for the summit climb up Ptarmigan Ridge and day five is spent descending and celebrating. "Winter II" is offered for intermediate climbers, the instruction incorporated in a classic winter alpine climb, the ascent of 13,911-foot Mount Meeker.

The school also offers a five-day "Introduction to Cross-Country Skiing." The first two days are devoted to learning the basics and days three through five are spent using and refining skills on a cross-country ski tour through mountain back country. If you have intermediate to advanced cross-country skiing ability plus summer backpacking experience, you can enroll in "Cross-Country Skiing Camp II," a five-day tour that combines skiing with winter camping.

If you don't have five days to spare, take advantage of one of the school's one-day courses that focuses on a particular aspect of climbing or skiing. A half-day course called "Snowshoeing: Getting Started" is also offered. Courses run from late November through late April.

COST: Fees for "Winter I" and "Winter II" and the two cross-country ski courses are $515 per person for a group of 5–6 people, $545 for four, $595 for three, $625 for two, and $175 per day for one person. This covers instruction, all community and technical gear, and breakfasts and dinners on the climb. Add $48 for three nights' lodging for "Winter I" and "Winter II" and $64 for four nights' lodging for the ski courses. Fees for the one-day climbing and skiing programs run from $70 to $155, depending on group size. The snowshoeing course is $55.

OUTDOOR DISCOVERIES

P.O. Box 7687
Tacoma, Washington 98407
(206) 759-6555

When you sign on for an experiential learning course with Outdoor Discoveries, you give yourself the opportunity to become totally involved in every aspect of the adventure ahead, starting with the planning phase. You will be asked to set personal goals about what you hope to accomplish and how you would like to apply your new knowledge to other areas of your life. The outdoors is "the ultimate learn-by-doing classroom" and Outdoor Discoveries instructors know how to use the environment to provide participants with opportunities to make choices, solve problems, practice teamwork, and develop new skills.

"The Balanced Climber" course supports the staff's belief that technical rock climbing is well within the reach of most people. You will learn about climbing ropes and equipment, gripping and footwork skills, and rappelling. You will also be introduced to relaxation, centering, and visualization techniques, all useful in maintaining mental and physical balance on and off the rock. The course is offered at the basic and intermediate levels and lasts from two to five days. It is open to those sixteen years and up. To participate in this program you should be in average or better physical condition, regularly involved in running, swimming, bicycling, or some other type of cardiovascular exercise.

If you want to take a family vacation that involves kids and parents learning outdoor skills together, enroll in a "Family Adventure Quest." The course is designed for two-parent and single-parent families with children ten years and older who want to experience supervised backpacking so that they can later make trips on their own. Participants of all ages learn about trip planning, equipment, campsite selection and setup, and back-country cooking. With the guidance of experienced instructors, you will learn to function as a team in the wilderness. Two-parent families can bring along three children. Single parents can bring two. Groups are limited to a maximum of ten participants.

Outdoor Discoveries also organizes many other expeditions, including "Teen Adventure Quests" and "Adventure Quests," specifically for adults. Those who enroll in the adult courses typically fall into the range between eighteen and fifty years of age, with the majority in their twenties and thirties. Depending upon the specific quest, these courses might involve backpacking, rock climbing and rappelling, sea kayaking, wilderness solos, and peak ascents.

Working in groups of five to ten with one or two instructors, you will learn about minimum-impact camping, outdoor cooking, safety procedures, route finding, map and compass navigation, and first aid. Typical of these is an eight-day expedition in the Olympic Mountains, open to those age twenty-one and up.

COST: The fee for "The Balanced Climber" is $140 for the two-day basic course; $200 for the three-day basic and beyond; and $325 for the five-day intermediate. The eight-day "Adventure Quest" in the Olympic Mountains costs $725.

Course fees cover group equipment and meals. You provide your own sleeping bag, pad, and rock-climbing shoes, or rent them from Outdoor Discoveries.

Natural History

THE YELLOWSTONE INSTITUTE

P.O. Box 117
Yellowstone National Park, Wyoming 82190
(307) 344-7381, ext. 2384

The Yellowstone Institute is an educational field program offering short courses in cultural and natural history as they relate to Yellowstone National Park. About half the courses take place at Buffalo Ranch in the Lamar Valley area of the park, where the Yellowstone Institute makes its headquarters. Rustic cabin and kitchen facilities are available for students, and the atmosphere tends to be convivial, with lots of communal meals. For classes that take place a distance from the ranch, students camp out or stay in park lodgings or motels.

The courses tend to be relaxed and informative, each one limited to ten to fifteen students. Most require at least some walking at higher elevations. Some involve backpacking, horse packing, and canoeing and are more demanding. The majority of the courses are scheduled from late May through October. The Institute offers about seventy-five choices, each lasting two to five days, taught by more than forty different instructors. The topics studied include wildflowers, grizzly-bear ecology, birds, geology, nature photography and writing, art, fly fishing, lake canoeing, philosophy, and native American and mountain-man history. Some of the courses involve back-country experiences using llamas and horses.

"Geysers, Mudpots, and Hot Springs" is a three-day course that explores the spectacular geothermal features of Yellowstone. Hikes are planned to coincide with the eruption of some of the less common geysers. Enroll in "Llama Trekking in the Tetons" and experience a four-day trip into high alpine lake basins. Students participate in all aspects of the trek, including cooking, setting up camp, and packing and leading llamas. You will also learn (and experiment with) the use of animal fibers for spinning and cordage making. "Characters of Yellowstone" is a two-day introduction to the biographies and hangouts of a dozen hermits, heroes, and other characters who have frequented the park through the years.

In the winter, courses are offered in snow ecology, wildlife ecology, photography, and winter back-country camping. A wide range of winter camping skills is taught during "Back Country by Ski" a four-day adventure that includes a two-day, two-night ski trek into the Fawn Creek back country. You will learn about travel over snow, food preparation, shelter building, cold-weather clothing, and the hazards of cold environments. All camping and ski equipment is provided by the institute. Previous ski experience is recommended although not required. It is important, however, to be in good physical condition.

COST: Tuition for "Geysers, Mudpots, and Hot Springs" is $100. Tuition for "Characters of Yellowstone" is $80. The fee for "Back Country by Ski" is $205, with one night's cabin lodging, food, and other equipment as described above. Cabin space is $8 per person per night (bring your own sleeping bag).

AUDUBON ECOLOGY CAMPS AND WORKSHOPS

National Audubon Society
613 Riversville Road
Greenwich, Connecticut 06831
(203) 869-2017

If you would like to search the desert for spadefoot toads, dredge the ocean floor for sea cucumbers, or listen to coyotes call under a moonlit sky, consider attending summer camp. The National Audubon Society operates several permanent adult camps as well as additional workshops that change from year to year. The sessions combine field studies in the company of distinguished naturalists with outdoor recreational activities. Sessions run six to eighteen days and are open to those eighteen years of age or older.

Situated in a glaciated valley seventy-five hundred feet high in Wyoming's Wind River Mountains against a backdrop of thirteen-thousand-foot snow-capped peaks, Audubon Camp in the West hosts six one-week field ecology camps each summer. The focus is on gaining an understanding of the mountain environment by studying the birds, mammals, insects, wildflowers, and other vegetation that live here. During a typical week, campers learn how the mountains were formed, how slopes and shadows affect plant communities, and how bighorn sheep, elk, mule deer, and other mammals survive in the rugged terrain. They hike through different parts of the valley, choosing from more and less strenuous options, always in the company of a well-informed instructor.

Campers also choose from classes in nature photography, ancient rock art, field sketching and keeping a field journal, basket making, beginning birding, daytime astronomy, animal behavior, environmental activism, and other subjects. Early morning bird walks, canoe expeditions, storytelling sessions, square dancing, canoeing, volleyball, and a float trip down the

Snake River in Grand Teton National Park are all part of the experience.

The Audubon Camp in Maine occupies a 333-acre wildlife sanctuary on Hog Island in Muscongus Bay, the southernmost outpost of many northern birds and marine mammals. During the six one-week summer camps, different weeks are set aside to study Maine coast field ecology, field ornithology, and marine biology. Each session is limited to fifty-five participants, who are divided into field groups of ten to fifteen to allow more personal instruction.

The ecology camp week includes approximately thirty-five hours of scheduled field experiences and classroom activities, with ample time for informal discussions, as well as swimming, volleyball, stargazing, and square dancing.

The marine biology week incorporates field trips, lectures, discussions, laboratory investigations, a session aboard a research vessel, and an all-day sea mammal and seabird excursion. A typical day begins with an exploration of the intertidal zone using nets and seines or a bottom-dredging trip in the bay aboard one of Audubon's two Coast Guard–licensed boats. Afternoons are spent in the laboratory or on field trips.

The field ornithology camp focuses on the breeding biology of birds, with special emphasis on warblers and colonial seabirds. Activities include early morning bird walks, workshops on bird identification, bird-banding demonstrations, a slide lecture on seabird conservation, programs on bird ecology and conservation, and an all-day field trip to offshore islands. The session incorporates approximately forty hours of field instruction and lecture/discussion and includes opportunities for those with beginning, intermediate, and advanced levels of knowledge.

COST: The cost of the one-week camp sessions in Wyoming and Maine, including accommodations, meals, and all instruction, is $650.

NATIONAL WILDLIFE FEDERATION CONSERVATION SUMMITS

1400 Sixteenth St., N.W.
Washington, D.C. 20036-2266
(703) 790-4363

Each summer the National Wildlife Foundation sponsors a series of week-long residential "Conservation Summits" at its centers in California, North Carolina, Montana, and Colorado. While the recreational facilities and the geography differ with the setting, each summit offers a combination of outdoor recreation, nature study, and environmental learning.

The California Summit takes place at the Asilomar Conference Center, a one-hundred-acre site at the tip of the Monterey Peninsula. Here sand dunes, beaches, and secluded forest form a living laboratory where participants learn about the delicate ecosystems of this coastal environment. Field trips and special activities include marine-life cruises, bird walks, and tide-pool explorations.

At the Blue Ridge Summit in North Carolina, Appalachian history and folklore are featured along with environmental issues specific to the area. Special activities at the Big Sky Summit in Montana include field trips to Yellowstone National Park to study geysers and hot springs, native American studies, and wildlife classes on elk, bison, and grizzly bears. The Educators' Summit at Estes Park, Colorado, introduces teachers to resources and methods that will enable them to teach about the environment with confidence.

After you register for a summit, you'll be sent a program handbook listing all the options. Most of the classes meet once, for 1½ or two hours. Some take the form of all-day field trips. A full schedule for the week consists of about forty hours of instruction, but participants sign up for as many or as few classes as they wish to take. Classes are scheduled all day long, from bird walks at dawn to photo walks at sunset to evening stargazing sessions.

Choose from classes like "Celestial Navigation," "Enviromental Health," "Nature Photography," "Wildlife Gardening Basics," "Marine Mammals," and "California Geology: Land of Fire and Ice." Live music, contredanses, theatrical performances, and slide lectures liven up the evenings.

The conservation summits are family oriented, offering special daytime programs for children. While parents and grandparents go to class, 13–17-year-olds can participate in the "Teen Adventure Program." Designed to challenge mental and physical abilities, the schedule incorporates instruction in outdoor skills and orienteering with day hikes and natural history field trips. For 5–12-year-olds, the "Junior Naturalist Program" features bird walks, outdoor games, stream studies, nature hikes, and arts-and-crafts sessions. Your "Big Back Yard Preschool Program" introduces 3–4-year-olds to the environment through micro-hikes, touch-and-feel expeditions, and nature crafts.

COST: The fee for most of the conservation summits is the same: $235 for adults, $160 for teens (ages 13–17), $160 for youths (ages 5–12), and $80 for preschoolers (ages 3–4). For adults, this covers all classes, special afternoon and evening events, and some field trips. The teen and youth programs run from 8:30 A.M. to 3:00 P.M. each day. The preschool program runs from 8:30 A.M. to 12:00 noon. Housing rates, which include all meals, vary according to the accommodations chosen.

SAN DIEGO
NATURAL HISTORY MUSEUM

P.O. Box 1390
San Diego, California 92112
(619) 232-3821

The San Diego Natural History Museum organizes scientist-led expeditions and camping trips focusing on specific aspects of natural history. "Dig Dinos" is a nine-day summer paleontology trip to unusual fossil sites such as Egg Mountain, famous because of the dinosaur eggs, embryos, and nests discovered there in 1978.

Under the leadership of an experienced paleontologist, participants spend four days learning, digging, and hiking at fossil sites. Evenings are spent stargazing and bedding down in Blackfeet tipis. Then the group boards a bus for Canada to explore the Royal Tyrrell Museum of Paleontology and Dinosaur Provincial Park.

The museum also offers a series of classes and field trips. Some take place entirely within one day, while others involve a classroom session followed by a field trip a day or two later. Still others are organized as a series of four or five sessions held once a week. "Butterflies and Moths of San Diego County" involves four weekday-evening classes, during which participants examine preserved specimens and discuss classification, identification, and insect lifestyles, and a Saturday field trip to observe Lepidoptera in their natural habitat. Led by a paleontologist/geologist, "A Faulty Field Trip" is a one-day excursion designed to introduce you to faulting, kinds of faults, and the seismic setting of southern California.

The museum also conducts classes, nature walks, and night hikes for children and families.

COST: The fee for "Dig Dinos" is $1,450. This trip is open only to museum members; annual membership costs $30 for individuals, $40 for a family, and $15 for seniors over sixty and full-time students. The fee for "Butterflies and Moths of San Diego County" is $59 for members, $69 for nonmembers. "A Faulty Field Trip" costs $29 for members, $36 for nonmembers.

WINGS, INC.

P.O. Box 31930
Tucson, Arizona 85751
(602) 749-1967

WINGS organizes and leads birdwatching tours to destinations all over the world, including an excellent selection of trips within the United States. In 1993 WINGS trips visited Alaska, Maine, Washington, Oregon, California, Utah, Arizona, New Mexico, Wyoming, Nebraska, Texas, South Carolina, and Florida. Most trips run from one to three weeks. The itinerary and timing of each trip is determined by ornithological considerations to maximize birdwatching opportunities. For example, "Platte River, Nebraska: Cranes, Waterfowl, and Grouse" is a week-long March tour of the Platte River region in south-central Nebraska, an area used at this time of year by several million birds (including 80 percent of the world's population of sandhill cranes) as a stopover on their northbound migration.

WINGS also offers "Weekends," short trips geared to those with a restricted budget or limited time. Scheduled throughout the year, these tours provide a good introduction to organized birdwatching. In July, you might travel to Arizona on a four-day weekend trip planned to coincide with the start of the summer rains, a time when many lowland birds come into full song and birdwatching is at its best in the mountain canyons. An October weekend tour to Duluth, Minnesota, is scheduled to coincide with peak numbers of northern goshawk, red-tailed and rough-legged hawks, and, at night, long-eared and saw-whet owls. In February sign on for a Florida weekend trip that explores the distinctive habitats of Everglades National Park or a Texas trip that travels by boat to view the wild whooping cranes who winter along a small stretch of the central Texas coast.

WINGS takes care to keep group sizes manageable. Regular tours accommodate six to twenty participants, plus the leaders. Weekend trips are run on a ratio of fifteen people per leader, with a maximum group size of twenty-four. In addition to being highly experienced birdwatchers, all trip leaders are knowledgeable about natural history. Trip leaders carry Questar telescopes for the use of tour participants.

While the tours are not particularly strenuous, birdwatching does involve a good dose of physical activity and some prebreakfast starts since birds are most active in the early morning hours. All trips require some gentle walking, sometimes for as long as four hours. Most trip participants have considerable birdwatching experience, own their own binoculars and know how to use them, and are familiar with at least the basics of watching birds. For those who have never watched birds before, WINGS will suggest ways of preparing for your trip. The company publishes a thick, handsome annual catalog that contains day-by-day itineraries for the longer tours as well as detailed descriptions of the weekend ones.

COST: The fee for "Platte River, Nebraska: Cranes, Waterfowl, and Grouse" is $810. The Arizona extended July weekend costs $200 and the Duluth, Minnesota, October weekend costs $150.

Trip prices cover travel as noted in the itinerary, lodgings, trip materials, and the services of the leaders. Meals are not covered for U.S. tours and lodgings are not included in the price of the "Weekends."

PINE BUTTE GUEST RANCH

The Nature Conservancy
HC58 Box 34C
Choteau, Montana 59422
(406) 466-2158, (406) 466-2621

Owned and operated by the Nature Conservancy, an international nonprofit conservation organization, the Pine Butte Guest Ranch is located in the peaks of Montana's rugged East Front, where the Rocky Mountains rise dramatically from the Great Plains. The ranch is surrounded by land that is protected for wildlife, including the Nature Conservancy's private eighteen-thousand-acre Pine Butte Swamp Preserve, home to bears, badgers, coyotes, and many other animals.

Like most guest ranches, Pine Butte offers daily guided rides into the surrounding country. There is also a heated pool for swimming. What distinguishes Pine Butte from other guest ranches is its in-depth natural history program, directed by a resident naturalist. A large cabin serves as a Natural History Center, stocked with books, photographs, maps, and fossils.

During the summer, the naturalist conducts daily treks that focus on the plants, animals, geology, and paleontology of the East Front. Guests hike the edge of an alpine lake searching for shaggy mountain goats or seeking a glimpse of a beaver gliding through the water. At the nearby Freeze Out Lake Waterfowl Refuge, guests sight white pelicans, blue-winged teal, and marsh hawks feeding, flying, and tending their young. There is also an opportunity to search for dinosaur egg fragments at the preserve, which shelters one of the world's richest dinosaur bone beds. After supper, guests watch slide shows about the diverse flora and fauna, discuss the day's sightings, and plan tomorrow's adventures.

Every spring and fall, the ranch offers week-long natural history workshops, led by the resident naturalist together with a variety of regional experts. A bear biologist teams up with the naturalist for an intensive week spent studying

Montana grizzly bears through slide shows, lectures, and daily hikes. Another week is set aside for nature photography and still another for a workshop on mammal tracking. The "Dinosaur Dig" workshop provides guests with the rare opportunity to learn and dig with experts at a site that has yielded more dinosaur eggs and nests than any other in the world.

The ranch can accommodate up to twenty-five guests in ten rustic yet comfortable cabins, each outfitted with fireplace and private bath. Meals are served family style in the main lodge.

COST: The rate for a one-week summer stay is $875 for adults, $700 for children 1–12. This includes room, board, naturalist program, riding program, use of all ranch facilities, and transportation to and from the Great Falls International Airport two hours southeast of the ranch.

WILDERNESS SOUTHEAST

711 Sandtown Road
Savannah, Georgia 31410
(912) 897-5108

A nonprofit organization specializing in wilderness nature-study tours, Wilderness Southeast conducts a lively schedule of adult and family educational adventures. Tours travel to Okefenokee Swamp, the southern Appalachians, coastal Georgia and South Carolina, the Everglades, and destinations in the Caribbean and Central and South America.

Committed to the conservation of wild places, all programs minimize human impact on wilderness areas. The trips are active but most are suited to anyone in good health.

Explorations of the Okefenokee Swamp are a twenty-year tradition with Wilderness Southeast. Paddling through the Okefenokee National Wildlife Refuge by canoe for five days in the company of knowledgeable naturalist guides, you will become attuned to the sights and sounds of the swamp, which was once covered by the Atlantic Ocean. The completely outfitted expeditions operate during the fall, winter, and spring months.

The first day is devoted to exploring the prairie boardwalk, the pine forests, and the restored cabin of one of the families that homesteaded here. The next four days are spent paddling through open lakes and beneath the domes formed deep within the swamp by towering moss-draped cypress trees, discovering the peat prairies, cypress forests, pine woods, and hardwood hammocks of this unique natural area. On sunny days, ripple-backed alligators and yellow-bellied turtles can be seen sunbathing. During a typical day, you will spend six to seven hours paddling, covering a distance of nine to twelve miles. Evenings are spent making camp on the periphery of the refuge or on large, raised wooden platforms or forested islands deep within the swamp.

Those who prefer not to camp can opt for the three- and four-day cabin/canoe trips. You will explore by canoe, paddling a maximum of eight miles each day and returning to a comfortable cabin complete with full kitchen and shower in Stephen Foster State Park each evening. Some cabin/canoe trips are designated as photo workshops; during these a Nikon representative offers informal instruction designed to enhance your nature and wildlife photography skills.

The outfitter provides canoes, paddles, life jackets, seat cushions, and paddles, all meals (including a cup of wine at dinner), tents, commissary gear, first aid and safety equipment, a reference library of field guides, and shuttle service to and from the Savannah Airport. Sleeping bags and pads are available for rental or you can bring your own. Previous canoeing and camping experience is not required. Each trip is limited to fourteen participants, with a recommended minimum age of fourteen years for the camping trip and eight years for the cabin trip, except for the photo workshops, which have a suggested minimum age of eighteen years.

Confident swimmers who are physically fit and have some previous canoeing experience can sign on for the "Everglades Ten Thousand Islands Paddle/Hike." Two days are spent hiking sawgrass prairies and wading thigh-high in a cypress strand, exploring the terrestrial and freshwater habitats of the northern Everglades and searching for epiphytic orchids and signs of the endangered Florida panther. The next five days are spent paddling canoes or sea kayaks (depending upon the program you choose) through the twisting mangrove creeks and open bays of the saltwater portion of the Everglades, observing herons, ospreys, and eagles and perhaps the endangered West Indian manatee. You will sleep at primitive campsites, carrying in drinking water, digging latrines, and carrying out all trash. The recommended minimum age for this trip is sixteen. Houseboat/canoe expeditions of the Everglades are another option, particularly suited for those who do not wish to camp.

Wilderness Southeast also offers several summer adventures just for teens.

COST: The fee for the five-day "Okefenokee Wilderness Canoe Trip" is $400–$420. The fee for the four-day cabin/canoe trip is $390–$400. The fee for the seven-day "Everglades Ten Thousand Islands" trip is $570–$590 (canoe) or $665–$790 (sea kayak).

BEAR MOUNTAIN GUEST RANCH

P.O. Box 1163
Silver City, New Mexico 88062
(505) 538-2538

For a very inexpensive learning vacation that combines nature study with opportunities for fishing, boating, and exploring ghost towns, Bear Mountain Guest Ranch fits the bill. Owner Myra McCormick has welcomed guests at her ranch for well over thirty years. She enjoys teaching her visitors about the two hundred native species of birds found locally and cheerfully points out the best spots for rock hunting, canyon exploring, spelunking, and the like. If you let her know of your interest in advance, she will also arrange a guided excursion to archaeological sites occupied by the Mimbres Indians between the years 1000 and 1500.

The ranch offers a six-day-long "Lodge and Learn Program," which revolves around two courses, "How to Use Your Bird Guide Book" and "How to Identify Ranch Trees, Shrubs, and Wild Plants." Each course is taught for an hour and fifteen minutes daily Monday through Thursday. Sited at an elevation of 6,250 feet on a 160-acre spread abutting the Gila National Forest, the ranch is a perfect laboratory for natural history studies. The program is open to anyone twenty-one years or older and tends to attract a strong following of mature travelers.

Built in traditional 1920s southwestern style, providing cool rooms in summer and warm ones in the winter, the two-story ranch house is full of sun-spaces where flowers bloom all through the winter. Up to forty guests at a time are accommodated both within the ranchhouse and in three other buildings on the property. The atmosphere is friendly and informal. Meals, featuring home-baked breads and desserts, are served buffet style. After dinner, an area specialist delivers a fifteen-minute talk usually focusing on a natural history topic.

COST: The fee for the "Lodge and Learn Program," including five nights' lodging, meals, and the two courses, is $275.

VERMILION ENVIRONMENTAL STUDIES

**1900 E. Camp St.
Ely, Minnesota 55731
(800) 657-3609**

The heart of the largest wolf range in the continental United States, Ely is the home of the International Wolf Center and of Vermilion Environmental Studies. Exhibits at the center include a captive wolf pack and lively displays designed to introduce the wolf's family system, as well as a six-thousand-square-foot exhibit called "Wolves and Humans." In cooperation with the center, Vermilion Environmental Studies organizes a variety of year-round field trips to study the wolves in their natural habitat.

Join a "Winter Wolf Weekend" and explore the Superior National Forest of northern Minnesota on skis, snowshoes, and by dog sled. The trip is headed by wolf biologists who demonstrate research methods and lead participants on a howling foray in search of the elusive predator. You will observe wolf tracks as well as moose and deer killed by wolves. During an aerial tour, you may even see a whole wolf pack. The field work is supplemented by audiovisual presentations and group discussions focusing on wilderness and wolf ecology and the management of wolves in the Great Lakes region. The program takes place from January through March and is based in a modern resort.

For a more intense experience, join experienced biologists

on a "Wolf Research Expedition," a trip through the boreal forest, immersing yourself in a week of actual wolf research. You will be trained to operate radio-telemetry equipment to radio-track wolves. As you investigate wolf behavior and the impact of human activities on wolves, you will learn to use a compass and map to plot bearings and you will become adept at entering data into computers. The program is led by college instructors and biologists and integrates presentations on wolf ecology and management with opportunities to hear wolves and observe tracks and other signs of their presence. This program is offered in June, July, and October.

"Winter Wolf Odyssey," a four-day field trip highlighted by a two-day dog-sledding course including an overnight dog-sled and cross-country ski trek into the wilderness, is another possibility. You will learn about winter wilderness travel skills and camping, as well as about wolf ecology, research, and management. All equipment (for skiing, snowshoeing, dog sledding, and camping one night on the trail) is provided, along with instruction on what to do with it. The program is offered in February and March.

Vermilion Environmental Studies, in cooperation with the Audubon Center of the Northwoods, also offers "Eagle Survey and Ecology," a week-long trip through the Boundary Waters Canoe Area Wilderness. You will learn about eagle ecology and survey techniques and you will also develop canoeing, low-impact camping, and map and compass skills. The program is offered in June.

COST: The fee for the "Winter Wolf Weekend" is $295, which covers lodgings, all meals, demonstrations, field trips, and snowshoe and ski rental and lessons. The fee for the "Wolf Research Expedition" is $620. "Winter Wolf Odyssey" costs $455, which covers all meals and lodgings. These three programs also feature an optional aerial tour for an additional

$30. "Eagle Survey and Ecology" costs $560, including all meals and all camping and canoeing equipment.

EYE OF THE WHALE
MARINE/WILDERNESS ADVENTURES

P.O. Box 1269
Kapa'au, Hawaii 96755
(800) 657-7730

Eye of the Whale owner/operators Beth Goodwin and Mark Grandoni combine their knowledge, skills, and enthusiasm for the outdoors to provide a unique blend of nature study, adventure, and relaxation on three different Hawaiian islands.

They offer three trip options. "Whale Tales" features five days of sailing aboard a forty-two-foot Morgan ketch with a focus on marine mammal biology. You'll be involved in photo-identifying individual humpback whales and recording their mating songs as part of an ongoing nonprofit research project.

"Earth, Fire, and Sea" begins with three days of land exploration, highlighted by a presentation on volcanology followed by a hike across the floor of Kilauea, the world's most active volcano. The second half of the expedition features three days aboard a sailing ketch, with the emphasis on coral reef exploration and sailing techniques.

"Hawaiian Hiking Odyssey" is a ten-day expedition that takes you to three different islands. There are fine opportunities for birdwatching, flora identification, and volcano and rainforest hiking. Highlights also include a visit to a former leprosy colony and an exploration of some of the ancient petroglyph fields of early Hawaii. For this expedition and for the land portion of "Earth, Fire, and Sea," accommodations are provided in comfortable bed-and-breakfast establishments. Swimming, snorkeling, and sunset barbecues are important components on all three trips.

To ensure individual attention and minimal impact on the environment, each expedition is limited to a maximum of ten participants. The three trip options are designed for healthy, adventurous people of all ages and levels of experience. Beth and Mark describe their philosophy as follows: "We encourage hands-on experience and group participation in all aspects of the trip, from taking photographs and recording vocalizations of whales and porpoises to hoisting sails and taking the helm while sailing. In this way, participants will maximize their learning experience, develop a sense of group unity, and form many long-lasting friendships."

COST: The fee for "Whale Tales" is $950; "Earth, Fire, and Sea" is $975; and "Hawaiian Hiking Odyssey" is $1,575. The fee includes all lodging, and most meals, activities, and instruction. It also covers interisland airfare where applicable.

CAMPALASKA TOURS

P.O. Box 872247
Wasilla, Alaska 99687
(907) 376-9438

CampAlaska Tours offer an inexpensive way to learn about one of our most remote and spectacular states. The tours attract active adults looking for a unique way to experience Alaska. Married couples and people traveling with friends often sign up, but most participants are single people who join on their own. Instead of staying at hotels (a costly proposition in this area), groups check into a campground at the end of the day. Tents and all other necessary community equipment are supplied. All you need to bring is a sleeping bag.

The trips are designed for first-time campers as well as experienced outdoorsmen. When it comes to making meals and taking care of camping chores, everyone pitches in. Each group member contributes to a "food kitty," which covers the cost of most meals during the trip, with the exception of those eaten in restaurants and on ferries. There's plenty of opportunity to shop for fresh foods and to refine your campfire cooking skills.

Each tour is led by an experienced guide who knows the best trails to take and who is chosen for his or her leadership qualities. Your guide, who coordinates activities but never leads you around like a pack of tourists, also drives the fifteen-person van that provides basic trip transportation. Since the group is limited to twelve and since all gear is stored on a covered roof rack, you will travel in relative comfort. Because travel days include sightseeing and hiking stops, long drives are rare.

Each tour incorporates a variety of activities, but most feature a three-night stop at Denali National Park. There is plenty of opportunity to explore the park and observe its wildlife, as well as the option of signing on for a Mount McKinley scenic flight or a white-water raft trip on the Nenana River. CampAlaska offers about ten different itineraries, some of which travel to the Yukon and the Canadian Rockies. Trips vary in length from six to twenty-two days.

CampAlaska publishes a detailed booklet with day-by-day tour itineraries. At the end of each description, you will find a list of included features and a list of optional (additional cost) highlights. Options include scenic flights, rafting trips, Alaska salmon bake, dog-team demonstration, museum visits, scenic cruises, ocean kayaking, canoeing, sailing expeditions, fishing trips, gold panning, horseback riding, hot springs visit, aerial tram, and helicopter flights.

In the past few years, CampAlaska has expanded its programs by developing a set of tours called "Alaska Travel Alternatives." True to the original CampAlaska philosophy, these are also small group tours with relaxed, flexible itineraries. "Adventure Tours" incorporate multiday wilderness trips into the traditional camping tours. The adventures include fly-in rafting, bicycling, kayaking, and canoeing. Two adventures are usually combined within one itinerary. Hiking is accented throughout all of these tours. Experience is not required to participate but you must be in good physical condition. Complete instructions and safety procedures are discussed before beginning any adventure component.

For those who prefer more creature comforts, CampAlaska Alternatives now also offers hotel/lodge tours. These tours maintain the flexibility and relaxed pace of the original CampAlaska Tours, but the group is limited to ten, leaving plenty of elbow room in the van, and instead of camping out you will sleep in hotels and wilderness lodges.

COST: "The Scout," a seven-day CampAlaska itinerary traveling to Denali National Park, Fairbanks, and Prince William Sound, costs $600 plus $55 for the food kitty. Additional expense depends upon the optional activities chosen. "The Pathfinder," a thirteen-day expedition incorporating a four-day kayak trip and a three-day fly-in raft trip, costs $2,000. "Glaciers and Gold," a ten-day hotel trip to Juneau, Glacier Bay, the Yukon, Prince William Sound, and Anchorage, costs $1,650.

Marine Life

SHOALS MARINE LABORATORY

G-14Y Stimson Hall
Cornell University
Ithaca, New York 14853
(607) 256-3717

A cooperative venture of Cornell University and the University of New Hampshire, the Shoals Marine Laboratory is North America's largest marine field station focusing on undergraduate education. Dedicated to sharing information about the marine environment with the general public, it also offers adult and family education programs unmatched by any other marine facility.

The lab is located on Appledore Island, largest of the nine Isles of Shoals that lie several miles off the New Hampshire and Maine Coasts. Complex, diverse, and unspoiled, the island is at once accessible and isolated. More than 125 species of pelagic and inland birds use Appledore as a migratory resting spot. A colony of harbor seals breeds nearby and whales, porpoises, and dolphins are annual visitors. All in all, it is hard to imagine a more ideal setting for marine studies.

The summer population of Appledore is limited to about one hundred people at any one time, which includes no more than sixty program participants. The size of the group and the residential nature of the program foster the development of a sense of community, which transforms the seminars into heady intellectual and educational experiences.

Noncredit seminars, most of which last about a week, are open to any interested person over the age of twelve (participants under age eighteen must be accompanied by an adult). The programs are geared to intelligent, curious individuals, but no prior experience is required.

During your stay you will live in shared rooms in modern dormitories. Program facilities also include dining and lecture halls, a darkroom, a library, and several laboratories. The main laboratory has bench space for sixty people and is equipped with both compound and dissecting microscopes. The lab maintains a small fleet of boats including inflatables, Boston whalers, a nineteen-foot sailboat, and the forty-seven-foot *R/V John M. Kingsbury*, a coastal research vessel. Boat excursions are integrated into all of the programs.

Seminar topics are fairly consistent from one summer to the next. If you enroll in "Marine Mammals," you will spend the week learning about the behavior of whales, porpoises, seals, and other sea mammals. As part of your study, you will join whale-watching expeditions.

"A Fine Kettle of Fish" provides an introduction to edible marine invertebrate and vertebrate species by following the saga of fish and shellfish from the sea to the table. Field trips include an on-deck trawling experience, a whale watch, and visits to commercial fish processors. "Colonial History and Archaeology" focuses on Appledore's rich seventeenth- and eighteenth-century history. Activities involve excursions to the islands and examinations of foundation ruins and artifacts discovered during excavations.

COST: The all-inclusive seminar fee is $775, which covers tuition, room, board, field trips, and roundtrip ferry transportation between Portsmouth, New Hampshire, and Appledore Island.

OKEANOS OCEAN RESEARCH FOUNDATION, INC.

278 E. Montauk Highway
P.O. Box 776
Hampton Bays, New York 11946
(516) 728-4522

Named after the father of all sea life in Greek mythology, Okeanos is a nonprofit environmental research and education organization with interests in marine life and ocean ecology. Okeanos is the only group in New York State authorized under federal and state law to handle marine mammals and sea turtles, assisting live stranded animals and examining dead ones to gather data for studies on both human and animal health problems. In addition to its stranding/rescue program, the organization conducts research projects designed to learn more about the biology of the marine animals and sea-turtle species that live in New York's waters, waters that carry some of the heaviest commercial boat traffic in the world.

For the public, Okeanos runs one-day whale watches, opportunities to study the whales as they feed in the waters off eastern Long Island. Each trip is staffed by a naturalist who gives a lecture focusing on the characteristics and behavior of the whales and other marine life likely to be encountered. The purpose of these trips is to observe the animals in their natural environment, so sightings cannot be guaranteed, but fin, minke, and humpback whales, dolphins, porpoises, sea turtles, and sharks are frequently seen. The cruises usually last about 4 ½ hours but because all trips are research oriented, the length may vary on occasion.

Okeanos also offers guided natural history tours and inshore bay investigations, evening seminar programs, and tours of the foundation's animal rehabilitation facility, where you will see rescued animals being prepared for their return to the wild.

Whale-watch cruises take place from late May through September.

COST: The fee for the whale watch is $28 for adults, $15 for children twelve and under.

BIOLOGICAL JOURNEYS

96 Ocean Drive
McKinleyville, California 95521
(707) 839-0178

Biological Journeys operates small-group natural history cruises to marine and land wilderness areas in North America, South America, and Australia. The trips provide an opportunity to observe wildlife close up, yet in comfort and security.

The trips are characterized by unhurried cruising, moderate hikes, and nightly anchorages in secluded coves. Trip leaders are experienced researchers and teachers, trained to provide sound and accurate information. Because of the small group size, travelers have ample access to the naturalists, adding to the educational value of the trips.

During the summer months, the company offers natural history cruises in southeast Alaska. You will live aboard the small, comfortable eight-passenger *Delphinus*, enjoying a snug bed, hot showers, gourmet food, and informative, illustrated evening lectures. Daily shore excursions accompanied by your professional naturalist guide provide the chance to explore your surroundings up close.

All of the *Delphinus*-based Alaska trips include a one-hour float-plane flight over the glaciers and wilderness areas in a fully restored 1947 vintage SeaBee complete with camera ports in the windows. Depending upon the specific trip chosen, you may also visit one of the restricted wilderness areas accessible only to groups of twelve or less, such as Pack Creek Bear Reserve on Kootznahoo Island, a superb area for viewing grizzly bears. While cruising, there will always be time for some excellent whale watching.

During the winter and spring months, Biological Journeys offers a variety of seven- to twelve-day Baja California cruises out of San Diego and La Paz. While cruising the Baja seas you can expect to see whales, dolphins, sea lions, birds, and manta rays. Shore excursions to desert islands offer the opportunity for land exploration and for snorkeling with the tropical fish. Depending upon the specific trip you choose, you might search for only-in-Baja land birds like Xantus' hummingbird, snorkel with the sea lions of Los Islotes, or observe the mating rituals of elephant seals at San Benitos Island. No matter which itinerary you choose, experienced, knowledgeable naturalists provide a solid, relevant natural history education.

COST: Trip fees for the 7–11-day Alaska cruises range from $2,695 to $3,895, which includes all expenses, accommodations, meals, naturalist guide services, and transportation while aboard the vessels. A less costly week-long southeast Alaska cruise aboard a forty-passenger vessel is $1,695.

OCEANIC SOCIETY EXPEDITIONS

Fort Mason Center, Building E
San Francisco, California 94123
(800) 326-7491, (415) 441-1106

A nonprofit organization built on the belief that responsibly conducted nature tourism can contribute to conservation efforts, Oceanic Society Expeditions offers ecotours that emphasize the protection of wildlife and the preservation of habitat. All trips are led by competent naturalists familiar with general ecology and conservation issues as well as with the natural history of the flora and fauna particular to the trip.

The society has an extensive selection of trips to choose from, including both land- and water-based options. There are small-boat whale-watching expeditions, wildlife safaris, rainforest and reef explorations, wild dolphin research trips, and SCUBA and snorkeling forays.

"Dolphins and Whales in Monterey Bay," one of the most popular programs, provides the opportunity to contribute to an ongoing research project centered on the study of Pacific white-sided dolphins in Monterey Bay, California, and surrounding waters. The bay contains the Monterey Submarine Canyon, over two miles deep and sixty miles long, which supports one of the most diverse populations of marine mammals in the world. Working aboard a fifty-five-foot motor vessel under the guidance of Oceanic Society researchers, participants collect data on the ecology and sounds of the dolphins. If you choose this trip, you are likely to see Risso's dolphins, northern right whale dolphins, minke whales, and Dall's porpoises; other possibilities include killer whales and Baird's beaked whales.

During the week-long program, expect to spend an average of eight hours a day on the water. The trip is headquartered at a comfortable lodge on the Monterey Peninsula, where slide and video presentations on marine animals are shown each evening. Each group is limited to ten participants and no prior experience is required for participation. The staff will teach you what you need to know.

For quite a different experience, sign on for a midwinter trip to Florida to swim with the West Indian manatees. You'll spend the days snorkeling with these huge, gentle endangered mammals in the waters of the Crystal River National Wildlife Refuge under the guidance of an experienced manatee biologist.

The Oceanic Society publishes an annual catalog of expeditions that describes all the expeditions offered both in the United States and abroad. Once you've limited your interest to one or two possibilities, you can request a detailed trip description complete with a day-by-day itinerary. The trips are open to those eighteen years and older. Depending upon age and experience, some trips may be suitable for children accompanied by a parent or legal guardian.

COST: For participation in "Dolphins and Whales in Monterey Bay," $1,090; $925 for "Florida Springs Manatees." These fees include accommodations, most meals, naturalist services, and boat excursions.

NATURAL HABITAT WILDLIFE ADVENTURES

One Sussex Station
Sussex, New Jersey 07461
(800) 543-8917

Observe animals close up in their own natural habitats under the guidance of seasoned program leaders by signing on for a trip with Natural Habitat Wildlife Adventures. Committed to the principles of ecotourism, this company seeks to approach wildlife as closely as possible without disturbing the animals. On most adventures, program leaders are joined by local guides with intimate knowledge of the region visited.

Natural Habitat runs trips to several different parts of the world. North American adventures include a trip to Alaska to observe moose, caribou, dall sheep, sea lions, whales, porpoises, sea otters, puffins, and the world's largest concentration of bald eagles. The thirteen-day itinerary includes a cruise of the Kenai Fjords and stays in Denali National Park and Katamai National Park, where travelers spend time on protective platforms just feet away from brown bears fishing for salmon.

During a trip to Massachusetts and Maine, travelers can expect to sight seals, puffins, loons, bald eagles, razorbills, and other marine animals and birds. Much of the trip takes place on the water. The eleven-day itinerary includes two days of whale watching, day trips by ferry and sailing schooner, and an opportunity to track moose in Baxter State Park.

Working in cooperation with the International Fund for Animal Welfare, Natural Habitat Wildlife Adventures operates Sealwatch, a series of thirteen tours scheduled from late February through mid-March, the time each year when a quarter of a million harp seals enter eastern Canada's Gulf of Saint Lawrence to bear their young on the vast floating ice fields off the Magdalen Islands of Quebec. The pups are born with snowy pelts, which they shed, turning gray in just a few weeks. The tours are instrumental in preserving the lives of these seals because they provide an economic alternative for the Magdalen Islanders who once hunted the animals for their pelts.

The basic Sealwatch tour runs five or six days. Travelers are based for the most part in the Magdalen Islands. The program includes trips to the harp seals, presentations on seals and wildlife given by leading scientists and naturalists, workshops on taking photographs in icy environments, guided cross-country ski and snowshoe treks, and guided day and moonlight nature hikes. The package includes the use of an expedition suit designed for arctic explorations when you travel by helicopter to the ice floes. Here you can walk safely among the seal pups, getting close enough even to pet those animals who are willing.

All of the Natural Habitat tours offer outstanding photography opportunities, but some are designated as special "Photo Tours." Led by world-renowned photographer and photography teacher Robert Winslow, these trips are designed for both amateurs interested in receiving instruction and professionals who are attracted by their structure (for example, additional "setup" time).

Natural Habitat adheres to the philosophy that nature can

be experienced in relative comfort. Accommodations are usually the best available hotels and lodges in the area, though at times these can be far from luxurious. The trips attract people of all ages and physical abilities who share in common their interest in animals and their desire to view wildlife in its own environment.

COST: The fee for the thirteen-day Alaska trip, which originates in Anchorage, is $3,795; airfare to Katmai is included. The fee for the eleven-day Maine/Massachusetts trip, which originates in Boston, is $2,495. Rates begin at $1,595 for the five- and six-day Sealwatch packages, including hotel, some meals, airfare from Halifax, Nova Scotia, to the Magdalen Islands, and other trip activities as described above.

Scientific Research

EARTHWATCH

680 Mount Auburn St.
Box 403
Watertown, Massachusetts 02272
(617) 926-8200

"The mission of Earthwatch is to improve human understanding of the planet, the diversity of its inhabitants, and the processes that affect the quality of life on earth." To implement its mission statement, the organization seeks volunteers willing to serve in an environmental EarthCorps, working alongside scientists for two- to three-week periods on research projects scattered across the globe.

Anyone sixteen years and older is eligible to join. No special skills are required, only a willingness to invest time and money in exchange for the opportunity to contribute to research relative to critical environmental issues. "What Earthwatch volunteers lack in training and formal background," observes a scientist who has directed volunteers for the past twenty years, "they make up in enthusiasm and willingness to learn." The actual tasks you will undertake as a volunteer differ widely according to the project chosen.

Within the United States, projects are currently underway in twenty different states. If you are interested in human adaptation to change, you might join a crew at the "Bison Kill" project based in Crawford, Nebraska, where 9,800 years ago a band of paleo-Indian hunters drove 1,000 head of buffalo over an embankment and then butchered the disabled animals. As a volunteer, you will assist in excavating skeletons, establishing the bone bed's boundaries, and in using ground-penetrating radar and coring techniques to search for the yet undiscovered campsite where the hides and meat were processed.

If you are interested in bird conservation, you might volunteer for "Loons," a project underway in Michigan, Wisconsin, and Minnesota to determine why 40 percent of the breeding pairs in the Upper Peninsula have disappeared. Stationed on the Lake Superior shoreline, teams work night shifts from boats, capturing, banding, and weighing loons, and taking blood and feather samples.

Last year over 3,400 volunteers ranging in age from sixteen to eighty-five helped staff 142 Earthwatch projects in fifty countries. Projects vary widely in terms of living conditions. Crews may live in tents at remote campsites, in cabins, school dormitories, or local nature centers. Volunteers pay their own airfare to the project site. They also make a tax-deductible contribution ranging from $800 to $2,200 to help fund the expedition they join, covering food, accommodations, field support, and equipment.

The best way to learn about the projects is to become a member of Earthwatch Expeditions. Membership entitles you to a subscription to the handsome bimonthly publication, *Earthwatch*, which contains articles, interviews, and announcements relative to the organization's mission, along with a catalog of upcoming project opportunities.

If you have difficulty choosing a project and want to know more about one or several before making a selection, you can order detailed expedition briefings for $25 each (up to $50 will be credited toward the project you join). Approximately forty pages long, each briefing describes the history of the project, its research mission and expedition goals, and the background of the principal investigators and staff. Also included is a description of the daily itinerary, volunteer assignments, and field logistics. Reference maps, information about the area, and a bibliography for additional reading are also part of the package.

COST: Each volunteer participant contributes $1,295 to the "Bison Kill" project and $1,195 to "Loons."

SAVANNAH SCIENCE MUSEUM

4405 Paulsen St.
Savannah, Georgia 31405
(912) 355-6705

For the past twenty years the Savannah Science Museum has operated the Caretta Research Project in cooperation with the U.S. Fish and Wildlife Service. The project seeks to learn more about the population levels, trends, and nesting habits of the threatened loggerhead sea turtle (*Caretta caretta*) and to enhance the protection of eggs and hatchlings on a nesting beach where loss to beach erosion and predators has been high historically. Another goal of the project is to involve the public in its work. It does this through an intensive volunteer program, which runs for eighteen weeks each year, mid-May to mid-September. Volunteers register for one or more weeks.

During the egg-laying season, which runs up until mid-August, volunteers spend most of each night patrolling six miles of beaches, searching for huge female turtles crawling out of the sea to nest. Each turtle is tagged and important data, including measurements of both the turtle and her path to her nest, are gathered. Volunteers also assist in transplanting some nests and protecting others with screen wire. Hatching season (late July into September) is devoted to monitoring the nests and escorting hatchlings down the beach and into the surf. During the day, volunteers help out with housekeeping chores and the upkeep of the project's vehicles. They also check the beaches for the carcasses of dead sea turtles.

To participate, you need only be in good health and at least fifteen years of age. There is no maximum age limit. Be prepared to walk two or three miles each night in the dark (use of flashlights on the beach is prohibited since it may scare the turtles). The most important qualification is a flexible, upbeat attitude, and a willingness to "cheerfully endure close quarters, insects, rain storms, and the heat and humidity of a week in the subtropics without air conditioning."

COST: The registration fee for participation on a project team is $395 (mid-May through mid-August) and $350 (mid-August through mid-September). This covers all food, housing, leadership, boat transportation to and from the island, and transportation while on the island.

THE YELLOWSTONE PROJECT

P.O. Box 6640
Bozeman, Montana 59771-6640
(406) 587-7758

The Yellowstone Project organizes research vacations, providing opportunities to join professional scientists in their efforts to protect and preserve the Greater Yellowstone Ecosystem (GYE) for future generations. All of the programs are "ecosystem specific," focusing on the eighteen million acres in Montana, Wyoming, and Idaho (including Yellowstone and Grand Teton national parks) that make up the GYE. As a participant, you will work side-by-side with the researchers, gathering data related to a wide range of studies covering predator–prey relationships, bird populations, riparian zones, and the impact of human activities (mining, logging, fire control policy).

Participation is open to people of all ages who want to commit their vacation time to increasing our understanding of the environment. Anyone who likes to work hard and has a lively intellect and a genuine interest in the environment is welcome to join one of the programs. Research teams frequently include physically fit seniors, midlife professionals seeking a meaningful vacation, and students interested in learning firsthand about the demands of environmental research.

Each research vacation is actually a multiday residential field research program. As a volunteer, you make a set cash contribution to help underwrite the cost of the project and to cover your food, accommodations, and transportation during the program. Programs run ten days to four weeks and operate consistently with the standards of low-impact wilderness travel. As a volunteer, you will be expected to share in daily camp chores. You will receive intensive training in research techniques, both traditional observation and sampling methods and state-of-the-art technologies. (The specific techniques you learn will depend upon the project you join.)

Programs vary tremendously in terms of physical difficulty and training complexity. Many are repeated each year, providing long-term continuity that will eventually shed light on even the most subtle changes taking place in the study area.

If you have four weeks to contribute, you could join "Coyotes and Canid Culture," a study that seeks to understand the complex social interactions of Canidae. The work involves recording coyote behavior around dens, using spotting scopes, hand-held computers, and video cameras. The program is labeled "easy to moderate," with long day hikes, lots of sitting, and dormitory accommodations. Four participants serve on the team. Labeled "moderate to strenuous," "Where Have the Songbirds Gone?" is an eleven-day program. Teams of ten volunteers study riparian habitats near Grand Teton National Park, identifying and quantifying songbird populations. Activities include mist netting, bird banding, vegetative analysis, and the use of global positioning devices. Living conditions involve primitive camping with hiking over altitudes above seven thousand feet.

COST: Fees run as follows: "Coyotes and Canid Culture," $2,700; "Where Have the Songbirds Gone?" $1,395.

FOUNDATION FOR FIELD RESEARCH

P.O. Box 2010
Alpine, California 91903
(619) 445-1893

A nonprofit organization founded in 1982 to coordinate research expeditions, the Foundation for Field Research supports projects in archaeology, architecture, biology, ethnography, paleontology, mammalogy, marine biology, ornithology, and primatology. Volunteers, who have ranged in age from fourteen to eighty-six, contribute financial and physical support to the research efforts sponsored by the foundation.

Projects take place all over the world, including the United States. In 1992, volunteers documented the impact of recreational use on prehistoric and historic native American sites in Idaho's River of No Return Wilderness Area. Other volunteers assisted in an archaeological survey on the Zuni Indian Reservation in New Mexico. In Arizona, one team gathered data relating rock art to the native American view of the solar system, while elsewhere in the state another team documented the abundance of desert plant and animal species.

Previous experience is not required to become a volunteer field assistant. When you sign up for an expedition, you will be sent a comprehensive preparatory booklet describing the research subject, the methodology that will be used, and field conditions. Once in the field, participants receive instruction from the scientist who heads the team.

Each participant is required to make a set financial contribution that supports the principal investigator's expenses and stipend and covers the cost of the preparatory booklet, shared accommodations, and all meals during the project dates, ground and water transportation as required during the expedition, and the use of necessary research equipment and expendable supplies. Preparatory booklets, which can help you decide whether you want to commit yourself to a particular project, can be ordered in advance for $20; the fee is deducted from the expedition contribution if you decide to join.

In joining a research project, it is important to be ready to accept some hardships in the field. Tented base camps, consisting of two-person tents, field kitchen, table and chairs, hot-water shower, and enclosed toilet, are used for projects in Arizona, New Mexico, and Idaho. Living and working conditions are subject to change due to weather and equipment breakdowns.

COST: The contribution required for participation in

"Astronomers of Ancient Arizona" is $495 (one-week experience). The contribution for "Archaeological Survey on the Zuni Indian Reservation" in New Mexico is $665 for the first week and $250 for each additional week.

UNIVERSITY RESEARCH EXPEDITIONS PROGRAM

University of California
Berkeley, California 94720
(510) 642-6586

For the past fifteen years, the University Research Expeditions Program (UREP) has invited laypersons to join with the scientific community as participants in field research expeditions both in the United States and abroad. The program "was built upon the conviction that curiosity about the world is not limited to scientists in lab coats or academics secluded in ivory towers," explains Jean G. Colvin, the director of UREP. The organization reaches out to men and women from all walks of life who embrace the challenge that underlies all research—the need to understand.

Depending upon the focus of the research, the expeditions are divided into the following categories: animal behavior, archaeology, arts, environmental studies, and social sciences. A recent catalog lists three expeditions within the United States. Team members assemble in Ely, Nevada, for "Fremont Settlements: The View from Above," a project based in the Great Basin National Park, where the Fremont, a group of prehistoric native Americans, lived 700–1,500 years ago. This project seeks to identify the survival strategies used by the Fremont to stay alive in an inhospitable environment. Hiking each day at elevations of 5,000–13,000 feet, team members collect and analyze surface artifacts and map and photograph various sites in an effort to identify food-gathering strategies used by the Fremont. This expedition is best suited to those with a strong interest in native American archaeology who are comfortable hiking over uneven terrain. The team will first camp at lower elevations, gradually moving up to higher elevations as the members become acclimated to the altitude.

Participants in the environmental studies program "Alien Plant Invasion of Hawaii's Woodlands" assemble in Hilo, Hawaii, in preparation for their work in Hawaii Volcanoes National Park. They will prepare plots of land for a "controlled burn" in an effort to learn why alien grasses live more successfully in these habitats than native grasses and to identify the influence of fire in these forests. They will also be involved in vegetation mapping and in taking core samples before and after the burn to measure soil nutrients and the number and variety of seeds present. Team members are accommodated in a simple dormitory. San Francisco is the assembly point for the expedition titled "Preserving Northern California's Coastline." Based in Tomales Bay just north of the city, the team studies the role that eelgrass plays in serving as a nursery for fish and invertebrates important for both a healthy ecosystem and a healthy local fishing economy. Participants wear chest-high waders as they measure and map eelgrass beds and observe the larvae that rely on them. Dormitory-style accommodations are provided.

A good way to learn more about the program is to attend one of the "UREP Nights," informational slide/discussion programs that are held in half a dozen states. If there is no UREP night scheduled in your area, you can contact the closest field representative (listed in the UREP catalog), who will put you in touch with a nearby expedition alumnus who would be happy to talk with you. Once you have applied to and been accepted by an expedition, you will receive full details on the project objectives, field techniques, and site conditions. Ongoing instruction in field methods will be provided at the site. Most U.S. expeditions run from ten days to two weeks and are open to participants of all ages.

COST: Each participant contributes $945 to the Nevada project, $920 to the Hawaii project, and $890 to the California project. Your contribution to the expedition underwrites the cost of the research and covers meals and shared lodging, ground transportation, camping and field gear (except sleeping bags and personal items), research equipment and supplies (except diving gear), and orientation materials.

6

Mind and Body

New Age

OMEGA INSTITUTE

Route 2, Box 377
Rhinebeck, New York 12572
(914) 338-6030, (914) 266-4301

The Omega Institute for Holistic Studies is built on the belief that "a sane world begins with healthy and loving people." Its mission is to encourage us to cultivate our creativity as we rise to the challenges we face today, both as individuals and as members of a society.

The Omega campus occupies eighty acres of rolling woodlands and lawns in the Hudson River Valley. Tree-lined paths accented by an abundance of flower gardens link the classrooms, meeting halls, cottages, café, craft shop, bookstore, and other buildings. Campus facilities also include a Wellness Center offering massage and body work, nutritional counseling, wellness evaluations, other holistic health therapies, sauna, and flotation tanks. Canoes and rowboats are available for use on the lake and there are tennis, volleyball, and basketball courts. Cars are not allowed on campus, further adding to the serenity of the environment.

Each summer an eclectic faculty is drawn to Omega to conduct over 250 workshops designed to nourish your ability to seek positive change and a healthy balance in your personal and professional lives. Participants from all over the world, representing many age groups, professions, and backgrounds, gather to deepen their understanding of themselves and their world and to become part of this fifteen-year-old learning community.

Omega's curriculum falls into five major areas of learning: Self, Others, Expression, World, and Wisdom. Workshops focus on many aspects of music, dance, theater, the fine arts, and writing. Others center on environmental and social concerns, spiritual understanding, business and work issues, and gender, relationship, and family subjects. Still others explore the nature of play, intuitive development, martial arts, yoga, addictions, aging, and many aspects of psychological development. And that's just an overview. There are both weekend and week-long sessions.

One of the most popular offerings is the "Omega Wellness Program," a comprehensive approach to holistic health that covers the interactive roles of diet and nutrition, prevention, exercise, fitness, lifestyle, attitude, and time perception.

The summer session runs from early June through September. Omega also offers programs throughout the rest of the year. In addition, "Omega Journeys" offer opportunities for personal growth in the context of an adventure travel experience. Most trips last about a week and all are accompanied by skilled guides. Recent journeys have included "Pecos Wilderness: Rite of Passage for Women" and "Utah Canyonlands: Questing for a Vision," each of which incorporated a wilderness solo experience.

COST: Tuition for the week-long "Omega Wellness Workshop" is $260. A variety of housing options are available on campus, including single- and double-occupancy cabin rooms with private and shared bath, dormitory space, and camping. A seven-day package including all meals and a double cabin room shared with a roommate (bath shared with adjoining room) costs $350.

ESALEN INSTITUTE

Big Sur, California 93920
(408) 667-3005

Located on the magnificent Big Sur coast overlooking the Pacific with the Santa Lucia Range rising dramatically behind, "Esalen Institute is a center to encourage work in the humanities and sciences that promotes human values and potentials." Through its seminars, conferences, research, and related programs, the institute expresses its commitment to the exploration of religion, education, philosophy, and the physical and behavioral sciences.

A good way to become acquainted with the institute is to request a copy of its current catalog, a substantial booklet published three times a year ($5 contribution appreciated). Here you will learn about the programs and the different ways to experience the institute, ranging from an overnight visit to a long-term stay. The standard route for learning the methods leading to personal growth taught at Esalen is through enrollment in the large selection of weekend and five-day residential workshops offered.

A weekend workshop for first-time visitors, "Experiencing Esalen" is designed to familiarize participants with a variety of approaches to deepening self-awareness. You will become familiar with practices including sensory awareness, gestalt, group process, guided fantasy, meditation, and massage. You can then pursue in subsequent specialized seminars those approaches that you find most attractive.

A sampling of seminars described in a recent catalog provides insight into the Esalen experience. The weekend program "Finding My Place: A Workshop for Men," is for men who want to grow beyond the traditional definitions of manhood. "Massage Intensive for Couples" is for partners who want to learn to massage each other. "Letting Go—Moving On" uses dream work, massage, dance, group process, and intensive body work to help participants release old defenses that can interfere with spontaneous feelings in present relationships.

Examples of five-day seminars include "Exploring Dimensions of Healing," "Biodrama: Know Yourself, Live Your Self," and "The Body and Zen." "The Practical Art of Creative Risk Taking" uses traditional psychological practice and non-traditional innovative approaches in body work, kinesthetic retraining, music, and guided imagery to break away from old habits and fears and to develop a more adventurous way of living.

The Esalen Institute recognizes that some of its programs may prove difficult for some people, particularly those who have experienced psychiatric problems: "Since we are a center for experimental education, we ask that persons come to our programs out of an educational interest. We ask that no one come whose interest is 'cure.'"

As well as attending your workshop, you may wish to attend the occasional forums in which writers and thinkers from within and outside the institute discuss their ideas. Lectures, films, and dance performances are often held on Wednesday evenings. During your stay you can enjoy the natural hot springs on the property. Bathing suits are optional in the hot springs, massage area, and swimming pool.

Seminar participants are accommodated in shared housing, two or more persons to a room (couples are always assigned to doubles). Meals feature herbs and vegetables from Esalen's organic garden along with breads and pastries baked on the grounds. The institute's "Gazebo School/Park Early Childhood Program" provides child care while parents are attending workshops.

COST: The fee for the weekend workshops described above is $350. The fee for the five-day workshops is $675. These fees cover tuition, room, and board.

KUSHI INSTITUTE

P.O. Box 7
Becket, Massachusetts 01223
(413) 623-2102

A nonprofit educational center devoted to teaching about the role of macrobiotic practice in the quest for a peaceful, healthful world, the Kushi Institute reaches out to those who wish to learn about both the practical and philosophical aspects of macrobiotics. For over forty years founders Michio and Aveline Kushi have taught students how to find balance in their lives by adopting a more natural way of living and eating. Here you will learn how different foods affect your health and how you can become actively involved in deepening your understanding of the relationship between body, mind, and spirit.

The institute offers courses for both beginning and experienced practitioners of macrobiotics. The most popular program at the institute is "The Way to Health Program," a week-long stay that incorporates daily hands-on cooking classes with lectures and discussions on the macrobiotic way of life. Some of the topics addressed include how different foods affect your health, how to choose the right foods, menu planning, and the role of diet in cancer prevention. The program is for both those who seek an introduction to macrobiotics and those who are seeking help with a specific health concern. Each session is limited to eighteen participants.

The institute is located in a peaceful, rural area in the Berkshires. Facilities include a spacious country home with simple rooms and a separate dormitory building with library, meditation chapel, and dining hall. During your stay, you will be served macrobiotic meals prepared by experienced cooks who rely on the freshest ingredients and food products, many produced right on the premises.

COST: The all-inclusive fee for The Way to Health Program is $958.

THE FEATHERED PIPE FOUNDATION

P.O. Box 1682
Helena, Montana 59624
(406) 442-8196

For the past sixteen years, the Feathered Pipe Foundation has offered programs designed to help participants become healthier in mind, body, and spirit. As the foundation brochure explains, "The ranch is named after the feathered pipe, the ceremonial pipe which Native Americans have used to receive direction from the Great Spirit and to connect all beings within the circle of life."

Nestled in the Montana Rockies, this seminar center specializes in intensive yoga sessions for both beginners and advanced practitioners. Representative week-long seminars include "The Fullness of Yoga," "Astrology Intensive," and "Radiant Health." In "Women's Wisdom," participants explore their own sources of inspiration and creativity. "Fire in the Belly" offers men the opportunity to explore the myths, stories, and hidden assumptions that shape their lives in the 1990s. Seminars are scheduled from May through September.

Accommodations at the ranch vary from large dormitory rooms in natural stone and log buildings to tipis, tents, and yurts. Bathroom facilities are located in a cedar bathhouse that also contains a hot tub, sauna, and massage rooms staffed by professional massage therapists. The ranch serves a vegetarian menu, along with some poultry and fish dishes, and the emphasis is on fresh, organically grown products.

COST: The price of each program includes all instruction, lodging, and meals. Seminars run three to ten days and cost $150–$1,150.

GANAS COMMUNITY

135 Corson Ave.
Staten Island, New York 10301-2933
(718) 720-5378

Established in 1980 by the Foundation for Feedback Learning, a nonprofit, nonreligious, educational research organization, the Ganas Community describes itself in its literature as "a New York City group living experiment in open communication committed to the union of reason and emotion in the service of learning how to make the dream of direct democracy a working reality."

The community began with six people and has grown to include more than sixty. Members of the community occupy seven attractive multifamily dwellings and three commercial buildings located in a lower middle class neighborhood just a ferry ride from Manhattan. The houses are connected by walkways bordered with flower and vegetable gardens. With a playground, small swimming pool, outdoor fireplaces, and porches, it has quite a rural feel, all within view of New York Harbor.

Amenities include video, music, and book libraries, an equipped exercise room, ping-pong and pool tables, a sewing room, and laundry facilities. Residents and visitors can also take part in a variety of workshops, feedback learning groups, and an English as a Second Language (ESL) program at no cost. Other equipment, including computers and software, video cameras, copy facilities, and a carpentry workshop, can be made available by special arrangement.

The community maintains three retail stores. One sells household items, books, toys, and arts and crafts. Another sells furniture and the third sells clothing. The stores, like the housing, are well organized, attractive, and efficiently run.

About twenty people work in the stores. Another fifteen work at tasks involved with food preparation, gardening, housekeeping, administration, and maintenance. Those who work full-time cover their share of the community's expenses and also receive $200 a month and a share of the profits. Another twenty-five people work outside of the community and pay their expenses through a monthly fee.

Ganas has a long-term economic plan that calls for making its businesses profitable to the point of providing each person an income comparable to or higher than what they would make in the general market. At the same time, there is a commitment to expand the occupational choices available to those who want to live and work in the community and to develop new, socially valuable businesses proposed by members.

The social and political structure of Ganas revolves around three complementary groups. A core group of nine serves as the board of directors. These people have pooled all their resources, including time, talents, and material possessions, and are committed to doing whatever needs to be done for the well-being of the community. They are also committed to exchanging thoughts and feelings and performance feedback with one another. Members of the extended core group (about twenty-five people) share some aspects of the Ganas philosophy but do not share their resources and are not necessarily involved in exposing themselves emotionally. Many of them do, however, choose to participate in community discussions and most join in the consensus process involved in almost all planning and decision making. The third group (25–30 people) consists of those who live at Ganas for perhaps six months to several years, attracted by its affordability and convenience and by the supportive atmosphere. Although their input is almost always solicited before any important issue is resolved, they tend to be only peripherally involved with the community's goals and activities.

The majority of those who live at Ganas are in their thirties and forties, although residents have ranged from one to eighty. The population is very diverse, reflecting many races, nationalities, religions, professions, educational backgrounds, and life views. People live in considerable harmony, perhaps because the community is committed to resolving conflicts before they escalate into major differences.

Ganas welcomes visitors who want to learn about the community and how it functions. All you need to do is to call at least a day ahead to make arrangements. You can visit for a day, stay overnight, or for a week. It is also possible to arrange a longer stay.

COST: There is no charge for a one-day visit; just offer to help with the dinner dishes. Those who stay less than a week are asked to pay $15 a day and to help out where they can. Those who want to stay longer pay approximately $500 a month, prorated for the length of stay. This covers room, meals, laundry facilities—just about everything except telephone expenses.

HIGH WIND ASSOCIATION

7136 County Road U
Plymouth, Wisconsin 53073
(414) 528-7212, (414) 528-8488

A nonprofit educational organization dedicated to appropriate technology, environmental sustainability, and alternative governance, the High Wind Association works to restore the delicate balance between the earth and the people who inhabit it. High Wind was started by a group of people who banded together in southeastern Wisconsin in the mid-1970s to share common concerns. As their literature explains, "We felt an imperative to live in greater harmony with nature and with one another, to honor the earth and cease exploiting it, to move from talking to doing; to live our vision more directly."

Today the High Wind Association has several components. High Wind Farm, 128 acres and growing, is the site of an evolving "ecological village," with privately owned land and houses, where eighteen people make their permanent home. High Wind Learning Center focuses on public programs. The association also operates High Wind Books in Milwaukee, which offers books, tapes, periodicals, and other materials related to advancing the evolution of a humane, sustainable planet.

The farm opens its doors to visitors on the third Sunday of each month. An information program with staff and residents is followed by a tour of the land and solar buildings. Those who are looking for a simple retreat can spend a few days simply living at the farm.

The High Wind Learning Center offers seminars and workshops, many in conjunction with the University of Wisconsin, that explore ways for people to live in harmony with nature and with one another. As its governing statement explains, "The purpose of the High Wind Learning Center is to develop transformational leadership and to offer opportunities for personal growth and planetary change." Representative offerings include "High Wind Houses: A Day with the Designers and Builders," a weekend workshop called "In Search of the Sacred," and "Waldorf Art and Eurythmy: New Approaches to Color, Painting, and Movement," a week-long course.

COST: The fee for "Waldorf Art and Eurythmy" is $435, which includes tuition paid to the University of Wisconsin and a food-and-lodging charge paid to High Wind. Similarly, fees covering tuition, food, and lodging at the farm for "In Search of the Sacred" total $195. For those who wish to experience the farm without enrolling in a formal program, the charge for overnight accommodation and community-prepared vegetarian meals is $40 per day.

MALACHITE SCHOOL AND SMALL FARM

ASR Box 21, Pass Creek Road
Gardner, Colorado 81040
(719) 746-2412

A nonprofit educational organization dedicated to developing and teaching socially responsible and environmentally sound ways of living, the Malachite School and Small Farm reflects the founders' belief that our future is tied to the soundness of our agricultural practices. Through its courses and workshops, Malachite strives to fashion healthy relationships between people and the planet. Here the land is the classroom. Vistors come to Malachite to learn about all aspects of the farm's organic food production. They also come to learn about the region and about themselves through a variety of educational experiences.

"Mountains and Myths" is a family-oriented weekend program for those who want to explore the geology and lore of the surrounding Sangre de Cristo Mountains. A weekend program for adults, "The Well of Nourishment," introduces students to a variety of meditation techniques drawn from different traditions.

Still another option is to enroll in "An Introduction to Malachite," which involves spending up to seven days as a working member of the farm community, actively engaged in the daily work of caring for the gardens, greenhouses, and animals. By arrangement with Elderhostel, the school also offers a selection of programs for those sixty and older, including "Returning Culture to Agriculture: An Intergenerational Farm Experience," for those who want to share Malachite with their grandchildren, and a one-week program incorporating three classes: "Climate and Global Change," "Edible and Useful Plants," and "Adobe—Native Building Material."

Overnight visitors are welcome any time of the year, for any length of time. Accommodations at the farm are in men's and women's dormitory rooms with shared bathrooms. Private rooms can be arranged if you make plans well ahead of time. Campsites are also available. Meals are served family style and the menus feature salads, grains, vegetables, breads, pasta, and dairy products incorporating foodstuffs produced on the farm, along with farm-raised eggs, rabbit, chicken, pork, and grass-fed beef.

COST: The fee for "Mountains and Myths" is $225 for adults, $175 for children under twelve. The fee for "The Well of Nourishment" is $225. Meals and housing are included.

BREITENBUSH HOT SPRINGS RETREAT & CONFERENCE CENTER

P.O. Box 578
Detroit, Oregon 97342
(503) 854-3314

A worker–owner cooperative corporation, Breitenbush Hot Springs is a community of people who live their lives consciously supporting values of energy conservation, personal accountability, and interpersonal honesty. The community supports itself partly by hosting workshops and conferences and by welcoming guests who seek a personal retreat.

Named for the hot springs found in its forests and meadows, Breitenbush Hot Springs is in many ways reminiscent of the rustic health resorts popular in the early part of the century. Guests come to savor the curative powers of the springs, which carry some thirty minerals and have served as the site of native American rituals and ceremonies. They also come to share in the spiritual practices of the community by joining in morning meditation as well as sessions in yoga (for everyone, beginner to advanced), and special classes offered by visiting artists and teachers.

Guest facilities include the Medicine Wheel hot tubs (three large hot tubs of different temperatures and one cold tub), natural hot springs in the form of mountain pools, a swimming hole, a 1930s vintage lodge (complete with dining hall, library, and sitting room), a greenhouse, health care center, and many wilderness hiking trails. Healing arts offered at Breitenbush by appointment include massage, hydrotherapy, herbal sheet wraps, aromatherapy, and metaphysical counseling. Visitors are accommodated in cabins with heat and electricity (some with their own sinks and toilets, other using shared facilities), or you may rent a tent complete with mattresses or bring your own tent. The community is open to guests from May through October.

Courses and workshops focus on relationships, spirituality, healing, meditation, movement, music, dance, nature, and related subjects. They are conducted by a wide variety of experts. A newsletter describing specific sessions is published three times a year. Samples of workshops listed in a recent edition include: "Walking the Spirit Path" (five-day course jointly led by leaders in psychology and in the spiritual traditions), "Dance to Glory!" (week-long program for beginning, intermediate, and advanced dancers, focusing on sacred dances), and "About Men: For Women and Men" (weekend experiential workshop exploring the forces that shape boys into men).

Throughout the season, the community frequently hosts Elderhostel courses, which are open to those sixty years or older and their spouses. Recent topics have varied from "Natural History of Mushrooms" (six-day course focusing on the identification and classification of higher fungi, combining lab sessions, lectures, and field study) to "Hispanic Culture and Language for Beginners" (six days).

COST: For personal retreats, cabins are available for $40–$75 per adult per day, depending upon size, amenities, and the day of the week. This includes all meals and use of facilities and waters. Fees for workshops described above run as follows: "Walking the Spirit Path," $495; "Dance to Glory!" $680; "About Men: For Women and Men," $245. The fee for the two Elderhostel programs is $270 each. Fees cover tuition, cabin, all meals, and use of facilities and waters.

Diet and Lifestyle

STRUCTURE HOUSE

3017 Pickett Road
Durham, North Carolina 27705
(800) 553-0052

People of all ages come to Structure House to lose weight quickly and safely, to develop positive feelings about themselves, and to learn the skills needed to maintain a healthy and desirable weight back home. Through an in-depth residential treatment program delivered in a highly supportive environment, guests learn to change self-defeating patterns and to not only lose weight but keep it off.

A systematic approach to weight control based on an individual's personal experience instead of on a rigid set of rules, the Structure House program helps guests discover their reasons for overeating. By choosing to attend, guests remove themselves from the situations and people that directly influence their overeating and substitute instead a positive, supportive atmosphere. Here they begin to understand that weight is primarily a psychological problem. As they learn to identify their own difficulties related to nutrition, exercise, and lifestyle, they gain insight into when and why they turn to food. At Structure House, guests learn a problem-solving approach to dealing with their own unique weight problems.

The program is highly individualized. In addition to medical consultation services, Structure House offers individual and group psychological treatments, exercise and fitness instruction, and dietary reeducation. Over one hundred activities are offered each week, including workshops devoted to assertiveness training, lifestyle change, stress management, understanding body image, behavior modification training, life and time management, nutrition, menu planning, and many other topics. Other activities include a supermarket tour accompanied by a dietician, practice in restaurant eating, and cooking demonstrations.

Opportunities for physical fitness include exercise classes and low-impact aerobics, pool exercise, instruction in the use of Nautilus, stationary bike, free weights, and related equipment, supervised aerobic walk/jog sessions, open gym for basketball and badminton, and more. Facilities include indoor and outdoor swimming pools, fully equipped fitness center, walking trail, and an activity center complete with counselor and physician offices, dining rooms, meeting rooms, and social areas.

Located on its own twenty-acre campus in Durham, Structure House enjoys a mild climate conducive to year-round outdoor activity. Guests are accommodated in private luxury apartments complete with TV, washer/dryer, maid service, and private deck, patio, or balcony. In recognition of its many Jewish guests, Structure House observes Jewish holidays and can always provide a modified kosher diet. At Passover, Jews and other guests enjoy a calorie-controlled seder.

COST: The fee for the recommended four-week stay is $4,800. This covers program, meals, and private, single-occupancy one-bedroom apartment. The program can also be attended for periods of one ($1,200), two ($2,400), and three weeks ($3,600). Charges are somewhat lower for guests who wish to share a two-bedroom, two-bath apartment. A spouse, family member, or other support person may attend for $340 per week. Additional fees are charged for individual counseling, massage therapy, and some medical services.

WILDWOOD LIFESTYLE CENTER AND HOSPITAL

Wildwood, Georgia 30757
(404) 820-1493, (800) 634-9355

Evidence from long-term health studies indicates that the majority of lifestyle-induced disease and health disease can be reversed. During the past fifty years, the doctors, nurses, counselors, and other staff members at the Wildwood Lifestyle Center and Hospital have helped guests achieve maximum health benefits and make permanent changes in their lifestyles resulting in continued improvements in health and well-being.

Specializing in preventive medicine, Wildwood helps guests experience renewed vigor and marked health improvement by replacing an unhealthy lifestyle with a healthy alternative. Wildwood's philosophy is to concentrate on the causes of disease rather than the symptoms. Since stress is recognized as a major contributor to poor health, guests are taught effective stress-management techniques.

Through the center's program, many guests lose weight and keep it off. Others successfully stop smoking or overcome other unhealthy habits such as caffeine addiction. Guests see their high blood pressure fall to normal and experience dramatic drops in cholesterol and triglyceride levels. Many find that they can successfully reduce or eliminate medications. Hundreds of guests have enjoyed health improvements in areas including being overweight, heart disease, arthritis, high blood pressure, diabetes, depression, hypoglycemia, allergies, and emphysema.

Wildwood offers seven-, fourteen-, and twenty-two-day programs, which include complete medical history, physical exam, chest x-ray, blood chemistry profile on admission and discharge (on admission only for seven-day program), electrocardiogram (EKG)—exercise stress test, lung function, periodic physician consultations, jacuzzi, sauna, limited massage, health and nutrition lectures, food demonstrations, guided walks, meals, and lodging. The results of the medical studies determine the specifics of each guest's conditioning program. Although operated by Seventh-Day Adventists, the program at Wildwood is nondenominational and nonsectarian.

During your stay you will live in á pleasant room overlooking the mountains with your own patio for relaxing. The meals, all built around fruits, vegetables, legumes, and grains, are served buffet style. Dairy products, fish, and meat are not served.

COST: The all-inclusive rate is $2,495 for the twenty-two-day program, $1,895 for the fourteen-day program, and $1,195 for the seven-day program. A participating spouse or other immediate family member receives a 25 percent discount. A supportive companion (nonmedical) receives a 50 percent discount. Wildwood also offers an inexpensive get-acquainted visit for those who would like to visit before committing themselves to the program.

HARTLAND WELLNESS CENTER

P.O. Box 1
Rapidan, Virginia 22733
(703) 672-3100, (800) 763-9355

Located in the foothills of the Blue Ridge Mountains in Virginia, Hartland offers "Lifestyle to Health," a residential program designed to help participants make positive, permanent changes in the way they take care of themselves. For some guests this translates into learning to reduce and manage their weight. For others, it means that they stop smoking. For still others it involves working toward diabetes control or the reversal of hypertension or heart disease.

Managed by a team of Seventh-Day Adventist professionals, including nurses, massage and hydrotherapists, nutritionists, and health educators, the center "provides the opportunity to renew the body and the spirit in a relaxing, Christian environment." People of all faiths are welcome to enroll in the ten- and eighteen-day-long program.

The program is based on the premise that diseases are often the result of lifestyle choices we make. When we alter our approach to living by tuning in to the natural rhythms and demands of our bodies, we experience better health. "Lifestyle to Health" affects these changes through an intensive series of health education and stress-management lectures as well as hands-on cooking classes and personal counseling. A supervised exercise program is still another component of the experience. Facilities include sauna and sun deck, indoor lap-swimming pool, complete hydrotherapy department, exercise room, and cooking lab. Sessions are offered year-round.

COST: The fee for the ten-day program is $1,500 and $2,500 for the eighteen-day program. A discount is given when two members of a family attend together.

THE PLANTATION SPA

51-550 Kamehameha Highway
Ka'a'awa, Hawaii 96730
(800) 422-0307

Hawaii's only full-service spa, the Plantation Spa is a premier vegetarian retreat located in a magnificent Polynesian setting. Sited on the slopes of the Koolau Mountains overlooking the Pacific Ocean, the spa occupies one of Hawaii's historical estates. Owned and operated by Swedish nutritionist Bodil Anderson, it is associated with the renowned Halsohem Masesgarden spa near Stockholm.

Plantation Spa accommodates only fourteen guests at a time, assuring high-dosage individualized attention. While most guests come to lose weight, many also arrive wishing to learn how to live a healthier life generally, and they do not leave disappointed. "The goal," Anderson explains, "is really to teach people to take care of themselves—to take the consequences of what they are doing and to develop positive attitudes."

The daily routine begins with the ringing of the morning bell at 7:00 A.M., followed by an hour of group wake-up exercises ranging from yoga to Energetics to walking on the beach. Breakfast follows. After that, guests participate in a broad variety of activities, including not only structured exercise sessions but outdoor hiking and canoeing excursions that enable them to immerse themselves in the island's natural beauty. Other classes and activities include stretching, toning, pool exercise, hydrotone, posture class, t'ai chi, low-impact aerobics, water volleyball, croquet, badminton, weight lifting, and brisk beach walking. You can enjoy the waterfall-fed swimming pool, the jacuzzi, and sauna.

During evening lectures you will learn about topics ranging from positive thinking to practical health hints and self-improvement techniques. An instructor frequently visits from the Polynesian Cultural Center to teach lauhala weaving, lei making, and silk-screen printing. Lectures on diet and nutrition are often presented by guest speakers.

Guests enjoy a lacto-vegetarian cuisine, featuring luscious tropical fruits and fresh vegetables and herbs. Bodil Anderson specializes in teaching the proper way to fast and introduces both juice and broth fasts to those who are interested. Alcohol, caffeine, meat, and smoking are all banned from the spa.

Plantation Spa has been in operation for five years. In that time, guests have ranged from sixteen to eighty years of age. The most typical guest is a middle-aged woman and 20 percent of the visitors are men. The spa has attracted a fair number of celebrities, eager for spiritual and physical renewal in a relaxed atmosphere. The staff aims to send all guests home "feeling energized and refreshed with ideas you can incorporate into your daily life."

COST: The fee for a full spa program, including six nights' lodging, meals, all classes and activities, plus several special treatments, is $1,450 per person double occupancy, $1,750 single occupancy. The spa will match you with a roommate if you like. Shorter stays can also be arranged. Additional fees are charged for therapeutic body treatments.

NEW AGE HEALTH SPA

Neversink, New York 12765
(800) 682-4348, (914) 985-7601

The New Age Health Spa caters to both those who want to slow down and unwind and those who want to rev up, preparing for new athletic challenges. You will begin your stay with a brief consultation with the health coordinator to discuss your current health status, expectations at New Age, and long-range health goals. There is also a nutritionist available to help you decide which of the spa's three different nutrition plans—the "Rotation Diet," "Juice Fast," and "Spartan Diet"—best complements your personal goals. The use of cigarettes, alcoholic beverages, caffeine, and drugs is off-limits.

Set on 155 acres of rolling hills and forests in the Catskill Mountains, the spa offers opportunities for cross-country skiing, snowshoeing, and hiking in addition to the use of its tennis courts, indoor and outdoor pools, steam and sauna rooms, and weight and exercise facilities. Here guests participate in the latest aerobic activities, from step classes to interval training to water aerobics. The core of the spa's fitness philosophy, however, centers on the "New Age Power Walking Program." Rain or shine, guests walk three to seven miles each morning, setting out at 7:00 A.M.

Each day you can choose from an assortment of classes, lec-

tures, and lessons. A typical schedule starts out with Zen meditation at 6:30 A.M. and a power walk at 7:00 A.M. After t'ai chi
or yoga at 8:00 A.M., breakfast is served. After that, it's time for
a lecture and an instruction session, then a half-hour of low-
impact aerobics or water conditioning. Stretch class at 12:30
P.M. wraps up the morning. After lunch you might choose to
attend a fitness lecture, a water aerobics class, then a step class.
Take a break for afternoon tea and meditation before moving
on to a predinner lecture. After dinner, there's time for another
lecture and maybe time to watch a movie, too.

As a pleasant addition to your schedule, sign up for one or
more of the personal therapies and treatments offered, which
range from the familiar to the exotic, from ancient remedies to
high-tech analyses. A sampling of services includes herbal
wrap, facial, Dead Sea mud treatment, aromatherapy, reflexol-
ogy, hypnosis, body-fat analysis, and herbology.

COST: The overall rate covers accommodations, all
meals, full-day supervised program, and use of all facilities.
Personal services cost extra. Two-day minimum stay required.
The rate is $174 per person per day, or $1,099 per week, in a
single-occupancy room. Double occupancy runs $114 per
person per day, or $699 per week. The spa will be glad to
match you with a roommate. Service charge and sales tax are
additional. Personal services carry separate charges.

DEERFIELD MANOR SPA

R.D. 1 (Route 402)
East Stroudsburg, Pennsylvania 18301
(717) 223-0160

At the Deerfield Manor Spa, director Frieda Eisenkraft
purposefully gears her programs toward helping guests achieve
healthier lifestyles not only during their stay at the spa but

afterward, too, when they return home. "We ask our guests to consider their goals," she writes, "and then try to give them some ideas of how to achieve them through cooking lessons, individual exercise counseling, and lectures devoted to their diets." There are never more than thirty-three guests, allowing for plenty of individualized attention.

The spa sits on twelve acres of mountain woodlands and facilities include the guest cottage, exercise barn, heated outdoor pool, shuffleboard courts, and the main house, which contains lecture rooms, libraries, meeting rooms, Swedish sauna, and massage room. The atmosphere is informal and the accommodations comfortable. Each room is air-conditioned and has its own bathroom. Meals are handsomely served in the sun-drenched dining room where guests learn how to develop healthy eating habits through a daily introduction to a broad variety of low-calorie gourmet meals. Several choices of diet are available and cooking demonstrations are offered.

Guests come to the spa wanting to learn how to look better and feel better and how to handle stress more effectively. They also come seeking stimulating interaction, and to this end the staff has arranged evening lectures that cover subjects ranging from feminine anthropology to Japanese house planning to graphology to sex education.

On arrival, an individualized fitness program is developed for each guest, taking into account both present level of fitness and personal self-improvement goals. The emphasis is on moderation and guests are not pressed to participate in every activity. The options, however, are extensive: aerobics, aquatics, body toning, calisthenics, Dancercize, massage, mountain hikes, sauna, swimming, tennis, treadmill, stationary bicycle, Stairmaster, vigorous outdoor walking, yoga, and group discussions on exercise, weight control, nutrition, and maintaining a fitness program back at home. A full selection of personal services including several types of massages, facials, body treatments, and manicures and pedicures is also available.

COST: The spa is open from April through mid-

November. The fee for a full week's stay during the peak summer season, including meals, fitness program, and room, ranges from $760 to $1,060. Rates drop considerably at other times. Shorter stays can also be arranged. There are additional charges for personal services.

BIRDWING SPA

21398 575th Ave.
Litchfield, Minnesota 55355
(612) 693-6064

The first spa to take root in the upper Midwest, Birdwing is proud of the highly personalized experience it offers, blending rewarding programs, peaceful surroundings, and a European philosophy into an affordable spa vacation. Birdwing offers programs in weight loss and fitness, but the spa also welcomes guests who come purely for pampering. At Birdwing the atmosphere is safe and nurturing, making this an excellent place to begin to explore what is sometimes an intimidating process: fitness and weight control. With a capacity of eighteen guests, you are assured attentive service and a highly personal program. Because of the limited number of guests, the staff is able to accommodate special dietary requirements.

If you come because you want to address your weight, you will soon realize that the word "diet" is excluded from the spa vocabulary. Instead, you will learn how to take better care of yourself through health presentations, cooking classes, and a consultation with the spa's registered dietician.

The spa's fitness director will also meet with you to design a fitness routine to complement your particular interests, time constraints, and physical limitations. Your visit is a perfect time to experiment with a variety of fitness approaches, seeking out the ones that work best for you. Sample classes in low-impact aerobics, deep muscle toning, STEP aerobics, total body stretching, progressive relaxation, and visual imagery. In the summer you can go on bicycle and canoe outings and swim in the outdoor pool. In the winter you can go cross-country skiing.

For just plain relaxation and revitalization (not to mention the calorie-burning potential), it's hard to beat a brisk walk. The three-hundred-acre Birdwing Estate has fifteen miles of groomed hiking trails that wind through forests, border lakeshores, and cross prairies. As you walk, you may well sight white-tail deer, swans, white pelicans, and other kinds of wildlife.

Unlike many spas, Birdwing charges an all-inclusive rate that covers all meals, services, accommodations, and use of facilities. You won't be slapped with an unpleasantly large bill when you leave, because your massage, facial, and manicure are all part of your package.

COST: The all-inclusive fee for a weekend is $315 for double occupancy and $385 for single occupancy. For a seven-day stay, the fees are $1,095 and $1,195, respectively.

LAKE AUSTIN RESORT

1705 Quinlan Park Road
Austin, Texas 78732
(512) 266-2444

A peaceful and remote health retreat set in the rolling Texas hill country, Lake Austin Resort offers classes, programs, and weekly workshops to help guests learn to cope with the stresses of everyday life. Combining personal attention with highly varied programming, the spa strives to meet the needs of all guests seeking renewal and revitalization. This is a place to pay attention to yourself, body and mind.

Here you can plan your own daily schedule, choosing from

the broad selection of activities. If you want to improve joint mobility and muscular flexibility, you can join a stretching class. If your goal is to slow down and relax, you might explore options including visualization, yoga, meditation, t'ai chi, breath work, and water t'ai chi. Still other activities focus on muscular strength and conditioning. For those seeking aerobic exercise, choices run the gamut from hill-country hiking and cycling expeditions to step classes, country-and-western dancing to lap swimming. For just plain fun, you can participate in water games, volleyball, paddle boating, horseshoes, card-table games, or even a winery tour.

Lake Austin Resort also offers a rich selection of experiential workshops designed to provide a structure for self-discovery and to help you create a sense of balance in your life. Called "Insight" programs, these include cooking classes and demonstrations as well as sessions on eating behaviors and body image. There are also workshops focusing on relationship issues, self-awareness, and approaches to fitness. You can join an art class, learn about movement therapy or the use of vitamins, minerals, and herbs, take an adult cardiopulmonary resuscitation (CPR) course, or even enroll in a session called "How to Shop for Shoes." And that's just a sampling of the opportunities awaiting you.

You can also pamper yourself with European spa services, including a variety of body masques, facials, manicures and pedicures, and therapeutic body treatments provided by professional massage therapists. The services of a beauty salon and a makeover artist are also available.

The Lake Austin Resort is one of the only spas in the country to endorse a nondiet approach to weight management. Consistent with this approach, several times a year the spa hosts a special week-long program called "Overcoming Overeating," led by two well-known psychotherapists with extensive experience in the treatment of compulsive eating.

There are also many other special-interest week-long programs to consider, all them designed to address lifestyle issues and enhance self-discovery. "Men in Action" gives men the chance to explore men's issues together while learning about new health and fitness approaches. "Mother–Daughter Week" combines all the benefits of a spa visit with classes geared toward exploring the mother–daughter relationship. As participants in "Lessons in Love," couples learn how to strengthen their relationship and increase intimacy by developing effective communication skills. Other special weeks are organized around learning and experiencing in depth a particular activity such as hiking, yoga, or trail riding.

The resort, which prides itself on creating a warm, family-type atmosphere, has forty guest rooms. Each one enjoys lovely views of Lake Austin and the surrounding countryside. About 25 percent of the spa's guests are men.

COST: The standard rate for a four-day stay is $640 per person in a private room, $556 per person in a double room. All meals and most activities are included. For a seven-day stay, the rate is $1,120 and $973. Ten- and fourteen-day packages are also available, as are deluxe accommodations. Special weeks involve supplemental charges. All guests are charged an additional $22 per day gratuities and service charge. European spa services are extra.

WOODEN DOOR DIET AND FITNESS SPA FOR WOMEN

628 Mulberry Court
Milwaukee, Wisconsin 53217
(414) 228-8980, (800) 800-7906

This midwestern bargain proves that spas aren't just for the wealthy. Wooden Door caters to women of all ages interested in losing weight, improving overall fitness, getting started on an exercise program, or simply taking time out to get back in touch with themselves. "Our philosophy," explains owner Marsha B. Sodos, "is to offer a low-cost, yet professional program where you can stretch your mind as well as your muscles."

The exercise program incorporates both aerobic and non-aerobic options. Choices include walking, jogging, stretching and toning, dance aerobics, weight training, and yoga. Exercise classes, designed for just about every level of fitness, are held both in the air-conditioned gym and outdoors in the gazebo overlooking the lake. There is no pressure here. Exercise as much or as little as you like.

The spa also offers a broad selection of afternoon and evening programs. There are sessions focusing on self-aware-ness, self-defense, stress management, and nutrition, along with fashion and beauty workshops. During your free time, you can swim in the lake, relax in the sauna, fish, hike the twenty-six-mile lakefront trail, play tennis, shuffleboard, or volleyball, or treat yourself to a makeover session, personal training consultation, body wrap, facial, manicure, pedicure, massage, or one of the other personal services available. Live entertainment, speakers, and movies fill out the evenings.

Lodgings at Wooden Door are no-frills but comfortable. Guests are accommodated in bunk beds in spacious, heated cabins equipped with bathrooms. Each room accommodates two to four women. Meals, served cafeteria style, provide a one-thousand-calories-a-day diet high in fiber and carbohy-drates and low in sodium and fat. Supplements are available for those who need more calories. Guests get to know each other as they join together to eat in the dining room at tables that seat eight.

Wooden Door welcomes guests from April through October at its Lake Geneva facility. Additional sessions are sometimes held at other times of the year. The spa also main-tains a new facility fifteen miles to the north, Alpine Valley Resort, which offers the same women-only program as well as coed weekends. The resort is highlighted by a 127-room Swiss-style chalet and amenities that include nine- and eighteen-hole golf courses, indoor and outdoor swimming pools, sauna, whirlpool, and tennis courts. The Alpine Valley facility is open from June through October.

From time to time, Wooden Door offers special weekends and weeks planned around a particular theme such as "Mother–Daughter Relationships," "Healthy Heart," and "Stress Relief."

COST: The rate is $299 for a weekend, $679 for a five-day stay, and $899 for a seven-day stay, based on double occupancy (additional charge for single accommodations). This includes all meals and snacks, plus a wide range of exercise options and personal improvement programs. There are additional charges for massages, manicures, body wraps, and other personal services.

Cooking

THE NEW ORLEANS SCHOOL OF COOKING AND THE LOUISIANA GENERAL STORE

The Jackson Brewery
620 Decatur St.
New Orleans, Louisiana 70130
(504) 482-3632

Learn the secrets of authentic Creole cooking in a three-hour session at the New Orleans Cooking School, created by native New Orleanian Joe Cahn in 1980. Weaving together strands of Indian, French, Spanish, and African cooking styles, Creole cuisine reflects the city's history. As you watch Cahn and fellow New Orleans cooks demonstrate their techniques, you will also gain insight into the culture and attitude that characterize this upbeat southern city. The school "isn't just about food," Cahn explains. "It's a group of people coming into a Welcome Wagon meeting, sitting around drinking coffee, and learning about the state." Each session can accommodate about sixty students, who make themselves comfortable around tables covered with checked cloths.

During the jovial one-time three-hour class, students observe the scratch-to-finish preparation of dishes like gumbo, jambalaya, bread pudding with whiskey sauce, and pecan pralines. Printed recipes are distributed so that you can prepare the dishes back home, incorporating the tips you've learned.

The school is located in the Jackson Brewery, a busy shopping center in the French Quarter along the Mississippi River. The class is taught every day except Sunday and lunch is served, complete with beer and iced tea, so that you can sample the steaming jambalaya.

COST: It costs $15 to attend the class, which includes lunch.

TANTE MARIE'S COOKING SCHOOL

271 Francisco St.
San Francisco, California 94133
(415) 788-6699

Tante Marie's Cooking School offers year-round classes for people who are serious about cooking, both those who want to pursue a culinary career and those who want to learn to cook well for pleasure. Aspiring professional cooks can enroll in the six-month full-time culinary course and the six-month part-time pastry course. For visitors with limited time in San Francisco, the school conducts evening, one-day, weekend, and one-week courses on a variety of subjects. In general,

Tante Marie's teaches the principles and techniques of French cooking, applying them to contemporary California cooking. Here you will learn not only how to prepare food and present it beautifully but how to purchase ingredients and plan menus. Many specialty courses are offered as well.

Mary Risley, Tante Marie's founder, director, and primary teacher, has taught more than three thousand students how to cook over the past twenty years. Her efforts are supported by an impressive staff of Bay-area chefs and cooking teachers along with guest speakers such as cookbook authors, nutritionists, restaurant owners, and caterers. Local experts frequently conduct demonstrations, displaying their skills at specialties such as sausage and paté making, cooking fish and shellfish, and working with chocolate.

The school adheres to the philosophy that the best way to learn to cook is by cooking. Most classes, then, are participatory in nature. Using the school's two kitchens, each of which can accommodate ten people working together, students cook under the watchful eye of the chef/instructor. One of the kitchens converts into a demonstration area where visiting chefs and guest celebrities can make presentations to up to forty students.

During these sessions, students watch the chef cook and then have the opportunity to taste the results. Samples are offered for tasting. This is a time for taking notes, asking questions, and collecting recipes. Often students observe a demonstration one afternoon and then replicate the process themselves the next day.

Tante Marie's one-week courses attract people from all over the country. The recipes and demonstrations change from week to week, so you can plan your visit to coincide with a topic of particular interest. You can also enroll for two or more consecutive weeks and be assured fresh lessons each day. Classes run Monday through Friday from 10:00 A.M. to 4:00 P.M. In the morning, students prepare recipes emphasizing French cooking with a California interpretation. Together with your fellow students and teacher, you will sit down to enjoy the three- or four-course meal you have just prepared. In the afternoon you join the school's full-time students in observing a demonstration presented by a guest chef. (You can also elect to enroll only for the demonstration.)

Evening participation courses are another option. Called "The Basics," these meet once a week for six weeks from 6:00 P.M. to 10:00 P.M. You will prepare and eat dinner, focusing on topics like pastry, regional cooking, or cooking with wine. The series is offered throughout the year, alternating between three levels: beginning, intermediate, and advanced.

Tante Marie's issues a quarterly calendar detailing current course offerings. A sampling from a recent edition includes one-day participatory workshops in Mexican cooking and Asian cooking, weekend workshops focusing on light Italian cooking and entertaining ideas, a week-long course on California cooking, and demonstration sessions on recipe development, culinary careers, and chocolate desserts.

The calendar also describes the content of each class offering day by day. The school is quite flexible; assuming it is not filled, you are welcome to attend a single class even if it is offered as part of a series.

COST: Admission to an afternoon or weekend demonstration/tasting is usually $35. The fee is $175–250 for a weekend workshop and $450 for most one-week courses. A six-week evening course costs $390.

YOSEMITE CHEFS' HOLIDAYS

5410 E. Home Ave.
Fresno, California 93727
(209) 454-2020

Yosemite Chefs' Holidays combines a mini-vacation in a fabulous natural setting with the opportunity to learn about cooking from a prestigious collection of great chefs and culinary experts. Presenters include chefs from many well-known California restaurants, as well as cookbook authors, food and wine editors, and accomplished bakers and pastry chefs.

Sessions, which run Sunday evening through Tuesday night and Wednesday morning through Thursday night, are scheduled throughout January. The format combines receptions and demonstrations complete with tastings with an elegant banquet, a five-course feast prepared by the featured chef. During a typical session, you can expect to learn about cooking procedures, foods, and presentation techniques from four or five experts. Most events are held in the Ahwahnee Great Lounge, where large windows frame views of Yosemite in its winter glory.

Participants stay at either the elegant Ahwahnee hotel or the more casual Yosemite Lodge. Recreational opportunities include ice skating, skiing, naturalist programs, snowshoeing, sightseeing tours, museum exhibits, camera walks, and simply experiencing the grandeur of Yosemite National Park.

COST: The fee for the "Chef's Dinner" is $75. Because seating is limited, reservations should be made at the time you book your lodgings.

CAROLE BLOOM PATISSIERE COOKING SCHOOL

6832 Maple Leaf Drive
Carlsbad, California 92009
(619) 931-5920

If desserts are your passion and you would like to learn how to concoct elegant finales that range from fresh-fruit desserts to homemade ice creams and sorbets to classic cakes, enroll in a session at a California cooking school where the owner teaches all the classes. Trained at prestigious cooking schools in London, Paris, and Venice, pastry chef and candy maker Carole Bloom has practiced her skills at world-class hotels and restaurants in the United States and abroad. The author of a book on classic candy making, *Truffles, Candies & Confections,* (The Crossing Press, 1992) she shares her talents through regularly scheduled classes held in the professionally equipped kitchen at her home. Classes are held on Saturdays from noon to 5:00 P.M. throughout the year and each session is limited to twelve students.

In the two-part series that bears the same name as Bloom's book, students learn techniques for working with chocolate, preparing confections such as orange hazelnut chocolate clusters, white chocolate almond bark, and orange chocolate truffles. In "Puff Pastry and Croissants," you will learn to make these pastries from scratch and to use them as appetizers and main dishes as well as desserts. Other courses include "Caramel Desserts to Rave About," "Great Classic Desserts," "Chocolates for Your Valentine," and "Basic Wedding Cakes, A Blueprint for Success."

COST: The fee for each five-hour class is $75.

HOMECHEF COOKING SCHOOL

3525 California St.
San Francisco, California 94118
(415) 668-3191

Judith Ets-Hokin's cooking school emphasizes "the science of cooking—why and how things work." The instructors believe that everyone can learn to cook. They take the mystery out of creating delicious food by going beyond the preparation of recipes and focusing instead on the principles of cooking. Students learn why a recipe calls for a particular combination of ingredients or a certain method. For example, you will discover how spices, herbs, and other ingredients influence one another.

The fourteen-week-long basic course, offered three times a year, covers stocks, sauces, cooking methods, soufflés, pastries, cakes, soups, custards and mousses, and breads. Several recipes are demonstrated each session, with generous tastings provided, and students are given homework assignments to reinforce what they have learned in class. The course is extremely flexible in that each class is a self-contained lesson that can be taken individually. Each class lasts approximately two hours and takes the form of a finely tuned demonstration.

The school also offers one- to four-week demonstration sessions on topics ranging from food-processor techniques to wild mushrooms, bistro cuisine to holiday chocolate treats. If you prefer to roll up your sleeves, you can get some supervised hands-on experience by registering for one of the Homechef's workshops. The three-hour sessions focus on topics like pasta making, breads, and gingerbread-house construction. Seminars on subjects such as how to run a catering business or how to give successful holiday parties are also offered.

COST: The fee for the complete fourteen-week basic cooking course is $392. A single class or seminar is $35; hands-on workshops are $45. Assistants pay $185 for the basic cooking course, $15 for individual classes, and $20 for most workshops.

SANTA FE SCHOOL OF COOKING

Upper Level, Plaza Mercado
116 West San Francisco St.
Santa Fe, New Mexico 87501
(505) 983-4511

At the Santa Fe School of Cooking you can get a handle on the techniques involved in cooking southwestern food and enjoy a delicious regional meal, all by attending a single-session demonstration class. Depending upon the class you choose, you will learn to use indigenous southwestern ingredients to prepare either traditional or contemporary dishes.

The atmosphere is casual during the 2½-hour classes, which are offered four or five times a week. Students sit around tables in the airy kitchen, taking notes and sipping coffee while the instructor demonstrates food preparation techniques. The large overhead mirror angled above the work area makes it easy to follow along, keeping one eye on the chef and the other on preprinted recipes distributed at the start of class. As he or she works, the chef answers questions and divulges information about the history and cultural significance of the foods being prepared. Each class culminates in a complete meal, so you get to sample the goods.

The standard classes are "Traditional" (I, II, and III) and "Contemporary Southwestern Cooking" (I and II). You don't need to take them in any particular order. Just choose the one that fits your schedule best or features dishes you would most like to learn to prepare. "Traditional I" covers corn tortillas, red chile sauce, cheese enchiladas, green chile sauce, chicken enchiladas, beans, posole, and sopa (bread pudding).

"Contemporary I" teaches the preparation of lime-marinated grilled salmon, roasted corn and black bean salsa, New Mexican scalloped potatoes, Southwest stir-fried vegetables, and a southwestern dessert. The classes are taught by some of the city's most notable chefs, five of whom usually work on a rotating basis.

The school also offers occasional culinary tours, field trips to explore the foods in northern New Mexico's villages as well as in Santa Fe's finest restaurants.

COST: "Traditional I" costs $25. "Contemporary I" costs $38.

THE CAMBRIDGE SCHOOL OF CULINARY ARTS

2020 Massachusetts Ave.
Cambridge, Massachusetts 02140
(617) 354-3836

The Cambridge School of Culinary Arts offers courses for home cooks that are taught by some of the same staff members who teach in the school's ten-month professional chef's program. The school's mission is to expose both the novice and the accomplished gourmet to the world of food. Food preparation is taught in the tradition of European cooking, while accommodating today's varied lifestyles.

Hands-on classes, taught in fully equipped professional kitchens, are kept small to allow for personalized instruction. Most courses include practice and demonstration sessions and end in a full-course meal of the food prepared during the lesson. Students receive printed copyrighted recipes.

Three- to five-week-long courses, which meet once a week for four or five hours, focus on a variety of cuisines and techniques. A recent listing included the following choices: "Basic Baking," "Southwest Cuisine," "Flavors of Italy," "Provincial French," "Sophisticated Desserts for the Advanced Baker," "Regional American Cooking," and "Thai Cuisine."

An inventive selection of one- and two-day courses is also offered. In "Off the Hook" you will learn basic buying, handling, and preparation techniques for saltwater and fresh fish.

"Soup's On" concentrates on the preparation of homemade stocks and soups, while "Off Cuts" teaches the basics of preparing one-pot meals with affordable but often-forgotten cuts of meat. There are also short courses devoted to pasta preparation, Cajun and Creole cooking, brunch, pizza, vegetarian cooking, and various dessert techniques.

In addition to the classes, the school sponsors a Celebrity Chef series, featuring demonstrations by chefs from fine restaurants and by well-known cookbook authors. The sessions are 2½ hours long. Like the courses described above, they are scheduled for weekend afternoons or weekday evenings.

COST: The fee for "Southwest Cuisine," a three-week course, is $150. The fee for the five-week "Basic Baking" course is $230. Most one-day courses cost $50 and two-day courses cost about $100. The fee for each Celebrity Chef demonstration is $45.

7
Traveling

HOSTELLING INTERNATIONAL

American Youth Hostels (AYH)
Department 860
733 15th St., N.W., No. 840
Washington, D.C. 20005
(202) 783-6161

This book is chock-full of programs and places designed to expand your knowledge of a specific skill, whether it be fly fishing, square dancing, kayaking, or weaving. American Youth Hostel Discovery Tours teach a less specific but tremendously valuable skill: They teach you how to travel. These tours are more than vacation adventures. They are valuable learning experiences that put you in contact with new people and new environments. They also give you the opportunity to take part in daily decisions regarding activities and itineraries. They enable you to develop the skills and confidence that will serve you well when you strike out on your own on other adventures, in this country or abroad.

AYH Discovery Tours are moderately priced. They are intended for fit, healthy participants who are willing to pitch in with necessary chores. You will stay in hostels (dormitory-style accommodations with separate quarters for men and women, self-service kitchens, and dining and common rooms) and in campgrounds. Contrary to popular perception, AYH serves travelers of all ages. Discovery tours are divided into age groups. "Teen" trips are open to those 15–18, "adult" trips are for those eighteen and over, and "50+" trips are for—you guessed it—those fifty and over. There are also "open" tours, which welcome all participants over fifteen years of age, making them good bets for active families who want to travel together or for grandparents and teenaged grandchildren. All Discovery Tours feature small groups, usually nine travelers plus a trained tour leader.

There are two basic types of Discovery Tours in the United States: hiking and cycling. Each tour is rated according to ability, with options for beginners as well as for the experienced. On cycling tours you carry your own gear as well as a share of the group equipment and supplies. Whatever level tour you choose, it's advisable to train in advance to get some practice riding with full saddlebags. Tours are divided into five skill levels. The most demanding involve riding fifty or more miles a day over rough terrain. The least taxing average thirty-five miles per day on moderate terrain. The specific route is chosen by the group in consultation with the leader, and all participants follow it together.

The ten-day "Dutch Treat" is typical of the cycling tours. Offered as an "open" tour with a C rating (least demanding), the route explores Pennsylvania's Lancaster County and focuses on learning about the customs of the Amish and Mennonite people. The trip begins and ends in Philadelphia and combines hostel lodgings with camping. Other cycling tours explore the Pacific Coast, the Finger Lakes region of New York, the Northwest, Cape Cod, and several regions of California.

AYH Discovery Tours also include a series of hiking tours by van. These excursions are built on day hikes out of a base camp. The only equipment you need to carry on the trail is a water bottle and a day pack. After the group decides on the day's itinerary, your driver/leader will transport you to the hiking trail you've chosen. Tours are divided into four skill levels; the most demanding require hiking ten or more miles a day over mountainous terrain, while the least demanding involve hiking 4–7 miles per day with some moderately hilly terrain. Typical of these tours is "Southwest Parks—Red-Rock Country," which begins and ends in Las Vegas. During this sixteen-day excursion you will visit some of the Southwest's most spectacular national parks, participating in ranger-led interpretive programs. Day hikes will take you to rugged canyons, cliffside Indian ruins, and dramatic natural bridges and arches. The trip combines hostel stays with camping and separate tours are scheduled for adults and for those fifty or older.

To participate in the Discovery Tours, you must be a member of AYH. A membership application is included in the tour catalog.

If you would like to learn to lead educational or recreational hiking or cycling trips or simply to develop your own outdoor skills, you can enroll in an "AYH Leadership Training Course." The one-week sessions provide training in group dynamics, equipment maintenance, low-impact travel skills, and the art of hostel traveling. Following three days of demonstrations, discussion, and hands-on work, the group embarks on a four-day trip to get some practical experience. Upon successful completion of the course, you will receive official AYH certification in group leadership. The course is offered several times a year at locations throughout the United States.

COST: The fee for "Dutch Treat" is $460. The fee for "Southwest Parks—Red-Rock Country" is $900. Prices cover lodgings in hostels or campgrounds, group-prepared meals, tour leader services, a contribution to the group entertainment/activities fund, and transportation as noted. You are responsible for arranging your own transportation to and from the tour starting and ending points. The fee for participation in the "AYH Leadership Training Course" is $295, which covers all meals, lodging, tuition, and AYH membership.

Program
and Sponsor Index

Geographic Index